HARVARD STUDIES IN BUSINESS HISTORY XXXII

Edited by Alfred D. Chandler, Jr.
Isidor Straus Professor of Business History
Graduate School of Business Administration
George F. Baker Foundation
Harvard University

Managerial Hierarchies

Comparative Perspectives
on the Rise of the Modern
Industrial Enterprise

Edited by
Alfred D. Chandler, Jr., and
Herman Daems

HARVARD UNIVERSITY PRESS
Cambridge, Massachusetts
and London, England

78602

Library of Congress Cataloging in Publication Data

Main entry under title:

Managerial hierarchies.

(Harvard studies in business history; 32)
Includes index.
1. Industrial organization—History—Case studies.
2. Big business—History—Case studies. 3. Business
enterprises—History—Case studies. 4. Industry and
state—History—Case studies. I. Chandler, Alfred
Dupont. II. Daems, Herman. III. Series.
HD30.5.M34   658.4′02   79-20396
ISBN 0-674-54740-3

Designed by Mike Fender

Preface

THE SEVEN ESSAYS in this volume exemplify much of the new scholarly work undertaken in the United States and abroad on the coming of the large managerial enterprise and, with it, managerial capitalism. Drawing together current research in the field, the authors focus specifically on the rise of modern managerial hierarchies in each of four leading Western economies and consider some of the broader implications of this phenomenon.

Scholarly research on the history of large-scale modern business enterprise and managerial capitalism is still in its early stages. These essays, therefore, outline underlying trends and suggest tentative hypotheses. Much more work needs to be done before we can say with precision why managerial hierarchies arose when and in the way that they did, or why their evolution varied so much in different economies. Only after such further research can we fully understand the implications of these institutional changes for broad, concurrent political and social developments and for refining economic analysis and theory.

The essays brought together here were originally presented at a conference held at the Harvard Business School on September 11–12, 1977. Aspects of the development of managerial enterprise had already provided themes for conferences at the University of Leuven in 1973, for a major session of the Sixth International Congress in Economic History in Copenhagen in 1974, for a conference in London in 1975, sponsored by the British Social Science Research Council, and for conferences held at the Center for Interdisciplinary Research at the University of Bielefeld in 1976 and 1977.

The conference at Harvard took the standard academic form: papers were presented, followed by formal comments on the four area papers and extended discussion. Paul Uselding commented on the United States paper; Donald N. McCloskey, on the paper on Great Britain; Charles P. Kindleberger, on the one on France; and Lawrence G. Franko, on that on Germany. Rather than publish the papers, comments, and discussions in their original form, I felt that the purpose of the conference might be better served, and a more useful volume might result, if the authors were asked to rework their contributions on the basis of the formal and informal evaluations. Herman Daems, who had worked closely with me in organizing the conference, agreed to be coeditor of the volume.

Professor Daems and I are grateful to the commentators and discussants for their valuable contributions to the revised essays. We also want to thank Dean Lawrence E. Fouraker and Associate Dean Richard S. Rosenbloom for sponsoring the September 1977 conference and the Harvard Business School Division of Research, the Alfred P. Sloan Foundation, and the German Marshall Fund for providing funds for a broad research project of which the conference and this volume are a part. We also acknowledge with thanks Vandenhoeck and Ruprecht, Publishers, for permitting Morton Keller to use the material from his essay "Public Policy and Large Enterprise: Comparative Historical Perspectives," in *Recht und Entwicklung der Gross Unternehmen, 1860–1920,* edited by Norbert Horn and Jürgen Kocka, published in Göttingen in 1979.

Alfred D. Chandler, Jr.

Contents

Figures

Tables

Managerial Hierarchies

Introduction

Alfred D. Chandler, Jr., and
Herman Daems

THE LARGE BUSINESS FIRM and its managerial hierarchy
are essential for organizing modern industrial activity. By 1975,
one of every five industrial workers in the United States and
Europe was employed by a company structured in the form of
a hierarchy with at least six levels of management. Large-scale
business enterprises characterized by multiple operating units,
varied activities, and hierarchies of salaried managers are now
at the center of the leading market economies; historically, however, they are a recent phenomenon. The hierarchical organization typical of big business has had a long history in the military
and the state bureaucracies, but only since the late nineteenth
century has it been used extensively to organize industrial activity. Today, only a century after they first appeared, these administrative mechanisms have revolutionized the operation and
organization of many basic industries in technologically advanced market economies.

Scholarly response to this institutional and managerial revolution has been diverse. Most of the research on big business
so far has dealt with the effects of the giant enterprise on social
and economic structures. Adolf A. Berle and Gardiner C. Means,
in their pathbreaking *Modern Corporation and Private Property,* published in 1932, were among the first to point to the
shift in power from owners to managers, a change that led some
economists and sociologists—including William Baumol, Oliver
E. Williamson, Robin L. Marris, Edith T. Penrose, John Kenneth Galbraith, and Richard M. Cyert and James G. March—

to challenge the notion that the motive of corporate action was to maximize profits.[1] The theory of the managerial enterprise has also become an important and controversial topic, and economists have begun to be interested in the effects of the giant firm on allocative and dynamic efficiency (that is, on the degree of efficiency with which it allocates resources and adjusts to changing conditions). Among the many issues discussed in this literature are the impact of size on profitability, patterns of growth, and innovation.[2] Sociologists have looked at the alienation of workers and even managers in the large enterprise and have begun to study the sociology of organizations.[3] In addition, management scientists have built sophisticated mathematical models to study the optimal design of hierarchical organizations.[4] Finally, a group of scholars has steadfastly ignored the phenomenon and has argued that managerial hierarchies are irrelevant for economics.[5]

Most research in this area has viewed big business as static and has only rarely considered the questions of why and how the modern business enterprise developed. These issues have been taken up by some neo-Marxists, however, who see the managerial hierarchy as an ingenious social construction permitting capitalists to reap the labor-surplus value of the workers.[6] From a totally different perspective, theoretical economists have analyzed why firms began to internalize market transactions;[7] although their work is useful in outlining basic issues, this group has done little to test its reflections against the realities of the historical development of the modern large-scale business enterprise. Historians have recently turned their attention to the growth of managerial hierarchies. So far, however, their work has been devoted largely to describing and analyzing the United States experience; little is yet known about the evolution of the giant business enterprise in other Western nations.

The aim of the essays in this volume is to begin the important task of comparing the development of the modern firm in the United States and in the leading economies of Western Europe. From the data they provide, the general outlines of the rise of big business in the West emerge. First, it appeared with surprising suddenness. Very few giant enterprises existed in the 1870s; by the 1920s, however, big business had already become the most influential nongovernment institution in all advanced industrial market economies. Second, it developed primarily in industries and sectors where advancing technology permitted companies to provide goods and services in high volumes to large, geographically dispersed markets. Third, salaried managers in these areas took over basic economic functions that had previously been carried out through market mechanisms; they gradually came to coordinate the flow of goods among operating units, supervise their activities, and allocate resources. The substitution of the visible hand of management for what Adam Smith called the invisible hand of market mechanisms is evident in essentially the same areas of major Western economies; it did not take place, however, in other industries or sectors in the same countries. An explanation of when, why, and how managerial hierarchies developed in certain industries and rarely appeared in others remains a challenge to economists, sociologists, practitioners of management science, and economic and business historians.

Differences as well as similarities are nonetheless apparent in the evolution of managerial hierarchies in Western economies, particularly in the periods at which large corporate enterprise evolved in different countries. In the United States and Germany, managerial hierarchies sprang up in large numbers in the 1880s and 1890s; in both countries, they appeared first in the most technologically advanced industries: chemicals in Germany, mass-produced machinery in the United States, and electrical machinery in both nations. Management hierarchies gained early importance in food-processing industries in the United States and Britain, but not in Germany and France. Metal making was the only industry in which they were significant in all four nations before 1914. Thus the large modern enterprise, which was common in Germany and the United States before World War I, did not become a major force in the British economy until the 1920s and 1930s and not until after World War II in France.

In creating big business, entrepreneurs in the different countries relied on different types of institutional arrangements. Those in the United States used as the standard legal, financial, and administrative form the incorporated enterprise that directly controlled its operations from a central office. In Germany, businessmen more often made use of the cartel; in Britain, the industry-wide holding company; and in France, the industrial group tied together by financial holdings. By the 1970s, however, the centrally controlled, incorporated operating enterprise had become the normal instrument for carrying on big business in all four economies.

The modern, centrally controlled operating enterprise differed from its traditional forebears in that, first, it was almost always a corporation rather than a partnership, and second, it controlled a number of factories, offices, transportation lines, mines, or other operating units, rather than just one or two. Corporate executives coordinated and monitored these units and allocated resources among them. Direct lines of authority and responsibility ran from the highest-level managers in the central office to middle managers in departmental headquarters and to the executives in charge of each of the operating units.

Holding companies were corporations created for the purpose of holding stock in other incorporated enterprises. They, too, controlled many operating units, but, unlike centralized operating companies, they were initially only legal and financial, and not administrative, devices. Some holding companies held the securities of a number of subsidiaries within a single industry; others provided the financial glue that held together a group of companies in related industries. Until it established a managerial hierarchy, however, a holding company remained little more than a federation of autonomous operating subsidiaries. Although its central office had the legal power to determine policies for its operating units, to coordinate and monitor their activities, and to allocate resources for future production and distribution, it could not do so in practical terms until a staff had been created to implement its decisions. Until then, formulation of policy and allocation of resources normally resulted from informal agreements among the constituent firms.

Cartels, in contrast, were not legally incorporated enterprises. Rather, they were formal federations of legally independent enterprises whose decisions about policy and the allocation of resources had to be negotiated through carefully defined legal and administrative procedures. A cartel's function reflected the size of the staff—that is, of the managerial hierarchy—it established to carry out those decisions. In a tight cartel, managers were appointed to monitor policies and performance and often to coordinate the flow of raw materials and goods through the processes of production and distribution. The basic difference between it and a centralized operating corporation was, therefore, that policy and decisions about allocation were made by legislative processes rather than by administrative fiat. In a loose cartel, in contrast, no managerial hierarchy existed to carry out decisions or to supervise the activities of members. Such cartels were little more than contractual agreements to maintain a particular price or volume of output.

Dependence on one of these three institutional arrangements rarely precluded the use of the other two, and the same group of businessmen might employ all three. A large, centralized enterprise might hold stock in other companies over which it had little administrative control. It might join with others in loose or even tight cartels. Moreover, it might continue to rely on market mechanisms in obtaining many of its supplies and in selling its products. In advanced industrial economies, however, as the essays that follow demonstrate, managerial hierarchies have gained an increasing advantage over market mechanisms or multilateral negotiations in coordinating the flow of goods, monitoring economic activities, and allocating resources. Equally important, federations in the form of cartels and holding companies have proved to be transitional forms in the process by which managerial hierarchies have replaced market mechanisms.

Differences in the evolution of firms and the institutional arrangements adopted in the four nations discussed in this volume have reflected underlying economic conditions and have, in turn, brought about variations in their basic capitalist mode of operation. In the United States, the modern business enterprise came into existence in a revolutionary manner. It appeared first as an instrument for administering the new forms of transportation and communication—that is, the railroad and the telegraph. Then the giant manufacturing firm emerged in the 1880s, primarily in industries whose goods could not be distributed by existing marketing channels as quickly as they could be produced. Many manufacturers first expanded by integrating forward into marketing and distribution and backward to secure supplies of raw materials and semifinished products. Others grew large by mergers, creating combinations of small firms that placed control of production in a central administrative office and then integrated forward and backward. In order to administer their many units, the resulting enterprises developed large managerial hierarchies. By the time the United States entered World War I, management decisions had replaced coordination by market forces in many of the most critical sectors of the economy. The result might be termed managerial capitalism.

Comparable changes in Britain were more gradual, since existing market mechanisms were more efficient than in the United States; thus businessmen felt less incentive to integrate forward and backward. British firms also grew large through mergers; instead of creating managerial hierarchies, however, the resulting holding companies remained federations of smaller family firms for years, or even decades. Because fewer firms undertook vertical integration and because mergers did not result in centralized administrations, founding families continued to manage their enterprises actively long after they had ceased to do so in the United States; only in the late 1920s and 1930s did a managerial class begin to appear in Britain. Until World War II, the British economy was for the most part an example of family capitalism.

In Germany, as in the United States, the existing distribution network was unable to meet all the needs of the new large-scale producers, and changes in industrial organization were correspondingly revolutionary. In the 1880s and 1890s, the scale of operations of German industrial firms was comparable to that in the United States; the German enterprises were equally fully integrated and even more highly diversified. However, almost no large firms produced and distributed consumer goods for the domestic market; instead, major industrial enterprises concentrated on technologically sophisticated producer goods for international markets. Concentration on such products had two main consequences. First, competition abroad encouraged cooperation at home in the form of formal federations or cartels. Second, because the initial cost of the equipment required to produce metals, heavy machinery, and chemicals was much greater than for foodstuffs and light mass-produced machines and because the capital markets were less highly developed in Germany than in Britain or the United States, banks played a much more significant role in financing large-scale enterprise in Germany than they did in the other two nations. Financiers thus had a greater say in the management of firms. Industrial sectors dominated by big business in Germany are therefore examples of financial capitalism.

In France, the modern firm developed later than it did in the other three nations. Existing marketing and distribution mechanisms were able to handle much of the manufacturing output, as they were in Britain. The French were even slower than the British to follow the lead of the United States in developing mass-produced consumer goods and lagged behind the Germans in making technologically complex producer goods. When French firms began to move into these industries, they were handicapped, as the German companies had been earlier, by the absence of a large central capital market. In order to obtain essential funds, French industrialists created groups of firms in which the profits and credit of one enterprise assisted in supporting others. The strongest firm in such a group took substantial stockholdings or, to use the French term, participations, in the others. The resulting system might be considered a variation of family capitalism; unlike British firms, however, which continued to be run by individual founding families, large French enterprises were apt to be managed by groups of interrelated families. Their members had often attended one of the *grandes écoles* (a group of elite government-sponsored technological institutes) and had close ties to the financial community and the government. After World War I, salaried managers with little or no financial interest in the enterprise for which they worked began to play a role in directing the large enterprises not only in France but in Britain and Germany as well. It was only after World War II, however, that family and financial capitalism gave way to managerial capitalism in the sectors dominated by large modern firms in all three countries.

The essays in this volume fall into two broad categories. The first four explore the rise of the modern business enterprise in the United States, Britain, Germany, and France. In addition to suggesting the mechanisms and causes of the shift from market coordination to managerial hierarchies, they attempt to pinpoint cultural and economic reasons for the persistence of transitional forms of organization in Europe even after they had been superseded in the United States. The final three essays focus on topics rather than regions. The first describes different countries' legal and regulatory responses to the rise of big business and the second, the implications of the history of the managerial revolution for students of economic development and industrial organization. The final essay provides an overall analysis of the reasons why managerial hierarchies replaced market mechanisms and agreements among firms as devices for coordination and the allocation of resources in advanced market economies. Together these essays present a set of new perspectives on the rise of modern large-scale business enterprise in the West.

NOTES

1. Adolf A. Berle and Gardiner C. Means, *The Modern Corporation and Private Property* (New York, 1932). See also William Baumol, *Business Behavior, Value, and Growth* (New York, 1959); Oliver E. Williamson, *The Economics of Discretionary Behavior: Managerial Objectives in a Theory of the Firm* (Englewood Cliffs, N.J., 1964); idem, *Markets and Hierarchies: Analysis and Antitrust Implications* (New York, 1975); Robin L. Marris, *The Economic Theory of Managerial Capitalism* (London, 1964); Edith T. Penrose, *The Theory of the Growth of the Firm* (Oxford, 1959); John Kenneth Galbraith, *The New Industrial State* (Boston, 1967); Richard M. Cyert and James G. March, *A Behavioral Theory of the Firm* (Englewood Cliffs, N.J., 1963).

2. See A. Singh and G. Whittington, *Growth, Profitability and Valuation* (Cambridge, 1968); Alex Jacquemin and Wistant Saez, "Compared Performances of the Largest European and Japanese Industrial Firms," *Oxford Economic Papers*, n.s. 28 (1976):271–283; Edwin Mansfield, *The Economics of Technological Change* (New York, 1968).

3. See Anthony Downs, *Inside Bureaucracy* (Boston, 1967); William H. Starbuck, "Organizational Growth and Development," in *Handbook of Organizations*, ed. James G. March (Chicago, 1964); James D. Thompson, *Organizations in Action* (New York, 1967).

4. See, for instance, Mihajlo Mesarovic, D. Macko, and Y. Takahara, *Theory of Hierarchical, Multilevel Systems* (New York, 1970).

5. See, for instance, Armen A. Alechian and Harold Demsetz, "Production, Information Costs, and Economic Organization," *American Economic Review*, 62 (1972): 777–795.

6. See Stephen A. Marglin, "What Do Bosses Do? The Origin and Functions of Hierarchy in Capitalist Production," *Review of Radical Political Economics* 6 (1974):60–112; Katherine Stone, "The Origins of Job Structures in the Steel Industry," ibid., pp. 113–173; David Noble, *America by Design: Science, Technology, and the Rise of Corporate Capitalism* (New York, 1977).

7. See Kenneth J. Arrow, *The Limits of Organization* (New York, 1974); Ronald H. Coase, "The Nature of the Firm," *Economica*, n.s. 4 (1937): 386–405; H. B. Malmgren, "Information, Expectations and the Theory of the Firm," *Quarterly Journal of Economics* 75 (1961):399–421; Williamson, *Markets and Hierarchies*.

1/The United States: Seedbed of Managerial Capitalism

Alfred D. Chandler, Jr.

AS POINTED OUT in the introduction to this volume, major sectors of technologically advanced market economies have come to be dominated by big business. The managers of modern business enterprises are responsible for coordinating the day-to-day flow of goods through the processes of production and distribution and for allocating resources essential to future production and distribution. The market continues to generate the demand for goods, and the managers make their decisions on the basis of their estimates of market demand. The visible hand of managerial direction has replaced the invisible hand of market mechanisms, however, in coordinating flows and allocating resources in major modern industries.[1] The purpose of this essay and the three that follow is to describe and attempt to explain why, when, and how this fundamental transformation in the organization of the world's leading market economies occurred. The first step toward achieving that goal is to elaborate on the nature of modern business enterprise and modern capitalism, using concepts and terms briefly defined in the introduction.

Managerial Enterprise and Managerial Capitalism

The modern business enterprise is defined by two major characteristics (see figure 1.1). First, it contains many distinct operating units, each with its own administrative offices, its own full-time salaried manager, and its own set of books and accounts that can be audited separately from those of the larger enterprise. Theoretically, each could operate as an independent

9

Figure 1.1. *The basic hierarchical structure of the modern business enterprise (each box represents an office)*

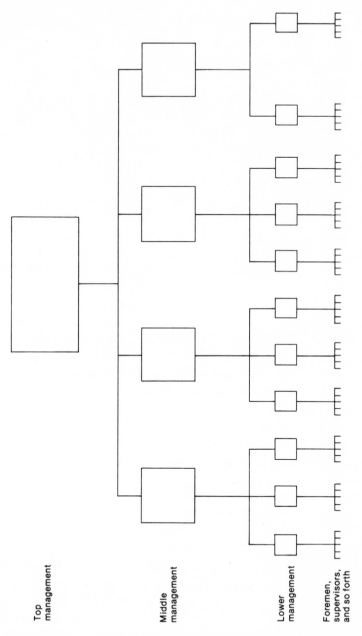

Top management

Middle management

Lower management

Foremen, supervisors, and so forth

Source: Alfred D. Chandler, Jr., *The Visible Hand* (Harvard University Press, 1977), p. 2.

business enterprise. The traditional firm was a single-unit enterprise, with an individual or a small number of owners operating a shop, store, factory, bank, or transportation line out of a single office. Normally, this type of firm undertook to fulfill only a single economic function, produced or sold a single line of products, and operated in one geographic area. Before the rise of the modern firm, the activities of these small, personally owned and managed enterprises were coordinated and monitored primarily by market and price mechanisms. The modern multiunit enterprise, in contrast, has come to operate in different locations, often carrying out a number of economic activities and producing or selling several lines of goods and services. The operation of its units and the transactions among them have been internalized within the firm. The activities of these units have come to be monitored and coordinated by the decisions of salaried managers rather than by market mechanisms.

The second salient characteristic of the modern business enterprise is therefore that it employs a hierarchy of middle- and top-salaried managers who supervise the work of the units under its control and who form an entirely new class of businessmen. As late as 1840, there were no middle managers in the United States and very few in Europe; that is, almost no salaried managers supervised the work of other managers and, in turn, reported to senior executives who were themselves salaried managers. Nearly all the top-level managers were owners, either partners or major stockholders in their enterprises.

This two-part definition of the modern business enterprise suggests the basic hypothesis about its initial appearance and continuing growth: that it began and expanded by internalizing activities and transactions previously carried out by a number of separate businesses. It emerged at the point when the businesses, or units, could be operated more profitably through a centralized managerial hierarchy than by means of decentralized market mechanisms. Administrative coordination by a managerial hierarchy gave enlarged enterprise several advantages. Routinizing the transactions among units lowered their costs, and the integration of units for production, purchasing, and distribution reduced the costs of information about markets and supplies. More important, the ability to schedule the flow of raw material and finished goods more closely and to standardize the processes involved made it possible for firms to use the resources of the individual units—their personnel, machines, and other facilities—more intensively; this ability thus cut the costs of production and distribution. (Scheduling and standardization made possible what can be termed economies of speed, a basic element in what economists normally call the economies of size or scale.) In addition, administrative coordination allowed product specifications and market services to be adjusted more rapidly to customer needs; in this way a steadier flow of goods was permitted and customer satisfaction increased. Such coordination also ensured a steadier flow of cash to the firm and therefore lowered the costs of credit. It became profitable in any economy, however, only after the development of technology and the growth of the market increased the economic activity to a speed and volume sufficient to make existing mechanisms of coordination by market forces cumbersome.

Once a managerial hierarchy had successfully increased profits by coordinating operations, it became in itself a source of power, permanence, and continued growth. The managers' basic objective was to keep their organization profitably employed; they did so by increasing the speed and volume of their activities and by internalizing more units or processes. As enterprises grew, and as the number of executives increased, managers became more specialized and more professional. They generally had much the same type of training, often attending the same group of schools. They joined the same professional societies and read the same journals. As their roles came to require more narrowly specialized expertise, they became increasingly independent of the owners of the enterprises. Salaried managers' specialized knowledge and their firms' ability to generate the funds necessary for continued expansion meant that they soon controlled the destiny of the enterprises by which they were employed.

By altering control within individual firms, the coming of the large, multiunit enterprise changed the nature of capitalism. If capitalism is defined as an economic system in which the means of production and distribution are operated by privately rather than publicly owned enterprise and in which decisions within individual enterprises are motivated by consumer demand rather than by a central plan, then varying types of capitalism can be identified by examining the relationships between those who make the decisions about the firm's operations and those who own its means of production and distribution. In traditional, personal capitalism, the owners and the decision makers were the same; owners made both the short-term decisions about current output and transactions and the longer-term decisions about investments in facilities for the future. In the large, multiunit enterprise, however, salaried middle managers, who have little or no share in its ownership, have come to be responsible for coordinating the flow of goods and supervising the operating units; owners rarely concern themselves with the work of middle management.

At the highest level, however, owners continued—often for extended periods of time—to have a say in critical policy decisions about products, services, volume of output, rate of return, and the allocation of resources. When the growth of the enterprise was financed from retained earnings—that is, when it was self-financed—the founding entrepreneurs and members of their families continued to own the controlling shares, and they or their representatives continued to be part of top-level management. When the enterprise relied largely on outside financing for its establishment and initial growth, bankers and other financiers participated in top-level management decisions. The first type of modern business enterprise can then be labeled the entrepreneurial or family firm (it was, naturally, enterpreneurial in the first generation and family-dominated thereafter); the second type can be called the financially dominated firm. An economy or sector in which entrepreneurial or family firms predominate can, furthermore, be considered an instance of family capitalism; one in which financially dominated firms are most common, an instance of financial capitalism.

Family and financial capitalism proved to be transitional stages in the evolution of the modern business enterprise and of modern capitalism. No family or financial institution was large enough to staff the managerial hierarchies required to administer modern multiunit enterprises. Because the salaried managers developed specialized knowledge and because their enterprises were able to generate the funds necessary for expansion, they ultimately took over the top-level decision making from the owners or financiers or their representatives. Unless the latter themselves became full-time professional managers, they soon participated in top-level management decisions only as members of boards of directors. At monthly or, more often, quarterly meetings, they had to make decisions on matters on which managers had been working every day, using information provided primarily by the managers. They rarely had the time, the information, or the depth of experience to propose alternatives; they could veto proposals, but they could do little else. If they disliked the managers' actions, they might hire others, but they could not manage the firm themselves. Family members, as a result, soon came to view their enterprise, as did other stockholders, from the point of view of rentiers; that is, their interest in the enterprise was no longer in its management but rather in the income derived from its profits. Firms in which representatives of the founding families or of financial interests no longer make top-level management decisions—where such decisions are made by salaried managers who own little of the companies' stock—can be labeled managerial enterprises; the economies or sectors where such firms dominated became parts of a new system of managerial capitalism. When types of capitalism are thus defined in terms of the relationships between owners and administrators of the means of production and distribution, it is clear that all advanced market economies have moved from traditional, personal capitalism toward managerial capitalism since the middle of the nineteenth century. The rapidity of the change has differed among sectors and nations, but managerial capitalism now dominates the central producing and distributing sectors of every major market economy.

The Rise of the Modern Enterprise in the United States

Before the coming of the railroad and the telegraph and the widespread availability of coal as a source of energy and heat, business activity in the United States economy was not extensive enough to create a need for multiunit enterprises or for a class of salaried managers. As long as goods were produced and moved by traditional methods and sources of energy—such as wood, wind and water, man and beast—the daily output of a production unit and the number of transactions carried out each day by a distribution unit could easily be supervised by the owners assisted by one or two managers. Using century-old business methods, traditional, small, owner-managed enterprises had little difficulty in carrying out production and distribution in the United States. Although the expansion of the United States economy in the early nineteenth century brought a rapid growth in the number of firms and spread the activities over a wide geographic area, it did not result in any increase in the size of firms. As business enterprises became more numerous, they became more specialized; most produced and distributed only a single line of goods, such as cotton, grain, hardware, or dry goods and carried out a single function, such as wholesaling, retailing, manufacturing, banking, or providing insurance. The activities of hundreds of thousands of these small businesses were coordinated almost entirely by the invisible hand of market mechanisms.

The coming of the railroad and the telegraph and the simultaneous availability of large quantities of coal quickly brought the modern enterprise to the United States—first in transportation and communications, then in distribution, and finally in production. The new technologies made possible much greater speed and volume in the production and movement of goods and necessitated the creation of managerial hierarchies to supervise, monitor, and coordinate the new processes of production and distribution. In transportation and communications, the managers of the railroad, telegraph, and steamship companies began to coordinate the movement of goods from one commercial center to another. In distribution, new mass-marketing enterprises, which relied on new means of transportation and communication, administered the flow of goods from processors or producers to retailers or ultimate consumers. In manufacturing, the new mass producers came to coordinate the flow from the extraction of raw material through production to distribution to retailers or final consumers. In sectors dominated by the new, large enterprises, the top-level managers of a few modern multiunit companies made the decisions that had previously been made by the owners of thousands of small firms.

TRANSPORTATION AND COMMUNICATIONS

The first modern business enterprises in the United States, the large railroad and telegraph companies, appeared in the 1850s. Because there were many more railroads than telegraph companies (by 1866 one company, Western Union, all but held a monopoly of telegraphic transmission), because scheduling, moving, and pricing wide varieties and large volumes of freight traffic was more complex than the transmission of messages by electricity, and finally because the railroads were much more costly to construct and operate than telegraph lines, the railroads became the nation's first big business. Unlike canals and turnpikes, railroads required centralized operating control, since trains moved at much greater speed than horse-drawn vehicles or boats. They did so on a single track, whereas roads and canals were wide enough to permit two-way traffic. The absolute necessity to centralize the scheduling of the movement of traffic meant that the railroads were the first common carriers to build and maintain their own rights-of-way. Up to that time, transportation firms had operated their carriages, wagons, or boats on the rights-of-way owned and maintained by other, often public, enterprises.

Managerial hierarchies first appeared in the nation's economy when the railroads began to operate more miles of track than could be personally managed by a single superintendent and his assistants. The basic operating unit of the new, large railroads was a geographic division that normally operated from 50 to 100 miles of track. The divisions, in turn, were divided into offices, each of which was responsible for a single function—the movement of trains, the flow of passenger and freight traffic, the maintenance of locomotives and rolling stock, or the construction and upkeep of the right-of-way. Once two or three such geographic divisions had been established—that is, after the railroad had become a multiunit enterprise—the work of the managers in charge of the functional departments within each division had to be carefully monitored and coordinated. Middle managers housed in the railroad's central office took on this responsibility; they supervised the activities of the lower-level managers in the divisions and reported to the full-time top-level managers—the general superintendent, the president, and, often, the chairman of the board of directors.

The effective operation of the larger railroad network required external cooperation among managerial hierarchies, as well as the perfection of their operation within the enterprise. In the years immediately before and after the Civil War, middle-

and top-level managers devised ways to move freight cars efficiently and without interruption over several different companies' lines. They standardized the width of track, or the gauge, equipment such as couplers and signals, and organizational procedures, such as the through bill of lading, interroad billing, and the operation of the car accountant's office (which kept track of the location of "foreign" cars carried on its road and of its own cars on other roads). This kind of technological and organizational standardization was planned and carried out by the quasi-professional association of managers. Such groups as the Society of Railroad Accounting Officers and the American Society of Railroad Superintendents helped make possible the movement of loaded cars from any part of the country to any other without a single transshipment—that is, without having to unload or reload from the cars of one line to another's. Before the coming of the railroad, freight moving from Philadelphia to Chicago had to be unloaded and reloaded as many as nine times. Once these cooperative techniques were perfected, railroad companies quickly took over, that is, internalized, most of the activities that had been undertaken by express companies, freight forwarders, and other specialized transportation enterprises, enterprises that had come into being in order to provide more certain delivery of goods to distant destinations on schedule.

Comparable cooperation among managerial hierarchies to control competition among railroads for the newly increased through traffic was, however, much less successful. To prevent what the managers considered ruinous competition and so to ensure a continuous flow of through traffic over their tracks, the railroads formed formal federations such as the Southern Railway and Steamship Association and the Eastern Trunk Line Association in the 1870s. These cartels allocated first traffic and then profits among competing roads. Even though they set up embryonic managerial hierarchies to enforce their policies, they nonetheless failed to maintain rates and to enforce traffic quotas both because the constant pressure of high fixed costs led companies to cheat on the pool by reducing rates to shippers through secret rebates and because these agreements could not be enforced as contracts in courts of law.

By the early 1880s, managers had decided, and representatives of investors on their boards had agreed, that the only way to ensure a continuous flow of traffic at profitable rates was to enlarge their enterprises by constructing new lines or buying existing ones to form giant "self-sustaining" systems; these networks provided their companies with their own tracks into the major commercial cities and raw material-producing areas in the regions in which they operated. By the mid-1890s, most of these systems had been built; thirty large railroad companies, administering lines 1,500 to 10,000 miles long, owned and operated two thirds of the railroad mileage in the United States.[2] Most areas of the country, however, were served by two or more systems. In order to obtain the massive financing they needed to build these systems, top-level managers had developed close ties with Eastern investment bankers with access to European sources of capital. These bankers increasingly replaced local and individual investors on the boards of the new systems.

The operation of these railroad systems required the creation of two or even three layers of middle management. In a company that had grown from 500 to 5,000 miles of track, several operating divisions were grouped together into geographically organized multiunit subenterprises; each was under a general manager, with his own set of functional executives. (The organization of these giant systems was strikingly similar to that of autonomous product and geographic divisions of the multidivisional industrial enterprise in the twentieth century.) The general managers reported to a corporate office made up of vice presidents with oversight of functional activities, the president, and the chairman of the board. The top-level management group concentrated on the road's strategies for growth and on allocating resources to achieve them. Because railroad building required unprecedented amounts of capital, top-level managers had to share strategic decisions with representatives of the investment banks, who provided the necessary funds.

Other transportation and communications enterprises followed the example of the railroads. Top-level managers allocated resources in consultation with financiers, and middle managers monitored the activities of operating units and coordinated flows among them. By 1900, nearly all the few United States steamship companies (largely coastal and river lines) had become parts of the major railroad systems. In the area of urban transportation, the expensive new electrical technology meant that middle managers of the one or two large companies providing this service in the leading cities supervised day-to-day operations, while top-level managers shared decisions about allocating funds with representatives of municipal authorities, as well as with investors. The new utility companies that provided the towns and cities with electricity were operated in much the same manner. Communications differed from transportation only in that monopoly rather than oligopoly was the norm. Both Western Union and American Telephone and Telegraph became dominant because their managers obtained control of the complex scheduling required to handle high-volume, long-distance, or through traffic.

By the beginning of the twentieth century, then, the nation's transportation and communications were operated by large, modern, multiunit enterprises administered by salaried professional managers. Although the financiers on their boards took no part in the middle managers' tasks of coordinating and monitoring the operations of individual units, they participated with top-level managers in allocating resources. These sectors thus became the best-known examples of financial capitalism in the United States. Even so, the financiers had little more than veto power, except during times of system building, since they rarely had the time, information, or experience to propose alternatives of allocating resources.

DISTRIBUTION

As the modern transportation and communications infrastructure began to take form, a revolution occurred in commerce. In the 1840s, traditional merchants marketed and distributed goods in much the same fashion as their counterparts had done for the previous five hundred years. In the United States, merchants were more specialized and were more likely to trade on a commission basis than those of fourteenth-century Florence or Venice, but they used the same kind of partnerships, the same kinds of contracts, and the same double-entry methods of bookkeeping. Yet barely a generation after the railroad and telegraph networks began to spread across the land, all the basic forms of modern marketing had appeared. In the 1850s, commodity dealers who bought directly from farmers and sold directly to processors quickly replaced factors and other types of commission merchants in marketing agricultural crops. The new dealers relied on the telegraph to transact business and on the railroads to deliver on a precise schedule. In the same decade, full-line, full-service wholesalers who bought directly from manufacturers and sold directly to retailers replaced commission merchants in marketing and distributing manufactured consumer goods. By the 1880s, the wholesalers were already beginning to give way, in their turn, to the new mass retailers—the department stores that sold directly to the consumer in the growing urban centers, the mail-order houses that sold to rural areas, and the first chain stores, which concentrated on retail trade in towns and smaller cities.

Each of these new types of distributors were similarly organized. Each had extensive buying and selling organizations. Commodity dealers had buyers in the farming regions and at commodity exchanges; wholesalers and mass retailers set up purchasing offices in the commercial and manufacturing centers of the United States and Europe. Each had a buying office for each major product line the enterprise handled. The buyers set price, quantity, and physical specifications (size, weight, and quality) of goods to be purchased; they also scheduled the shipments to the company's sales organizations, often working with the latter in writing advertising copy and setting up displays. In all cases, profit came from volume, rather than mark-up. The criterion for evaluating the degree of success achieved through administrative coordination was "stock-turn," that is, how many times stock turned over within a specified period of time. The greater the stock-turn, the more intensive the use of existing facilities and personnel and, therefore, the lower the unit cost of distribution.

Thus the visible hand of management came to coordinate the flow of goods from producers to retailers or consumers in a more efficient and profitable manner than had been achieved by market mechanisms. The nature of the necessary scheduling set limits to effective coordination and, therefore, to the extent of vertical integration of different economic functions. Distributing firms had little to gain by moving into manufacturing. Coordinating flows into and through the processes of production required very different types of coordinating procedures and skills, and distributors undertook to manufacture only when goods could not otherwise be obtained at the quality, quantity, and price desired. Once a stable source was assured, they nearly always sold out their interest in the manufacturing plant, or retained only a passive concern with that facility. In contrast, mass retailers had little difficulty in internalizing wholesaling transactions and coordinating flows directly from the manufacturer to the consumer. They quickly began to take over business from the wholesalers, whose share of the total distribution of goods declined from the 1880s on. Mass retailers grew, therefore, not by moving into manufacturing but by adding new lines of products for which they might use their existing purchasing organization and their coordinating skills.

The success of this kind of administrative coordination was dramatic. Wholesalers and the small retailers who purchased from them turned increasingly to politics in an attempt to obtain state and federal regulation to protect themselves from the mass retailers. Even though the latter's prices were low enough to generate protest, the profits they reaped from administrative coordination quickly placed their families—the Wanamakers, the Fields, the Filenes, the Kresges, the Strauses of Macy's, the Rosenwalds of Sears, Roebuck, the Hartfords of A&P, and others— among the wealthiest in the land. Because the cash flow generated by this kind of high volume, administratively coordinated distribution was so large and the necessary capital investment so small, these enterprises continued to be owned and controlled by their founders and their families, and family members normally continued to have a major say in top-level management decisions. The distribution sector of the United States economy therefore remained a bastion of family capitalism longer than other sectors.

PRODUCTION

The revolution in production was longer in coming than that in distribution primarily because far more technological development was required. The innovations in distribution were almost wholly organizational—responses to the opportunities offered by fundamental technological changes in transportation and communications. In production, the railroads and the telegraph encouraged technological innovations that increased output by making it possible for materials to pass through manufacturing plants more rapidly and with greater regularity, a process that was helped further by the new availability of coal as a source of power. Equally important, these new developments permitted several processes of production to be incorporated into a single factory or works. ("Works" can be defined as several factories at a single site.)

Three basic mass-production techniques—large-batch and continuous-process production methods and those involving the making of machinery by fabricating and assembling standardized interchangeable parts—were quickly perfected. Large-batch and continuous-process methods first appeared in the refining and distilling industries. Because the materials were liquid and semi-liquid and the processes were chemical, careful plant design and more intensive use of energy permitted a sharp increase in the volume of material processed and the speed with which it could pass through the refineries—that is, the "throughput" was increased. Within a decade of the discovery of oil at Titusville, Pennsylvania, in 1859, for example, petroleum was refined without ever being touched by human hands; labor was needed only for packing the product into barrels. At the same time, the more intensive use of coal-fired, superheated steam and high-pressure cracking processes further increased the yield for each unit of capital and labor and thus decreased the unit cost of production. Comparable developments took place in processing sugar, whiskey, beer, and cotton and linseed oils and in the production of acids, bleaches, and paints. Somewhat later, in the late 1870s and early 1880s, continuous-process machinery was developed for turning agricultural products into cigarettes, flour, breakfast cereals, and canned goods and for mass-producing matches, soap, and photographic film.

Mass production came somewhat more slowly in the metal-making and metalworking industries. Here both the technology and the organization of production were more complex. The first spectacular breakthroughs in metal making came in iron and steel production during the late 1860s and early 1870s, when energy was used more intensively, plant design was improved, and new machinery was developed in works that integrated at a single site the basic processes of production—the blast furnaces that produced pig iron, the Bessemer and open-hearth convertors that made steel in massive batches, and the rolling and finishing mills that produced rails, beams, and other final products. In the metalworking enterprises, where mass production involved the assembly of interchangeable parts, managers paid even closer attention to improving machinery and plant design and, above all, to the organization of the work force in order to ensure an even, steady flow of materials through the many fabricating and assembling processes in each manufacturing establishment. It was no accident, therefore, that the modern machine-tool industry was developed primarily for the metalworking industries and that modern "scientific" or systematic factory management was first devised there. New types of machines and new types of organization were necessary if metalworking factories were to produce goods in volume.

The new methods of mass production, however, did not in themselves lead to the creation of large, multiunit business enterprises. Monitoring and coordinating the processes internalized within a single establishment required the services of only a small number of salaried managers. The new mass producers became modern enterprises only when they integrated forward by creating their own extensive organizations for sales and distribution. They rarely adopted this strategy of growth, furthermore, unless existing marketers—specialized manufacturers' agents, as well as the new mass marketers—were unable to sell and distribute their output as quickly as it could be produced by the new techniques.

THE INTEGRATED INDUSTRIAL ENTERPRISE

In the 1880s, as the basic transportation and communications infrastructure neared completion and as procedures for its operation were perfected, enterprises that integrated mass production with mass distribution appeared quite suddenly in many different industries. They clustered in four types of industries with similar characteristics: mass producers of low-priced, semiperishable, packaged products, which had adopted large-batch and continuous-process technology; processors of perishable products for national markets; manufacturers of new mass-produced machines that required specialized marketing services if they were to be sold in volume (the products of these three groups of manufacturers sold in mass consumer markets); and the makers of high-volume producer goods that were technologically complex but standardized.

During the 1880s, pioneering enterprises—including American Tobacco in producing cigarettes; Diamond Match in matches; Washburn and Pillsbury in flour; Quaker Oats in breakfast cereals; Heinz, Campbell Soup, Borden's Milk, and Libby, McNeil and Libby in canned goods; Procter & Gamble in soap; and Eastman Kodak in photographic film—integrated mass production with mass distribution in the first set of industries. The managers of these enterprises continued to use the wholesaler to handle the physical distribution of goods, but they took over branding, advertising, and scheduling the flow of goods from the factories to the new mass markets.

In the same decade, the meat packers, including Armour, Swift, Morris, Hammond, Cudahy, and Swartschild and Sulzberger, and the brewers, including Pabst, Miller, Schlitz, and Anheuser-Busch, began to build national, and often international, networks of branch houses with refrigerated warehouses and distribution facilities, as well as fleets of temperature-controlled railroad cars and ships. Similar networks were formed in the 1890s by the precursors of United Fruit. These firms often bypassed the wholesaler completely, since their distribution services and facilities had to be so closely coordinated with production. At the same time, they, like the producers of semiperishable products, created extensive purchasing organizations to ensure a continuous flow of raw materials into their mass-producing facilities.

The third group, the makers of newly invented machinery produced by assembling interchangeable parts, also bypassed the wholesalers. To sell as many of their relatively complex and costly products as they could produce, they had to provide demonstrations, continuing service and repair on machines sold, and credit to consumers. Moreover, the weekly delivery of thousands of machines on schedule required the same kind of careful coordination as ensuring a high-volume flow through the factory. Nearly all these firms quickly built worldwide marketing organizations. The pioneers were the makers of sewing machines; Singer, the most successful, was the innovator in direct canvassing of customers, that is, in retailing as well as in wholesaling. Others, particularly the makers of agricultural implements, such as McCormick Harvester, Deering Harvester, John Deere, and J. I. Case, preferred the less expensive alternative of using franchise dealers supported by a strong, well-organized wholesale organization that permitted dealers to market aggressively and provide necessary services. The manufacturers of new business machines, Fairbanks Scales, Remington Typewriter, National Cash Register, A. B. Dick Mimeograph, Burroughs Adding Machine, and Computer-Tabulator-Recorder, used one or the other of these types of marketing organization but eventually came to rely on the franchise dealer. Nearly all these enterprises either built or perfected their sales departments in the 1880s.

During the same decade, makers of standardized heavy machinery created comparable worldwide organizations, which they normally staffed with college-trained engineers because of the technological complexity of their products and the uses to which they were put. These firms included the forerunners of General Electric and Allis Chalmers, as well as Westinghouse Electric, Westinghouse Air Brake, Western Electric, Otis Elevator, Worthington Pump, Babcock & Wilcox, and Morgenthaler Linotype. The fast-moving technology of the machinery makers, particularly that of the manufacturers of electrical equipment, required close coordination among salesmen, product designers, and manufacturing managers. Later, this kind of coordination would be significant in the growth of chemical companies.

For the new industrial firms that integrated high-volume production with national and international distribution, then, administrative coordination went beyond the careful scheduling and standardization that had characterized it in the railroad, telegraph, and mass-marketing enterprises and beyond exploiting the economies of speed. In the production of consumer goods, it meant the provision of specialized services and facilities; in the manufacture of technologically complex producer goods, it also meant the constant adjustment of the product to customers' needs. Existing wholesalers and manufacturers' agents rarely had the technological know-how or the financial resources to provide such services and facilities.

Thus the limits to effective administrative coordination and therefore to the growth of the industrial enterprise by means of vertical integration—that is, by the incorporation of successive processes of production and distribution—were directly related to scheduling and marketing needs. Mass producers, particularly processors of agricultural products, integrated backward, doing their own purchasing in order to control the flow of vast quantities of goods into their factories. Very few, however, integrated forward beyond wholesaling into retailing. In most cases they did so only when their managers believed that their wholesaling and distribution network could not ensure the effective scheduling of flows, the provision of services, the maintenance and expansion of sales volume, and the rapid remittance of payments to the central office by the franchised dealers or other retailers. Internalization of differing economic activities within a single firm proved profitable only when it permitted a more intensive use of personnel and facilities by maintaining a high-volume flow of goods through the processes of production and distribution.

Building the purchasing and marketing organizations that were essential to mass-producing and distributing many goods, in turn, created powerful barriers to entry by other firms into markets. New competitors had to set up comparable buying and wholesaling networks before they could achieve the volume necessary for competitive unit costs. As a result, industries where administrative coordination lowered costs and provided essential services quickly came to be dominated by a few large, integrated firms that competed with one another in an oligopolistic manner, that is, in a market they dominated but did not individually control.

GROWTH THROUGH MERGERS

In the 1880s, when many firms grew large by building extensive marketing and purchasing networks, a few others followed another route to size—that of merger. In this case a number of small, single-unit manufacturing enterprises managed by their owners personally merged into a single entity, legally defined as either a trust or a holding company, and then integrated forward and backward. Nearly all such mergers grew out of loose cartels established by manufacturers in the depression of the 1870s to control price and production in response to falling prices and increasing output. Both legal devices—the trust and the holding company—permitted a central board to acquire direct control of a number of operating subsidiaries. The merger was normally legally consummated by exchanging the stock of the operating companies coming into the merger for trust certificates or shares of the holding company.

The first to turn from coordination by agreement among firms to the more efficient coordination by a managerial hierarchy were the early mass producers in the refining and distilling industries. After legally consolidating, then centralizing the administration of their production facilities under the control of salaried managers housed at large main offices, usually in New York City, the creators of the Standard Oil, cottonseed-oil, linseed-oil, and lead trusts, and later the whiskey and sugar trusts, integrated forward into marketing and backward into purchasing and often into the control of raw materials. As they quickly learned, this route to growth reduced costs, increased profits, and raised barriers to entry far more effectively than their previous strategy of horizontal combination.

In the 1890s, mergers became increasingly popular. As was the case with the railroads, the number of firms involved and the problem of legally enforcing agreements among them made cartels difficult to maintain. Then the Sherman Antitrust Act was passed in 1890 and New Jersey's general-incorporation law in 1889. The first, a federal law, declared illegal any trust association or other combination in restraint of trade; the second permitted a company formed to hold stock in another to receive a charter simply by filing a form and paying a small fee. Before the New Jersey law was passed, such holding companies could be created only by a special act of the state legislature. In a series of decisions, the United States Supreme Court declared that associations setting prices and production schedules violated the federal law; it implied, however, that holding companies, such as those incorporated in New Jersey, did not. These decisions encouraged the few existing trusts and the many cartels operating through trade associations to become holding companies. Economic reasons were even more persuasive in encouraging mergers, however, since mergers permitted many manufacturers to follow the profitable example of the pioneering integrated enterprises of the 1880s. By the end of the decade, mergers had become a positive mania; this first, most significant merger movement in the United States persisted until 1903, when the market for new securities became saturated.

Although mergers occurred in every industry, few continued

to prosper unless they met two conditions. A merger was rarely successful unless it replaced a strategy of horizontal combination with one of vertical integration and unless it created a managerial hierarchy to coordinate, monitor, and allocate resources through its operating units. In carrying out these moves, the directors of the holding company set up a staff of mangers in a central office to administer the factories and other producing units of the company's subsidiaries. Then they integrated forward and backward by building marketing and purchasing networks staffed by salaried managers; and then they increased the number of top-level managers responsible for administering the enterprise as a whole. Even when a merged enterprise followed this course, it rarely continued to dominate its industry unless the technology of that industry permitted mass production and unless its products were sold in mass national and international markets. In those cases, the first firms to integrate usually continued to dominate, and these industries became and remained highly concentrated—that is they were controlled by a few large firms.

By 1917, the long-term effects of the merger movement of 1898–1903 had become clear; mergers that were going to fail had failed, and nearly all those that had survived would continue to prosper. A detailed review of the largest enterprises in all areas of production in the United States in 1917 shows that 278 had assets of $20 million or more.[3] Thirty of these were in mining, 7 in crude-oil production, 5 in agriculture, and none in construction, but 236 were in manufacturing, of which 171, or 72.5 percent, were clustered in six industrial categories according to the United States Bureau of the Census's Standard Industrial Classification.[4] Thirty-nine of these enterprises were in primary metals, 34 in food and kindred products, 28 in transportation equipment, 24 in nonelectrical machinery, 24 in petroleum and related industries, and 21 in chemicals. Only 23, or 9.7 percent, were scattered in seven other industrial groups— textiles, lumber and wood products, leather, printing and publishing, apparel, photographic and optical goods and scientific instruments, and furniture and fixtures. Nearly all the remaining 42 firms were in four-digit industries within the larger two-digit industrial categories of tobacco; rubber; paper; stone, glass, and clay; fabricated metals; electrical machinery; and miscellaneous industries that used modern mass-production technology to produce goods for mass markets.

Thus by 1917 the large enterprises were clustered in the same industries in which they had first appeared in the 1880s and 1890s and in which the turn-of-the-century mergers had been most successful. They had spread to such industries as chemicals and automobiles, where products made by means of capital-intensive, energy-consuming, continuous- or large-batch production technology went to a large number of customers and where marketing and distribution benefited from careful scheduling; from specialized facilities for storage and shipping; from such marketing services as demonstration, installation, after-sales service and repair, and consumer credit; and from adjusting product design to customers' needs. By 1917, over 86 percent of the 278 enterprises with assets of $20 million or more had integrated production with distribution.

As this review of the largest enterprises description indicates, the modern corporation evolved more slowly and failed to flourish in industries where the processes of production used labor-intensive methods that required little heat, power, or complex machinery. It was also slow to appear where existing middlemen were successful in distributing and selling the product. In the older, more traditional industries that produced and processed cloth, wood, and leather, in printing and publishing, and in industries making specialized, nonstandardized instruments or machinery, volume was rarely high enough or marketing requirements complex enough to encourage manufacturers to integrate production with distribution. The lesson here is an important one. In the United States, manufacturers internalized distribution functions only when internalization made possible services and scheduling that reduced manufacturers' unit costs. Only in those cases did vertical integration create large firms and concentrated industries. In other industries, where additional services and scheduling were unnecessary to maintain volume, mass marketers continued to distribute and sell consumer goods; manufacturers' agents, usually selling on commission, arranged for the distribution of goods to producers. In the former case, the mass retailers increasingly scheduled the flow of materials from the supplier to the producer as well as from the producer to the final customer.

Expanding the Managerial Enterprise

The relationship between ownership and control in the large, integrated mass-production firms, and therefore in their top-level management depended on the route by which the enterprise had expanded. On the one hand, those that became multiple-unit enterprises by first creating an extensive marketing and purchasing organization almost always built and enlarged their facilities with capital from retained earnings derived from high-volume throughput and stock-turn. The ownership of the voting stock remained in the hands of founders and their families, and family members continued to share in top-level decision making. Industrial enterprises that first grew large through mergers, on the other hand, quickly came to be dominated by managers. The process of merger itself scattered stock holdings; its effect was more obvious if the newly consolidated enterprise went to the capital markets a raise funds to rationalize its constituent companies' facilities. Often rationalization meant rebuilding a large part of the production and distribution facilities of an entire industry; in carrying it out, United States industrialists in need of financing turned for the first time, at least on an extensive scale, to the large and sophisticated capital markets, particularly those in New York, which had been created to finance the railroad systems. In a few cases, financiers dominated the boards after the merger; in most cases, however, two or three experienced manufacturers, advised by one or two financiers, became the core of the new top-level management. Although they were large stockholders, these managers rarely enjoyed a degree of control comparable to that of the founders of entrepreneurial enterprises. Soon, too, they were hiring salaried managers who owned no stock in the enterprise to head the firm's functional departments and central staff. Not surprisingly, the techniques of modern top-level industrial management were devised in the United States by the salaried managers in the central offices of these consolidated enterprises. The techniques of middle management, on the other hand, originated in the offices of the entrepreneurial firms that integrated forward and backward in the 1880s.

In the years following World War I, the great majority of the industrial enterprises founded before 1917 came to be controlled by managers, partly because of the passage of time. Even in entrepreneurial firms, the members of the founding families continued to have a decisive impact on top-level management decisions only if they had extensive managerial training and experience. Since they already received large incomes, only a few wished to devote the time and energy needed to mount the managerial ladder. During the same period, financially dominated communications and utility companies and, to a lesser extent, transportation enterprises increasingly generated their own funds, so financiers played a declining role in top-level decision making. Salaried managers from within the company soon replaced outside financiers on the boards of directors; by the 1930s, for example, American Telephone and Telegraph was already being described as the archetype of the managerial enterprise. In the few consolidated industrial firms where the boards were dominated by investment bankers who had financed the mergers, such as General Electric and United States Steel, the same thing occurred.

A further reason for the increasing power of managers was the continued growth of enterprises. Salaried managers planned and carried out the strategy of growth, which, in turn, increased the number of executives at all managerial levels within the enterprise. Most firms continued to grow by exploiting the increased profitability of administrative coordination. Mass marketers expanded by adding new lines or new outlets that enabled them to use their central buying organizations more intensively. Because new outlets were the most effective way to extend the range of administrative coordination, the chain store became the fastest-growing type of modern marketing enterprise after 1900. In addition, other types of mass retailers began to build chains. In the 1920s, the mail-order houses organized national chains of retail stores; department stores then began, though more slowly, to open outlets in the suburbs. As had been the case with the first mass marketers, these distributing enterprises only went into manufacturing when they could not find adequate sources of goods. Rarely did as much as 10 percent of their total profits come from their manufacturing facilities. Specialized coordinating skills and procedures continued to determine the paths and limit the growth of marketing enterprises.

The mass producers who had integrated forward into wholesaling and, in the case of producer goods, to making direct sales to other business enterprises and who had integrated backward into purchasing and often into obtaining and processing raw and semifinished materials, developed a wider range of business skills and thus a greater potential for growth. In order to exploit their facilities for distribution even more fully, they produced a "full line" of goods aimed at their basic markets; to get more out of their production facilities, they concentrated on increasing uses for the by-products of their manufacturing processes. Often, expansion in marketing led them to develop new processing or purchasing organizations. When meat packers began to sell eggs, milk, cheese, and other refrigerated products, for instance, they had to create an extensive buying staff to obtain these goods; after expanding their output to include fertilizers, glue, and soap, they had to set up new market organizations to sell these by-products, which could not be distributed through their primary marketing network.

After World War I, the large, integrated enterprises adopted an explicit strategy of diversifying beyond a full line into new products for new markets; they searched for products that made use of their technological, marketing, and managerial techniques and skills rather than those that used only existing purchasing, production, and marketing facilities. The strategy of diversification quickly caused administrative difficulties, however. Managerial hierarchies that had been created to coordinate, monitor, and allocate resources for one line of products had great difficulty in administering the processing of several sets of products for new and different markets. Middle managers were unable to handle the very different coordinating requirements of the several lines. Top managers were overwhelmed by the need to supervise and to allocate resources to many businesses that often varied greatly. The response was the invention of the multidivisional structure (see figure 1.2). In this type of organization the general managers of the several autonomous operating divisions become responsible for coordinating the flow of goods and supervising the operating units that produced and distributed one major product line to one major market; a general office and top-level executives with no operating responsibilities, assisted by a large general staff, concentrated on allocating resources to the various product divisions.

Figure 1.2. The multidivisional structure: manufacturing

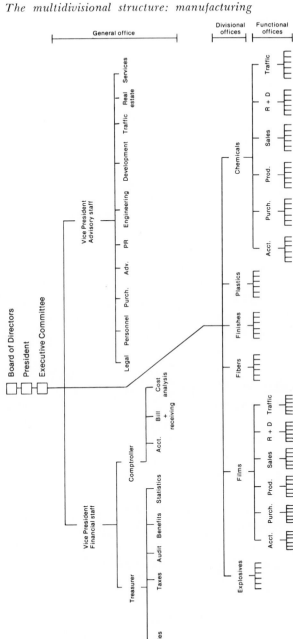

Source: Alfred D. Chandler, Jr., *The Visible Hand* (Harvard University Press, 1977), p. 458.

In the United States, the growth of these diversified divisionalized, managerial enterprises was largely self-financed, with new facilities being paid for from retained earnings. The executives who carried out this expansion relied to some extent on the New York and other United States capital markets, which remained as large and as sophisticated as any in the world, but they did so primarily to supplement retained earnings. They drew on commercial banks for working capital and on security markets for long-term funds. For the latter, they preferred to issue shares of stock rather than incur long-term debt by issuing bonds. By spreading out stock ownership even further, managers weakened outside control over their enterprises. Nevertheless, the representatives of family or other financial interests on the board rarely opposed the moves made by managers, since the carefully planned, ongoing growth of the firm provided the most prudent way to increase the value of their original investment.

As the integrated industrial enterprises grew larger and became both numerous and more diversified in their activities, their salaried managers became increasingly professional in training and outlook. Professionalization began, in fact, as soon as a strong demand appeared for managers to oversee production, marketing, financial, and other specialized activities. Shortly after the turn-of-the-century merger movement, some of the nation's most prestigious universities–among them Harvard, Dartmouth, and the universities of Chicago, Pennsylvania, and California—set up schools or courses of business administration to train managers. During the first two decades of the twentieth century, national professional associations of accountants, auditors, production engineers, marketing managers, and general managers were established; professional journals appeared to supplement their proceedings. The appurtenances of professionalism developed in industry in much the same way as they had evolved a generation earlier in railroading—to provide channels of communication through which managers could discuss mutual problems. By attending the same meetings, reading the same journals, and undergoing the same type of training, these managers came to see themselves as having a common outlook as well as common interests and concerns.

As the century moved on, the large managerial enterprises became more common and their managers more influential.

By 1947, the largest industrial enterprises, measured by assets, all of which were integrated and many diversified, accounted for 30 percent of the value added in manufacturing and 47.2 percent of all corporate manufacturing assets.[5] By 1963, when most of the firms were diversified as well as integrated, they were responsible for 41 percent of the value added and 53.6 percent of assets. By 1968, their share of assets had risen to 60.9 percent. By that time, they had become almost as powerful abroad as at home. The 200 largest industrial firms accounted for well over half the direct United States investment in Europe; their share rose from $1.9 billion to $24.5 billion between 1950 and 1970.[6] Thus in the central sectors of the United States economy, managerial enterprise had become the dominant business institution and managerial capitalism had triumphed.

THE RISE OF THE MANAGERIAL ENTERPRISE IN EUROPE

A comparable transformation has taken place in other advanced market economies, but more slowly and more recently. The modern multiunit industrial enterprise first appeared in Europe about the same time—in the late nineteenth century— as it did in the United States; equally important, it was clustered in only a few industries. With the exception of textiles in Great Britain, these were capital-intensive, energy-absorbing industries with an increasing need for professional managers. The manufacturers in these industries, however, made less extensive use of mass-production techniques, particularly the manufacture of machinery through assembling interchangeable parts, than those in the United States. Because coordination of the flow of goods was less complex, middle management was leaner than in United States firms. Even more important, owners continued to manage enterprises at the highest level. In Europe, entrepreneurs, their families, and representatives of banks and other large investors continued to make critical policy decisions about coordination of production and allocation of resources. As a result, the managerial class remained much smaller than in the United States and fewer signs of professionalism, such as schools, associations, and journals, appeared. Because the managerial enterprise and the class that managed it first flourished there, the United States experience often provided models and precedents for their evolution in other parts of the world.

Even the briefest look at the development of modern business enterprise in Europe, however, suggests a history quite different from that of the United States. In continental Europe, the central government played a much larger role in designing, building, and operating the transportation and communications infrastructure; even in laissez-faire Britain, the post office came to operate the telephone and telegraph. As a result, administrative techniques and personnel may have been transferred directly to business from government bureaucracies in a way that could not have been possible in the United States, where no large government offices existed before the beginning of the twentieth century. Like their counterparts in the United States, the Europeans created department stores and chains for mass distribution in urban markets, but more direct channels to rural and small-town markets, the full-line, full-service wholesalers and then the mail-order houses, came more slowly. Intricate and elongated networks of middlemen seem to have remained in operation longer in Europe than they did in the United States. The most important difference, however, was that mass production was less often integrated with mass distribution in Europe. The most dynamic form of modern enterprise, the integrated industrial firm, therefore had less chance to grow, to diversify, and to extend its operations to other countries. Such enterprises did appear, but those that developed in Europe were fewer in number and usually smaller than their counterparts in the United States.

One possible reason why the United States turned out to be the seedbed of managerial capitalism was the size and nature of its domestic market. In the second half of the nineteenth century, that market was the largest and, more important, the fastest-growing in the world. In 1880, national income and population were one and a half times the size of those of Great Britain; they were twice as large by 1900 and three times as large by 1920. As Simon Kuznets's data indicate, the rate of growth of the population and national product was consistently much higher in the United States than in other technologically advanced nations—France, Germany, and Great Britain—during the years between the Civil War and World War I.[7]

In Europe, mass markets developed more slowly. The relative oversupply of labor and the resulting low wages reduced potential consumer demand; income distribution may have been more skewed than in the United States; class and regional tastes were more strongly differentiated. For these reasons, the first large integrated enterprises in Europe were concentrated in primary metals, shipbuilding, heavy machinery, and chemicals, rather than in food, petroleum, and light standardized machinery, as in the United States. An important exception was the large, integrated food and brewing enterprises in Great Britain. Otherwise, most large British companies made goods for producers rather than for consumers. Even the dominant British textile firms produced thread or cloth to be processed, rather than finished goods. The products of the first large enterprises in Europe were therefore mainly nonstandardized or semifinished goods that went to a relatively small number of industrial firms; in the United States, in contrast, standardized finished products went directly from producers to millions of homes, offices, and farms. In addition, European firms provided most of the materials needed for building the transportation systems and establishing the basic industries in nations that were just beginning to industrialize; they also equipped the growing armies and navies of the rest of the world.

The smaller, slower-growing consumer markets in Europe reduced both manufacturers' interest in adopting new mass-production techniques and their incentives to build large marketing and purchasing organizations. In Great Britain and France, producers of consumer goods continued to rely on middlemen to handle their more traditional wares, such as food, apparel, and appliances for home use—products that were, in turn, produced in a traditional craft fashion. Where large, multiunit enterprises did appear, they remained small enough to be managed at the top level by a small number of owners. As a result, family capitalism continued to flourish. In Germany, where the integration of production with distribution was more common, smaller markets and cash flows reduced the opportunity to rely on internal financing and thereby increased the dependence on the large banks for outside financing. Managers continued to make top-level decisions in consultation with financiers, and financial capitalism thus continued to hold sway.

Cultural and social factors, particularly as expressed through legal differences, also appear to have played a role in delaying the coming of the large managerial enterprise and, with it, managerial capitalism. In the United States, individualistic values and the fear of concentrated economic power that might curtail equality of economic opportunity were reflected in the passage of the Interstate Commerce Act of 1887, which regulated the railroads, and the Sherman Antitrust Act three years later, which outlawed trusts and cartels. Ironically, this legislation hastened the growth of the large, centrally administered enterprises. Because it was the only nation that did not permit agreements among railroads to maintain rates by assigning traffic and profits, the railroad companies in the United States built their enormous self-sustaining systems of transportation, most of which were larger than any privately owned European railroad company. In Europe, family firms joined federations, which took the legal form of holding companies in Great Britain and cartels in Germany and France, in order to be sure of continuing profits for their small, single-function enterprises. Only a few of these firms employed middle or top-level managers. Instead, owners or their representatives made decisions about price, output, and coordination at weekly or monthly conferences. Even in the most sophisticated cartels and holding companies—those with staffs of salaried managers to handle day-to-day administration—basic policies were determined by vote of the constituent companies' representatives on a central board. In the United States, such federations were illegal. The Sherman Antitrust Act itself and the courts' interpretations of the law exerted powerful pressure, of a sort that did not exist elsewhere, to force family firms to consolidate their operations into a single, centralized enterprise administered by a hierarchy of salaried managers.

Class distinctions in Europe may also have made a difference in the way managerial capitalism evolved. Families identified themselves more closely with the firm that provided them with the income to maintain their status than did families in the United States. Even in large enterprises that integrated production with distribution and that took on middle managers to coordinate the flow of goods, family members continued to dominate top-level management. Often they chose not to expand the enterprise if it meant losing personal control; they continued to prefer negotiating within cartels to creating or expanding managerial hierarchies.

Since World War II, restraints on the growth of the firm have diminished, and the spread of managerial enterprise has accelerated in Western Europe. Greatly increased demand for goods during and after the war encouraged the adoption of new mass-production technology. Mass markets grew as national output rose rapidly, as income was distributed more equitably, and, above all, as full employment brought higher wages. The establishment of the European Economic Community further enlarged these markets. Laws passed in the 1950s and 1960s against monopolies and restrictive business practices discouraged the continuance of holding companies and cartels of family firms. At the same time, large enterprises with salaried middle managers have grown in size and increased in numbers; they have developed mainly in the same industries as in the United States—those in which administrative coordination is the most profitable. These firms have adopted administrative structures and procedures similar to those used by large United States firms. With the spread of the modern managerial business enterprise in Europe, all the paraphernalia of professional management have appeared—associations, journals, and training programs.

These comparisons of the development of modern multiunit enterprises at home and abroad are tentative and introductory. Large amounts of data are still to be collected and analyzed before a clear picture can emerge of growth patterns of the European enterprise, their procedures for internal organization, and the actual operation of the federations of firms in the form of cartels and holding companies. Existing information, however, does indicate that managerial enterprise, and, with it, managerial capitalism, is becoming the dominant form of organization and the dominant system of production and distribution in the central sectors of modern, technologically advanced economies. Clear differences nevertheless remain in the ways in which the flow of goods through the economy are coordinated and resources allocated for future production and distribution. Only by comparing the evolution of large-scale, multiunit enterprises in different economies can organizational imperatives be identified and the impact of the cultural attitudes and values, ideologies, political systems, and social structures that affect these imperatives be understood.

NOTES

1. Many of the statements in this brief chapter should be qualified. For a more complete discussion of broad generalizations and for the documentation that supports them, see Alfred D. Chandler, Jr., *The Visible Hand: The Managerial Revolution in American Business* (Cambridge, Mass., 1977).

2. Listed in Chandler, *Visible Hand,* table 3.

3. These firms—with their assets, extent of integration, and organizational structure—are listed by United States Bureau of the Census Standard Industrial Classification categories in ibid., appendix 1; see also pp. 346–348.

4. The United States Bureau of the Census classifies industries by a digit system. The broadest category, a "major group," is designated by two digits; as industries become specialized, digits are added. Thus food and kindred products is labeled 20; sugar and confectionary, 206; chocolate and cocoa products, 2063; and chocolate candy, 20634. The industries noted here are the twenty two-digit industrial groups listed by the bureau.

5. U.S. Federal Trade Commission, *Economic Report on Corporate Mergers* (Washington, D.C., 1969), p. 176.

6. Mira Wilkens, *The Maturing of Multinational Enterprise* (Cambridge, Mass., 1974), p. 330.

7. Simon Kuznets, *Economic Growth of Nations* (Cambridge, Mass., 1971), pp. 45–47.

2/ Visible and Invisible Hands in Great Britain

Leslie Hannah

THE DIVORCE of ownership and control in managerial capitalism and the operation of the "visible hand" of the integrated modern corporate enterprise are such ubiquitous phenomena that they seem almost to be part of the natural order of things. Thus, describing their evolution poses a special challenge to historians. Convergence theories, which have held the field in both popular and scholarly analyses until recently, portray the modern corporation as monolithic and universal, without variations among national economies. European economic historians have most often devoted their attention to the similarities between large corporations in Europe and those in the United States; they have failed either to analyze differences or to develop independent theories of historical evolution based on the kind of detailed and broad-gauged national case study Alfred D. Chandler, Jr., has undertaken for the United States.[1] This chapter represents an attempt to sketch the development of managerial capitalism in Great Britain and to test Chandler's theories by an examination of the contrasts between the British and United States economies.

THE ADVENT OF THE MODERN CORPORATION IN BRITAIN

Although the multidivisional organization that characterizes the modern corporation was relatively late in coming to European business, other statistical indicators suggest that many of its characteristics became dominant in British economic life no later than 1930 and continued to expand in importance thereafter.[2] Thus a strong case can be made, I believe, for dating European—or, at least, British—emulation of United States corporate patterns not from the years after World War II, where Chandler has placed it, but from an earlier period. The proportion of manufacturing value added accounted for by the 100 largest firms, which had reached approximately 22 percent in the United States by 1909, attained that level in Britain by the mid-1920s; this index of industrial concentration remained at about the same level in the two countries until about 1955; it rose in the late 1920s, fell discernibly in the 1930s and early 1940s, then rose again in the late 1940s and 1950s. Since that time, the 100 largest firms' proportion of value added has risen much less rapidly in the United States, while industrial concentration in Great Britain has grown to an appreciably higher level; in the early 1970s, the share of the top 100 stood at 43 percent in Britain, surpassing their 33 percent share in the United States.[3] These measures reflect, although only roughly, the combined effect of increases in the vertical integration of operations within individual firms—that is, the integration of production, purchasing, and distribution within a single enterprise—and of the expanded role of the visible hand of management in the horizontal control of markets.

Despite the higher level of concentration in Great Britain, the absolute size of British firms is, of course, generally lower than those in the United States. By international standards, however, Britain had its share of giants. In 1972, each of 30 British manufacturing enterprises employed more than 40,000 people; this is fewer than the United States' 89 but almost as many as all the original six countries of the European Economic Community considered together, though their combined population was more than three times that of Great Britain. Although difficulties arise in measuring industrial concentration in continental Europe—primarily because census definitions and financial structures differ—it is clear that the present level of concentration in Britain is higher than in Germany or the other European countries.[4] The large British corporations have also been active in adopting American management methods. The multidivisional structure and strategies of integration and diversification have been as firmly implanted in the United Kingdom as in Germany and France—even more firmly, in some respects.[5] This was not always the case. Comparable data on concentration for earlier periods are not available for Germany; there is no reason, however, to dispute Jürgen Kocka's view that, at least until the 1920s, the level of concentration and the strategy and structure of large corporations had advanced further on United States lines in Germany than in Britain.[6] At the turn of the century, for example, the largest British manufacturing firm was J. & P. Coats, a sewing-thread manufacturer of Paisley, which employed 5,000 people—only a third or less of the number employed in the largest German corporations at that time.

Merger and acquisition were major sources of growth for large corporations in Britain; certainly after 1950 and probably in the 1920s and 1930s as well, they were more important there than in the United States.[7] This difference was partly a consequence of the United States' discouragement of mergers through antitrust legislation; furthermore, the first wave of mergers in the United States, which began in the 1880s and reached its peak around the turn of the century, had already done much to build up the position of the giants in the United States economy. A movement toward merger took place at the same time in Britain, but both the number of firms involved and their assets were smaller, and it affected fewer and less rapidly growing industries.[8] The real equivalent of the United States merger wave came between 1916 and 1930 in Britain, when major modern corporations such as Imperial Chemical Industries (ICI), Unilever, and English Electric were formed in an unprecedented move toward combination. Compared with the earlier mergers, this second wave involved more "rationalization" of facilities for production and distribution and the creation of more extensive managerial hierarchies to coordinate, monitor, and allocate resources to the component companies or operating units.

Merger is no guarantee of retaining a large share of the market in a competitive economy, however, as the heads of many turn-of-the-century amalgamations in the United States discovered, but the corporations created in the mergers of the 1920s in Britain seem to have been at least as successful as those in the United States in retaining their dominant position in the market. Table 2.1 shows the proportion of the 100 largest British firms that changed or maintained their status between 1919 and 1948; it gives some indication of the chance a large enter-

Table 2.1

Stability and change in the 100 largest manufacturing firms in the United Kingdom, 1919–1969.[a]

	STATUS		
		ACQUIRED BY	
	STILL IN	FIRM STILL IN	NO LONGER IN
FIRMS	TOP 100	TOP 100	TOP 100
Top 100 firms of 1919 in 1930	52	17	31
Top 100 firms of 1930 in 1948	71	5	24
Top 100 firms of 1948 in 1957	71	3	26
Top 100 firms of 1957 in 1969	68	22	10

a. Size of firms determined by market value of securities.

prise had of remaining among the largest over time.[9] As table 2.1 suggests, many of the firms that dropped out of the top 100 during this period did so, not because their size diminished, but because they were acquired by another firm that remained in the top 100; in many cases, they would have remained in the top 100 in their own right if they had continued to be independent. This pattern was particularly prevalent from 1919 to 1930 and from 1957 to 1969. Whether one assumes that all acquired firms would have remained among the largest or that all would have fallen to lower ranks, however, the trend toward greater stability is notable. After 1930, at least two thirds of the largest firms survived undiminished over each period. Greater stability is also evident in the leading ranks of the largest enterprises after 1930; 6 of the "top 10" firms in 1930 were among the 10 largest in 1957 and 1969.[10]

Thus the kind of stability that has been identified among the leading firms in the United States economy beginning in the early 1920s was apparently established in Britain by the early 1930s. The underlying reasons for the increasing corporate stability in the two economies are no doubt similar. Some firms were among the few powerful leaders in an oligopolistic market; their positions were protected by barriers to entry, so that newcomers had great difficulty in dislodging them. On the basis of experience in the first wave of mergers, many large firms abandoned strategies that had earlier proved inimical to growth or even to survival; fewer mergers took place among large numbers of firms, for instance, and vertical integration was attempted less often in industries where it offered no competitive advantage over market coordination. More recently, large corporations in both countries, especially those in stagnant markets, have diversified their output so that they depend less heavily on demand in any single market for continued growth. Diversification has also been accompanied by improved managerial techniques and by the spread of multidivisional organization; thus the large corporations are now managed more effectively than many of their earlier counterparts. By adopting mass production and techniques to coordinate the flow of goods through the enterprise more effectively than was possible for smaller enterprises, the giants have delivered real economic benefits by reducing unit costs and, in the process, have maintained their positions.

The Industrial Breakdown of the Largest Corporations

Before examining the response of large British corporations to the problems of managerial capitalism, it is useful to examine their distribution among major industries. Chandler's analysis of the 50 and 200 largest British corporations before 1948, although incomplete, is the fullest analysis available of the broad dimensions of the structure of management in British companies during this period.[11] It covers the 200 largest manufacturing firms, measured by the market value of their capital, in 1919, 1930, and 1948.

Table 2.2 shows the breakdown of the top 200 firms according to the Standard Industrial Classification (S.I.C.) categories of the United States Bureau of the Census.[12] These enterprises vary greatly in size. In 1930, for example, the two largest firms were Unilever and Imperial Tobacco, each with capital valued at more than £130 million, or $650 million; each of the 100 smallest firms valued at less than £3.4 million, or $17 million; with the smallest worth only £1.3 million, or $6.5 million. The 100 largest firms in Britain were comparable in size to the 200 leading United States corporations by the 1930s, but the firms ranking lower than one hundredth in size included many that were significantly smaller than their United States counterparts;

Table 2.2

Industrial breakdown of the 200 largest firms in the United Kingdom, 1919–1948.[a]

Category[b]	Industry	1919		1930		1948	
		Number	% of top 200	Number	% of top 200	Number	% of top 200
19	Ordnance	0	0.0	0	0.0	0	0.0
20	Food and allied products	63	31.5	64	32.0	52	26.0
21	Tobacco products	3	1.5	4	2.0	8	4.0
22	Textile mill products	26	13.0	24	12.0	18	9.0
23	Apparel and allied products	1	0.5	3	1.5	3	1.5
24	Lumber and wood products	0	0.0	0	0.0	0	0.0
25	Furniture and fixtures	0	0.0	0	0.0	0	0.0
26	Paper and allied products	4	2.0	5	2.5	6	3.0
27	Printing and publishing	5	2.5	10	5.0	7	3.5
28	Chemical and allied products	11	5.5	9	4.5	15	7.5
29	Petroleum and energy products	0	0.0	0	0.0	0	0.0

SIC	Industry					
30	Rubber and allied products	3	1.5	3	1.5	2	1.0
31	Leather products	0	0.0	0	0.0	0	0.0
32	Stone, clay, and glass products	2	1.0	6	3.0	5	2.5
33	Primary metals	35	17.5	18	9.0	28	14.0
34	Fabricated metal products	2	1.0	7	3.5	8	4.0
35	Nonelectrical machinery	8	4.0	7	3.5	7	3.5
36	Electrical machinery	11	5.5	18	9.0	13	6.5
37	Transportation equipment	20	10.0	14	7.0	22	11.0
38	Instruments and allied products	0	0.0	1	0.5	4	2.0
39	Miscellaneous	3	1.5	4	2.0	3	1.5

a. Size of firms determined by market value of capital.
b. United States Bureau of the Census Standard Industrial Classification category.

this fact is not surprising in view of the relative size of the two economies.[13]

The problems of classifying firms with a wide range of different products by a single industrial category are obvious, but during the period between 1919 and 1930 they were not insuperable. Nonetheless, some lacunae require explanation. British ordnance output was large; much of it came from firms that do not appear under "ordnance" in table 2.2, since all were considered to be engaged primarily in other industries. The absence of certain firms under "petroleum and energy products" is equally misleading. Two of the seven world oil giants, Shell and Anglo-Persian Oil (the corporate predecessor of British Petroleum) were owned, respectively, by Anglo-Dutch and British companies; by the interwar years they held a strong position in British and other world markets for diesel fuel and gasoline. Since significant oil reserves had not yet been discovered in the United Kingdom, these companies were engaged in distribution rather than manufacturing in Great Britain, with their refining and crude-oil production carried on overseas. Thus they do not appear in this list as manufacturing concerns, although they were certainly large British corporations. After 1948, when they built refineries and chemical plants inside Britain, Shell and British Petroleum were among the largest manufacturing corporations in both that country and the world.[14]

Aside from such quirks of classification, the list of the 200 largest British corporations and comparable lists for the United States indicate that the large firms were clustered in much the same types of industry (see chapter 1, "The United States: Seedbed of Managerial Capitalism," for clustering in the United States). In particular, three of the six industrial categories with the largest number of firms were distinctly modern ones: transportation equipment, chemicals and allied products, and electrical machinery. At an early stage, firms in these categories often developed strategies and structures akin to those of their United States counterparts. Within the transportation-equipment group, shipbuilding accounted for more than half the firms in 1919, but automobiles and automobile equipment made up more than half by 1948; aircraft's share also rose. In both 1930 and 1948, the chemicals group was dominated by Imperial Chemical Industries (ICI), formed in 1926 by the merger of the four largest chemical companies in Great Britain. The relatively stable representation of manufacturers of electrical machinery among the top 200 firms conceals a substantial rise in the size of individual firms between 1919 and 1948.

Other industries also show a pattern similar to that in the United States. Some were dominated by giants such as Imperial Tobacco in tobacco products and the Dunlop Rubber Company in rubber and allied products. In such historically small-scale industries as apparel, wood products, furniture, and leather, few of the largest firms in Britain or the United States are represented. The main exceptions by 1948 were the large, vertically integrated mass-tailoring chains such as Montague Burton and Prices, which dominated the cheaper end of the trade in ready-made and custom-made men's suits and which controlled both production and retailing.

Elsewhere, substantial differences appear between the British patterns, indicated in table 2.2, and the industrial breakdown of the largest corporations in the United States. There were far fewer firms manufacturing nonelectrical machinery among the largest enterprises in Great Britain than in the United States, presumably because British factories, offices, and farms depended more heavily on skilled labor and less heavily on capital for their operation—that is, they were less capital-intensive and more skill-intensive; the market for nonelectrical machinery was correspondingly smaller.[15] The few large firms in this category produced textile machinery (a field in which British firms such as Platt Brothers dominated world markets) or imported United States machine technology. (The British United Shoe Machinery Company, for example, was a subsidiary of a United States corporation.) The largest British-owned company distributing or manufacturing nonelectrical machinery in all three years was Babcock & Wilcox, which had begun as a subsidiary of the United States boiler-making firm of the same name but had become financially independent of its parent in 1900. The British offshoot nonetheless depended heavily on the United States company for technical and manufacturing know-how and maintained close links with New York; it exploited the United States company's patents not only in Britain but in the rest of Europe, the British Empire, and other countries outside North America.[16]

Some of the industrial groups with the largest number of

representatives among the top 200 firms also showed significant contrasts to the United States pattern. Food and allied products, for example, accounted for almost a third of the firms in 1919 and 1930 and for more than a quarter in 1948—substantially more than it did in the United States. Over half these firms were manufacturers of alcoholic beverages in each of the three years for which data are given; their predominance is to some extent a statistical illusion resulting from the British approach to licensing public houses. In the late nineteenth century, the temperance forces obtained the enactment of laws that restricted the total number of outlets for alcoholic beverages; during World War I, the times they could remain open were also restricted. In any region, then, the number of pubs was limited, and it was crucial for a brewery to ensure their loyalty. Almost all the breweries met this marketing problem by acquiring pubs; thus, by the interwar period, only a small and decreasing number were owned by independent small businessmen. (The major exception to this strategy was Guinness, which chose advertising and national branding as an alternative.)[17] As a result, the large real-estate holdings of the breweries inflated the market value of their capital. Their dominance in table 2.2 would be significantly reduced if the top 200 were chosen on the basis of value added in manufacturing.

Nevertheless, the remaining firms in the food and allied products industry were also somewhat different from their United States counterparts. More British firms were makers of semiperishable products. Flour, sugar, and chocolate companies had United States counterparts in size and degree of integration. Unlike the United States firms, however, many were processors of imported agricultural products, and many native fresh products were handled by the smaller businesses. Milk combines appeared at an early stage; canners and bakers, later on. By 1928, one of the largest, United Dairies, owned a large number of retail dairy shops in Great Britain, as well as creameries and dairies in that country and in France. In 1919, a large number of fat processors made goods as varied as margarine and soap (they were similar to and competed with Procter & Gamble and American Cotton Oil), but by 1930 almost all had been united by the Unilever merger. The counterparts of firms like Armour and Swift in the United States—such companies as Union Cold

Storage, which had extensive meat-producing interests in Argentina and Australia—were mainly distributing firms in Great Britain, where they owned cold-storage plants and chains of retail shops. Because their manufacturing facilities were located in the colonies and in Argentina and North America, they do not appear in table 2.2. Manufacturing meat extract was the major business of Liebig and Bovril, two of the largest firms in 1919; they were still represented in the 200 largest firms at later dates.

Another more striking contrast with the United States appears in the dominance of textile mill products—not surprisingly, in light of Great Britain's share of the world cotton trade. Nor is it surprising that their importance declined as foreign competition grew; they accounted for 13 percent of the 200 largest firms in 1919, 12 percent in 1930, and 9 percent in 1948. Many of the largest textile firms in all three years were horizontal combinations organized as holding companies—that is, federations of small firms legally controlled by a single corporation—operating in one process of production such as bleaching or printing calico, or in special areas like the manufacture of cotton sewing thread. J. & P. Coats, the leading thread manufacturer, was ranked first in 1919 and fifth in 1930 and was still eighth in 1948. The modern textile sector was also represented; Courtaulds, the rayon manufacturer, was already the eighth largest firm in 1919, and British Celanese was in the top 50 throughout the period.

Another industry, primary metals, is also well represented, although no British firm was comparable in stature to Vereinigte Stahlwerke in Germany or to United States Steel.[18] A wide range of medium-sized iron and steel firms served the major industrial districts and maintained strong representation in the top 200 firms; the decrease in their numbers in 1930 resulted largely from the exceptionally adverse movement of stock market prices that reflected the severe depression in the steel industry in that year, compared with the booms of 1919 and 1948. In both 1930 and 1948, the representation of nonferrous metals in this category increase, although the absence of sources of raw materials in Great Britain meant that some of the large British-owned firms in these sectors operated mainly abroad and are not included in table 2.2.

Classifications of this kind make it possible to identify distinct similarities and contrasts between the industrial balance of the British economy and that of others, but they also conceal a great deal. The trend over time, for example, is only imperfectly captured in table 2.2. Although small increases in the proportion of firms in the top 200 in industries like electrical machinery are reflected, these industries' share measured in total output, rather than numbers of firms, increased much more dramatically between 1919 and 1948. Changes that had already taken place among the largest firms by 1930 are also understated in table 2.2. The 50 largest corporations show a clear trend toward the representation of the new growth-oriented industries, including electrical machinery and automobiles, by that date; table 2.2, on the contrary, shows a decline in representation.[19]

THE STRUCTURE OF BRITISH CORPORATIONS

The data available for determining other characteristics of the British corporate experience—whether or not management was dominated by owners and their families, whether firms served regional, national, or international markets, what internal structures existed for management, or to what extent production was vertically integrated—are less abundant than those on industrial classification. The histories of the majority of firms remain unwritten, and information must be inferred from *Stock Exchange Year Books* and trade journals, a method that leads to significant errors of classification. Before World War I, for example, the names of board members, the addresses of offices, and other information listed for the United Alkali Company imply that the firm was still owned by the family that founded it, was not administered by salaried managers, put out a single product, and was organized as a holding company—a representative of the old style, in other words. More detailed research indicates, however, that the number of professional managers in the higher echelons was increasing and suggests that the company was developing a more diversified range of products, was vertically integrated, was organized according to functional departments, and was centrally administered.[20] Until British business historians have produced a wider range of case studies, then, the generalizations made in this section, based on the imperfect data available, must be considered tentative.

Table 2.3 demonstrates the impact of the mergers of the 1920s on the 200 largest manufacturing corporations. In 1919 the single-unit enterprise was the norm; by 1930 the multiunit enterprise, most often organized as a holding company, clearly dominated. Little information is available on the internal management structures within these categories. Some firms identified as holding companies remained extremely loose federations, while others may have created extensive managerial hierarchies that operated through centrally administered, functional departments and in which subsidiary companies were not operating entities but merely legal forms. A few firms, such as ICI, can be identified as distinctly multidivisional by 1930; there were perhaps a dozen by 1948. It is not yet possible to refine the data further. What seems clear, however, is that in 1930 the looser holding company arrangement with only an embryonic managerial hierarchy was still dominant in Great Britain; in the United States during the same period, the centralized, functionally departmentalized structure predominated.[21] In 1948 the federated holding company was still strong in Britain, while the multidivisional organization had made more headway among the leading firms in the United States.

In other respects as well, British industry still conformed to older models. The separation of ownership and control, for instance, had not progressed far enough to displace founding or family directors from company boards; 110 of the 200 largest firms in 1919, or 55 percent, had family board members, as did 140, or 70 percent, in 1930, and 119, or 59.5 percent, in 1948.[22] These statistics do not imply, however, that the families represented on boards owned all, or even most, of the capital; indeed, it was the exception rather than the rule for them to hold the majority of the capital, at least among the larger companies, in the 1930s.[23] Nor does the persistence of family names on the board show that they exercised a dominant role in direction and management. Many were present as important minority shareholders; others, as the price of a merger agreement when their own firms were absorbed. In such cases, family influence was often dwindling in the face of the advance of professional management. In many sectors, however, particularly in brewing, shipbuilding, and food, founding families retained their directorial prerogatives. Many of the multiunit enterprises organized

Table 2.3

Organization of the 200 largest manufacturing firms in the United Kingdom, 1919–1948.[a]

Type	1919		1930		1948	
	NUMBER	% OF TOP 200	NUMBER	% OF TOP 200	NUMBER	% OF TOP 200
Single-unit enterprise	104	52.0	56	28.0	31	15.5
Multiunit enterprise	51	25.5	136	68.0	153	76.5
Unknown or other	45	22.5	8	4.0	16	8.0

a. Size of firms determined by market value of capital.

54

as holding companies remained federations of family firms. There the founding families still managed "their" subsidiaries, and decisions about production and distribution policies and about allocating resources were usually arrived at by negotiation.

The question of whether continuing family management was a brake on the development of modern management caused much contemporary debate and remains controversial. Where family management proved incapable of generating an adequate cash flow, its strength was, of course, reduced by the need to obtain capital to keep the firm going; the Du Cros family was ousted from control of the Dunlop Rubber Company in the crisis of 1921–22, for instance, and was replaced by professional managers from outside. In other cases family managers were skilled and innovative like the Pilkingtons, who were glassmakers, or like the Kenricks, who were hardware manufacturers, merely skilled at obtaining enough credit to survive even when their firms deserved to go under on general grounds.[24] Perhaps there is as much variation, if not more, within the two groups of firms—those still controlled by family and those run by salaried managers—as there is between them.

The continuing dominance of families in British board rooms is partly a function of the highly developed but diverse capital market. No real equivalent existed in Great Britain, at least before the 1930s, of the investment bankers of the United States or the industrial banks of Germany, which controlled new capital for transportation and industrial enterprises. Even for quite large British corporations, capital came from many sources. Reinvested profit was always a major source of funds, and new capital was raised from stock exchange issues, from private placings with stockbrokers, insurance companies, or merchant banks, and from families and managers themselves. Strong financial interests rarely appeared on the boards. It is, in fact, more difficult in the British context than in any other to distinguish among a founding entrepreneur and his family, the financial interest, and the managerial interest, simply because these roles were not clearly differentiated in Great Britain.[25] Family firms in the shipbuilding industry financed manufacturers of electrical machinery and automobiles and electric utilities. They might appear on their boards as family and might hold a large proportion or even a majority of the shares, but in some cases they were actually members by virtue of their skills in finance or management, rather than as representatives of a family interest. To classify the British entrepreneur who brought together finance, management, and technology as the creator of a family firm may blur the distinction between his services and those of the family directors of a firm inherited from past generations; the latter, of course, is the more traditional version of the family firm as a brake on progress.

In some areas of business, the distinction is clearer. In the electrical-machinery industry, for example, two of the three largest firms had been subsidiaries of General Electric and Westinghouse before World War I; in 1930 they were still controlled by United States capital. The same was true of two of the largest automobile makers, Ford and Vauxhall, the latter a subsidiary of General Motors; their boards, however, had come to be dominated by British managers. Large firms like ICI and Unilever, which still had some members of the original families on their boards in the 1930s, were also dominated essentially by managers and had wide ownership of shares.

In some of the largest firms, however, family management remained a real force; Imperial Tobacco, for instance, was a federation of family firms with little central direction over the two main family branches, the Willses and the Players.[26] Middle-sized enterprises tended to adopt similar federal structures. The history of the Metal Box Company is one of a gradual transition from a federation of family tin-box makers, merged in 1920–1930, to a more centralized structure, necessitated by its decision in 1930 to license can-making technology from the United States firm, Continental Can Company.[27] In the cases of Imperial Tobacco, Metal Box before 1930, and other holding companies that remained federations of family firms, the failure to create a managerial staff meant an inability to take full advantage of administrative coordination and monitoring or of more systematic ways of allocating resources.

Similar loose federations were numerous in the textile industry, where the Calico Printers' Association, Bradford Dyers, and Fine Spinners and Doublers remained horizontal combinations, and in the iron, steel, and metalworking industries, where Guest Keen and Nettlefolds, Stewarts and Lloyds, and Dorman Long remained loose-knit, vertical combinations. Even firms

dominated by financiers often preferred to remain loose holding companies that left only residual powers to their main offices.
Associated Electrical Industries, formed by merger of four firms
under United States ownership in 1926–1928, ran its two largest companies—Metropolitan-Vickers and British Thomson-
Houston—virtually as independent enterprises, despite the fact
that they had similar, and even competing, product lines.

The United States influence on large-scale enterprise in
Great Britain was especially noticeable in technology. The adoption of modern techniques of mass production and the development of science-based industries such as steel-rolling mills and
the manufacture of automobiles, electrical machinery, and chemicals have depended largely and increasingly in Britain on
links with large United States enterprises, through licensing
agreements, consultants, or direct impact on patterns of integration and on management structures. Modern tinplate mills,
for example, required larger and more fully integrated manufacturing processes, and the British firms that took them over
usually responded accordingly.[28] The multidivisional management structure also seems to have evolved in firms that were
aware of practices in the United States. Some of these were
United States subsidiaries; others, though independent, learned
about and emulated organizational innovations in United States
corporations like Du Pont and General Motors early in their
development. For example, ICI, which had close contacts with
Du Pont, had adopted a multidivisional structure by the late
1920s. Others, like Dunlop Rubber, which was managed by Sir
Eric Geddes, a former railway executive, apparently developed
an advanced, partially functional, partially multidivisional structure largely on their own initiative in the 1920s.

The spread of British business interests abroad can also
be seen at an early stage. In 1919, 21 of the 200 largest firms, or
10.5 percent, listed overseas subsidiaries in the *Stock Exchange
Year Book* and similar directories. This number had grown to
62, or 31 percent, by 1930, and to 73, or 36.5 percent, by 1948.
Since only overseas activities carried on by separately incorporated businesses, rather than by the companies' branch offices,
are listed for many firms, these statistics undoubtedly understate
the degree of British involvement overseas. In both absolute and
relative terms, Great Britain invested more extensively abroad

in the decades before World War I than the United States. Although much of its outlay was in securities, a substantial proportion was invested directly in operating businesses. Even though Britain's direct overseas interests exceeded those of the United States (at least by some definitions), the importance of United States-owned business abroad was probably somewhat greater in the manufacturing sector.[29]

Considering the probable omissions (particularly firms not listed in *Stock Exchange Year Books*) from this data and the relatively small size of many of the 200 largest British firms, the nation's degree of international involvement by 1930 is remarkably high. Some of these connections were long established, such as J. & P. Coats's and English Sewing Cotton's extensive networks of foreign manufacturing subsidiaries or Unilever's subsidiary, Lever Brothers, in the United States. The majority of listed overseas subsidiaries were new in the 1920s, however, and many represented an attempt to capitalize on newly acquired technology and skills by manufacturing outside Great Britain or by creating sales outlets in international markets. Another important motive for the expansion of British firms overseas was the search for raw materials. Vertical integration meant a move abroad more often for British than for United States firms, a pattern that obviously reflects the relative wealth of raw materials in the United States and Britain's poverty in this respect. Thus British steel firms integrated backward to Spanish ore mine and railways, and Turner & Newall, the dominant asbestos firm in Great Britain, acquired mines in Quebec, Swaziland, and Rhodesia.

Within the British economy, the extent to which successive mining and manufacturing processes were integrated and companies integrated forward by establishing marketing and sales capabilities is more difficult to assess. In some respects, integration had gone much further by the early 1920s in Great Britain than in the United States. Shipbuilders commonly owned steelworks; breweries controlled pubs; margarine manufacturers operated chains of retail shops (integration with retail chains was generally more common than in the United States); and newspaper barons owned newsprint plants. In cases where integration had occurred largely in order to assure outlets or sources of supply, however, and had produced holding companies that remained little more than federations of firms, with no central managerial hierarchies, vertical disintegration often came about in the 1930s. Mergers between shipbuilding and steel concerns and newspapers and newsprint manufacturers were dissolved when supplies became more readily available and when outlets proved to be unprofitable. Firms most often turned instead to horizontal combinations in a single industry, such as steel or newsprint, in an attempt to achieve some economies of scale by setting up a central managerial organization and reorganizing plants.

Other kinds of integration common in the United States were absent in Britain. Automobile manufacturers, for example, did not normally own steel-pressing or electrical-components plants; ironmaking was integrated only slowly with steelmaking and finishing; vertical integration between cotton spinning and weaving remained rare. Cases of integration similar to those in the United States do exist, however. Some manufacturers of electrical machinery and cables had substantial interests in the one-third of electric utilities that were not publicly owned. The development of modern road-based distribution, advertising, branding, and sales forces favored the closer interrelationship of manufacturing and distribution and increasingly replaced the earlier reliance on wholesalers and distribution by railway. These trends were clearly strong in the 1920s and 1930s, but the data that are presently available are inadequate as a basis for a statistical summary of their chronological development or for a meaningful comparison with the United States.[30] What is clear is that the choice between integrating vertically related production processes by way of the firm and integrating them by way of the market is revealed to be a complicated one; it depends on many factors, including the degree of monopoly that was achieved, the economies of scale that were possible at various successive stages, and changing technology. It is not surprising, then, that we see much diversity in the experience of different countries at different points in time.

Thus many gaps remain in our knowledge of the structure of the British corporate economy, but the broad picture can be tentatively sketched. In 1919, the characteristics associated with the modern corporate economy were rare in Britain. Large corporations were less common in almost all industries than in the

United States; in some sectors, such as electrical machinery and steel, there were also many fewer than in Germany. Nevertheless, by the early 1930s a substantial merger wave had increased the size of corporations, the number of multiunit enterprises, their degree of overseas involvement, and probably their degree of vertical integration. The degree of functional departmentalization and centralization are uncertain, as is the frequency of multidivisional organization. Both were clearly increasing, but this trend was less evident than in the United States. The loose holding company and the family firm remained much more common structures, despite the development of modern managerial enterprises among some of the largest firms in certain sectors. Corporate development in Great Britain showed distinctive national characteristics, but in the 1950s and 1960s British firms would evolve along a path more clearly similar to that followed in the United States. Substantial reasons remain, nonetheless, for identifying the foundations of the modern corporate economy in the interwar years; postwar evolution built on this already strong base.

THE CORPORATE ECONOMY IN BRITAIN AND THE UNITED STATES

How well does Chandler's framework of explanation for the contrasting experience of the United States and other countries fit the British case? In Britain there is little evidence of the influence of the central government on the evolution of the modern corporate economy. The local and national telephone services were run as a government department beginning in 1912, and high-ranking civil servants, ministers, and military officers were recruited to senior positions on the boards of large corporations, but state intervention in industrial development was rare before 1945 except in wartime. The major exceptions to this generalization in manufacturing were the activities of the central bank, which was privately owned but anxious to ward off government intervention in its affairs. In the 1930s the Bank of England helped to promote mergers and the creation of larger business enterprises, particularly in the cotton and steel industries. Tariffs, finally imposed in 1932, also contributed to large-scale organization by increasing the monopoly profits that could be gained from domination of the home market. This effect was already evident in Germany and the United States much earlier, however, and it was, in any case, a minor influence.[31]

As Chandler has suggested, the size and the rate of growth of the United States market explain many of the evident contrasts between its pattern of output, and its concomitant corporate structure, and that of Britain.[32] Regional and class tastes generally varied more widely in Great Britain than in the United States, although radio, national advertising, and national brands were already reducing these differences by the 1920s. Significantly, in business sectors in which tastes were probably more standardized and less ethnically differentiated in Britain than in the United States or continental Europe—in the food industry, for example—mass production and mass retailing grew rapidly and probably faster than in the United States.

Moreover, British wages were lower than those in the United States (though higher than in continental Europe); this factor limited the market for automobiles and electrical appliances before World War II. As already noted, low wages and a ready supply of skilled labor in Great Britain had affected the demand for capital goods as well. It was not always economical to substitute electric or mechanical power for manpower; thus the home market for power machinery was restricted, and fewer machinery firms accordingly appeared among the largest corporations. By the 1930s, however, wages and the standard of living had reached relatively high levels. Walt W. Rostow, in his now infamous classification of the stages of economic growth, dated the onset of the "age of high mass consumption" in Great Britain to 1935.[33] It was in the years between the wars that electricity was first installed in most homes and that the middle income groups could realistically aspire to automobile ownership. Appropriately, it was also during this period that the corporate economy emerged in Britain.

Yet the size and growth rate of the British and United States markets can explain the contrasts between the two nations only partially. In some periods the British market was better suited than that in the United States to the development of modern corporations, but they did not evolve. In the 1880s, for example, Britain was more highly urbanized and the nation thus required more street lighting and had a more highly skewed distribution of income (and thus more potential consumers of luxury electric lighting); infant United States electrical-machinery firms under Edison and Westinghouse made more of an arguably less attractive market for early development (though later new mass-market advantages proved greater).[34] No country had as large a market for dyes before 1914 as Great Britain, primarily because of its large, prosperous, and rapidly expanding textile industries, but it was the technically superior German chemical industry that took the opportunity offered by the need for dyes to found modern large-scale firms manufacturing fine chemicals. Historians disagree about the reasons for British entrepreneurs' failure to enter or succeed in these new science-based markets; foreign investment, imperialism, and the social and educational systems have attracted their shares of the blame, while some historians continue to argue that the choices made reflected Great Britain's comparative advantages and thus cannot be construed as mistaken, at least in the short run.[35]

More generally, however, the size or rate of growth of the domestic market is not the best indicator of potential or actual demand. Much more than the United States, Britain considered the world its marketplace, and it exported roughly a third of its output for most of the twentieth century. The major markets of the United States and Germany were in fact closed to it by tariff barriers, and the market made up by its own vast Empire was only partly developed and often not protected by tariffs against competition from third parties. Yet significant market opportunities remained: many United States-made goods, such as electrical machinery, were too expensive to compete in third markets, and chauvinism was often sufficiently strong to exclude German competitors at least from Empire countries. The market faced by British firms, then, was somewhat wider, especially in the white-settler dominions, than its domestic market alone might suggest. (The United States and Germany had also established economic relationships with Canada, Latin America, and central Europe, but these were smaller and less significant.) The rapidly growing British manufacturers of automobiles, chemicals, and electric machinery clearly saw Empire markets as a major field for growth during the interwar years, and the names of such newly formed giants as Imperial Chemical Industries were no accident. International cartel agreements, such as those among Du Pont, I. G. Farben, and ICI, also recognized Britain's claim to large overseas markets even in industries in which its technology was still relatively weak; moreover, attempts by the Soviet and United States governments during World War II to induce Britain to dismantle its Empire were based on the view that it was an economic unit of real significance.[36] In seeing their potential market as a wide one comprising the entire Empire, British businessmen were thus perhaps overly optimistic about the future, but they seemed realistic to their contemporaries.

Other factors made even the British home market larger than a simple comparison with the United States suggests. Especially in the heavier industries, where the cost of transporting goods inhibited competition among regional markets in the United States, the effective domestic markets for a typical British firm—in cement and steel, for example—might be larger than those for comparable United States plants. Market size is thus a complex phenomenon, which can explain only part of the differences between the two economies. The highly compact and urban nature of the British domestic market, however, explains the absence of some types of vertical integration evident in the United States. The economies of speed gained across the Atlantic by the visible hand of the manager were often readily available in Britain through the "invisible hand" of the market. Markets work well where the costs of information and transactions are low, and these are likely to be lowest in the kind of compact, industrialized urban region in which most British industries were located. Sheffield, for example, contained a large proportion of Britain's many ordnance and steel-blade firms, but the area in which they were concentrated was small enough for them to communicate effectively through well-developed, traditional market mechanisms.

Chandler has argued that energy- and capital-intensive industries require hierarchical structures for scheduling in order to ensure a steady flow of work, but similar changes in the nineteenth-century British economy, likewise brought about by the application of coal and steam to industrial processes and by the growth of a railway network, did not lead to an equally noticeable growth of large corporations. This difference resulted at least in part from the highly developed and efficient British system of markets for commodities, skills, and distributive and financial services, as well as for final products; thus efficient scheduling by market mechanisms was often possible. In Britain, existing institutions were able to obtain the benefits of competition and efficient dissemination of information, making transactions among firms faster and cheaper than before. Thus markets could offer advantages that outweighed the rival benefits of internal organization—primarily economies of scale and efficient scheduling of flows—at least in the short run. When tested by competition in the British context, the invisible hand was often apparently superior to the visible hand of the managerial firm.[37]

A highly developed national and international network of marketing middlemen—including trading companies, commission agents, wholesale and factoring houses, and consultants—was also available to British manufacturing firms. In many cases, they proved more efficient in delivering goods to the point of sale at lower cost than an internal administrative hierarchy.[38] In the absence of import tariffs, which were not imposed generally until 1932, Britain had virtually the status of a free port and was an international center for the exchange of goods and services; strong competitive forces thus created further pressure for efficiency within the market system. Significantly, investigations by the "new" economic historians of production efficiency under these conditions have generally yielded a favorable verdict; in the cotton-textile industry in Lancashire, for example, Lars Sandberg's view is that the market effectively coordinated the competing activities of many small, single-product firms and that the visible hand had a correspondingly small part to play.[39] The picture just sketched of a successful and effective British market system is, of course, complementary to that of Alexander Gerschenkron, developed further by Jürgen Kocka, which argues that continental European economies without similar advantages were obliged to substitute hierarchical coordination by industrial banks, by the state, or by large-scale enterprise in order to economize on scarce coordinating talents.[40]

Nonetheless, market mechanisms were not always superior to managerial hierarchies in Britain, and historians have identified cases of market failure in which hierarchical organization within the firm might have been more efficient. Whether the rate of development of corporate and market institutions in

Great Britain resulted from an optimal balance between the two or whether the nation erred on the side of conservatism in its reluctance to adopt the new hierarchical institutions is thus debatable. Modern corporate organization was yielding important gains in efficiency in the economies of countries such as the United States and Germany, although they were quite different. As already noted, Britain may have been mistaken in not developing new technology based on electricity and chemical production, and handling complex technical change is arguably a test that competitive market economies may fail.[41] Later, particularly in the years between the wars, British managers often adopted the view that patterns of organization overseas were more efficient. Indeed, in cases where Britain succeeded in developing new technology it did so through the medium of the integrated corporation; this was the case with British Petroleum and Shell in oil, Turner & Newall in asbestos, Courtaulds in rayon, or Dunlop in rubber. British firms' expenditures for research and development did not begin to rival those of industrial research laboratories in Germany and the United States until after World War I.[42]

Historians have also criticized the performance of the British capital market, especially in allocating resources to new industries. Despite the existence of a securities market in Britain that was more highly developed than similar markets in the United States or Germany, some maintain that market institutions performed their primary functions of bearing risks and encouraging innovation less efficiently than large corporations or industrial banks did elswhere.[43] The availability of consulting engineers, whose activities may be thought of as a market device for allocating skilled technical and managerial resources among small, unintegrated firms, has also been criticized as leading to the lack of standardization of plant design and equipment and to a failure to take advantage of economies of mass production in some sectors.[44] Whether or not faulty market mechanisms were responsible, even the old industries for which market organization had seemed ideal, such as coal and cotton, were experiencing severe economic difficulties by the interwar period. Competitive market forces might normally have been expected to enforce the required reduction in capacity through bankruptcies, but, in fact, important "barriers to exit" existed; the result was that attempts were made, not always successfully, to substitute the visible hand of administrative coordination by the state or by more concentrated ownership structures for the market processes that were considered to have failed.[45]

The existence of large, urban markets in Britain and the efficient market institutions it inherited not only served as an alternative to multilevel managerial hierarchies but also made it possible for organizations with a less hierarchical structure to coordinate and oversee operations and to allocate resources effectively.[46] The relative costs of market and mangerial coordination depended heavily on the creativity of the entrepreneurs in the economy at any given time and could not readily be predicted. In Britain, however, opportunities for profit through administrative coordination seem to have been more readily seized in distribution than in manufacturing. Retailing, in particular, was strong in the British economy, and Napoleon's gibe that the nation was one of shopkeepers was even more apposite at the end of the nineteenth century than when it was made. Although retailing has been relatively neglected by business historians, the movement to larger-scale operations was at least as vigorous there as in manufacturing.[47] Moreover, although the large retailing groups in the United States—groups such as the Atlantic and Pacific Tea Company and Sears Roebuck— did not generally integrate backward, they were seen in Britain as a natural base from which to build a manufacturing organization or to bolster its position. Thus such firms as Unilever, Union Cold Storage, United Dairies, the brewery combines in the food and drink industry, and Lever Brothers and the major subsidiaries of Imperial Tobacco in soap and tobacco had important distribution and retailing investments that strengthened their market positions.[48] Even in the technically oriented industries, some of the large British corporations developed backward from retailing. For example GEC (the General Electric Company, the major British-owned electrical-equipment manufacturer before World War I) began in the 1880s as a wholesaler and retailer of electric-lighting equipment; Boots, ICI's major rival in the fine-chemical trade, developed its assets, management skills, and cash flow from its chain of retail drugstores in major British towns.[49] In all these enterprises, except possibly the breweries, companies created managerial hierarchies to coordinate high-volume flows and to oversee operating units. Once again, certain industries in which hierarchical organization offered no special benefits in the United States tended to develop large corporations in Britain through the influence of sales; the market power of the British Shoe Corporation and of mass clothing retailers like Burtons depended to a large extent on their chains of High Street shops.

Another difference between Britain and the United States, as Chandler points out, was in their legal situations. Cartels and restrictive practices were legal in Britain, as they were in Germany and France, and effective legislation against them was not enacted until 1956. In important respects—particularly in coordinating sales policies and securing monopolistic control over prices—cartels were an alternative to merger that was open to European entrepreneurs but closed to their counterparts in the United States.[50] Firms that preferred to maintain a single-unit structure in Britain were therefore free to do so while, at the same time, reducing competition by joining a cartel; in the 1930s and during World War II, in fact, these arrangements were actively encouraged by the government. United States industrialists like Gerald Swope, the dynamic president of the American General Electric Company, accustomed to the antitrust tradition, were advised by bankers in Britain that they need not create large, centralized corporations through mergers for their European operations; market competition could be regulated by agreement with other firms, and there was thus no need to acquire them.[51] Such arrangements did not permit careful scheduling of flows among units, but they avoided the creation of large and sometimes overly bureaucratic structures of management; they therefore permitted firms to retain some of the flexibility of medium-sized enterprises.

Tax factors, on the other hand, were probably a more common encouragement to merger in Britain than they were in the United States. Until 1965, Great Britain had no capital gains tax but taxed income heavily; thus independent entrepreneurs or partners had strong incentives to convert the flow of future income from their enterprises into capital gains by allowing their firms to be acquired by corporations. When the former owner of a firm or his family could continue to operate it as an autonomous subsidiary within a federated holding company, merger became even more attractive.

The factors that encouraged mergers did little, however, to reduce the dominance of family directors on the boards of leading companies. As noted earlier, the pattern of family-dominated enterprise survived longer in Britain than in the United States; even when a family no longer controlled the majority of voting shares, they often retained positions on the board and sometimes took a leading role in management. They continued to be active in part because, as Chandler suggests, many of the enterprises were still small enough to be managed by family shareholder-directors and in part as a result of cultural factors. Still another reason was the relative age of the large British enterprises. In many corporations, such as Unilever, it was only after the death of the founder that professional managers took over leadership. The contrast between Britain and the United States in the 1930s and 1940s arises partly because pioneering entrepreneurs in the United States started their firms earlier and therefore died earlier than men like William Morris of Morris Motors. In some British corporations whose boards were dominated by family members, such as Courtaulds, significant numbers of professional managers already held executive positions by the 1930s; they were not able to consolidate their position, however, until after World War II.

The persistence of family control was not entirely determined by outside factors; it was also a matter of deliberate policy on the part of the controlling families. For example, proposals for a merger between Morris Motors and Austin Motors, the two largest British automobile manufacturers, and for their combined integration backward to steel pressing, were made throughout the 1930s. The pressures to join forces were much the same as those operating in the United States automobile industry. Because of the desire of Morris and Sir Herbert Austin to maintain their independence, however, the merger was not undertaken, and Morris had to abandon his plans for acquiring the Pressed Steel Company. It was not until the 1950s, when Austin and Morris had personally left the scene, that effective integration was accomplished.[52] In the steel industry as a whole, family trusts and family boards still inhibited horizontal and vertical mergers of the kind that were being made increasingly necessary by advances in production technology.[53]

The family firm was not symptomatic of an entirely irrational approach to industrial policy; rather, a case can be made for it on the basis of the alternative resources available for management. Although little is known about changes in the recruitment and training of managers in the twentieth century, the lack of professional development in the field cannot be traced solely to the low demand for managers. Business in Britain was proverbially less prestigious than politics or the professions; although the universities gradually responded to the needs of industry, a substantial gap in the supply of technically trained manpower for management probably remained.[54] Britain's earlier heavy reliance on its market-based industrial organization also led to an underinvestment in managerial talent in the early stages of corporate development. As a result, patronage had to replace professionalism. A young man who wished to learn the business of management could often envisage no better training than in the family firm, where many potential managers both within and outside the family sought it.[55] In some areas, larger, more fully integrated, managerially controlled organizations could probably have developed, but the response was not forthcoming from native British sources. One consequence was an influx of foreign investment, primarily from the United States in the 1920s and 1930s; it continued after World War II. One-sixth of British manufacturing is now foreign-owned and uses imported technology and managerial techniques and, less frequently, non-British managers; this proportion is higher than that in any other European country.[56]

RETROSPECT AND PROSPECT

Theories that the role of the visible hand of management developed in essentially the same way in Western economies, then, are only partially confirmed by an examination of the British case. Perhaps the contrasts between Britain and the United States, or between Britain and other European countries, can best be understood as resulting from a combination of factors that include cultural attitudes, values, ideologies, and social structure as well as the nature of markets and the available technology. Although the British experience broadly confirms Chandler's proposed model of comparative development, some modifications seems necessary if it is to fit the British case. Moreover, considerable further research on individual companies is required before the British corporate experience can be fully compared with that of the United States.

Two more general points are suggested by the data already described. First, a chicken-and-egg problem arises in international comparisons of economies that are continuously in evolution. The fact that the United States market was bigger and was growing more rapidly than European markets may genuinely have resulted from factors exogenous to the strategy and structure of corporations. It market size was, after all, a function of its already high standard of living, and market growth owed much to population increases resulting from immigration and the expansion of the frontier.[57] If, however, the increasing importance of the visible hand is seen as a source of substantial economies of scale, speed, and integration, then the developing corporate economy may be the cause as well as the consequence of rapid economic growth. Between the late 1890s and the 1920s, when Britain experienced the lowest rate of economic growth in its industrial history, the United States and German economies, which were developing large-scale corporations, grew more rapidly. This difference raised the question at the time, as it does now, of whether Great Britain was clinging too long to inherited market structures and failing to develop appropriate integrated and hierarchical coordinating structures in industries where they were being shown to have a comparative advantage in Germany and the United States. Imperfections in the market certainly made such suspicions plausible; and by the 1930s when Great Britain had developed its own large-scale organization, the international rankings in rates of growth were reversed and Britain's relative economic performance improved. The causes of Britain's economic success in that period are themselves to some degree external; the British standard of living, for example, benefited from the fall in world prices for primary products in the early 1930s. Yet it may also be true that the development of the British corporate economy, which allowed new economies of scale, speed, and integration, also contributed to favorable performance.[58]

A second point raised by the material reviewed in this chapter—one that conflicts to some extent with the first—is that the consequences of the visible hand of large-scale enterprise were not all benign. Without creating a managerial hierarchy, merger and expansion cannot reduce costs or improve service, a point Chandler has emphasized. Forward integration by breweries to secure pub outlets, motivated by the licensing laws, or merger undertaken for tax reasons may be neutral in their effects on efficiency. Other kinds of considerations, such as horizontal or vertical mergers undertaken to enhance monopoly power, may have negative effects. The arguments on this subject are well known, but economists may have defined them too narrowly. Equally or more important, increases in scale have had social consequences in the form of worker alienation and the loss of freshness and vigor as entrepreneurship has given way to bureaucracy.[59]

Large firms are aware of these problems, and modern multidivisional structures or job-enrichment schemes, for example, may do something to alleviate them, but difficulties clearly persist. On both sides of the Atlantic, there is overwhelming evidence that managers systematically overestimate the gains to be had from contemplated mergers. They undervalue the invisible hand of the market in coordinating activities and overvalue the visible hand with which they plan to replace it in their merged enterprises. Thus a large proportion of mergers are reported to be financial failures.[60] Of course, counterpressures discourage such managerial misconceptions—profit-related executive-compensation packages, stock options, the threat of takeovers or proxy fights for unsuccessful boards—but it is arguable that they work only imperfectly and in the long run.

The two countries with the most concentrated industrial structures and largest corporations since World War II, Britain and the United States, are also those with the least impressive economic performance. The balance between the negative and positive influences of the factors considered here is difficult to assess, and many other factors are involved in determining economic performance. Nonetheless, the questions raised in the 1890s by the early critics of the emerging modern corporations are still properly before us.

NOTES

1. See especially Alfred D. Chandler, Jr., *Strategy and Structure* (Cambridge, Mass., 1962); idem, *The Visible Hand* (Cambridge, Mass., 1977); idem, "The United States: Seedbed of Managerial Capitalism," this volume.

2. I have developed this theme at greater length in *The Rise of the Corporate Economy: The British Experience* (Baltimore, 1976).

3. Leslie Hannah and J. A. Kay, *Concentration in Modern Industry* (London, 1977).

4. See S. J. Prais, *The Evolution of Giant Firms in Britain* (London, 1976) pp. 155–162; but see *Economist,* October 8, 1977, p. 97, for data on the absolute size of German corporations, which grew even faster in the 1970s.

5. See Derek F. Channon, *The Strategy and Structure of British Enterprise* (London, 1973); Gareth P. Dyas and Heinz T. Thanheiser, *Emerging European Enterprises: Strategy and Structure of French and German Industry* (London, 1977); Alfred D. Chandler, Jr., and Herman Daems, introduction to *The Rise of Managerial Capitalism,* ed. Herman Daems and Herman Van der Wee (The Hague, 1974).

6. See Jürgen Kocka, "The Rise of the Modern Industrial Enterprise in Germany," this volume; see also Robert A. Brady, *The Rationalization Movement in German Industry* (Berkeley, 1933).

7. Hannah and Kay, *Concentration,* chaps. 5, 6.

8. Leslie Hannah, "Mergers in British Manufacturing Industry 1880–1918," *Oxford Economic Papers* 26 (1974):1–20.

9. For a more complete discussion, see Hannah and Kay, *Concentration,* pp. 103–105.

10. Richard C. Edwards, "Stages in Corporate Stability and the Risks of Corporate Failure," *Journal of Economic History* 35 (1975):428–457; see also Chandler, *Visible Hand,* pp. 371–372.

11. Chandler's preliminary analysis of the data for the 50 largest firms was published as "The Development of Modern Management Structure in the U.S. and U.K.," in *Management Strategy and Business Development,* ed. Leslie Hannah (London, 1976); improved information has led, however, to the reclassification of some of the firms listed there. The extension of Chandler's work is based on estimates of firm size and a list of the 200 largest firms prepared by Margaret Ackrill for the study reported in Hannah and Kay, *Concentration;* the analysis of industrial groups and other characteristics was carried out by Peter Grant.

12. Like the comparable list of United States firms in Chandler's *Visible Hand* but unlike those for Germany prepared by Jürgen Kocka and Hannes Siegrist, that on which table 2.2 is based includes a few subsidiaries of foreign corporations for all three dates. Firms such as Boots Pure Drug Company and Associated Electrical Industries have passed from British to United States ownership and back in the course of the twentieth century. To include only British-registered and British-owned companies would thus have distorted the overall picture and have led to the inclusion of

many companies that operated principally abroad. The criterion for inclusion—an operational standard, rather than one depending on ownership—was that a substantial proportion of a company's assets be in British manufacturing.

13. For a list of the largest United States firms in 1917, see Chandler, *Visible Hand,* appendix A.

14. British Petroleum was still quite small in 1919, however; see Ronald W. Ferrier, "The Early Management Organization of British Petroleum," in *Management Strategy,* ed. Hannah.

15. For a discussion of this industry in the nineteenth and early twentieth centuries, see Samuel B. Saul, ed., *Technological Change* (London, 1970); C. Knick Harley, "Skilled Labour and the Choice of Technique in Edwardian Industry," *Explorations in Economic History* 11 (1974):391–414.

16. Information supplied by Babcock & Wilcox, Ltd.

17. See John Vaizey, "The Brewing Industry," in *The Effects of Mergers,* ed. P. Lesley Cook and Ruth Cohen (London, 1958).

18. See Shin-ichi Yonekawa, "The Strategy and Structure of Cotton and Steel Enterprises in Britain, 1900–1939," in *Strategy and Structure of Big Business,* ed. Keiichiro Nakagawa (Tokyo, 1977).

19. See Hannah, *Rise of the Corporate Economy,* chap. 8; see also Chandler, "Modern Management Structure," pp. 33–35, 41–43. Given the size difference between the two economies, it may be more appropriate to compare the 50 or 100 largest firms in Britain with the 200 largest in the United States.

20. For this example I am grateful to Yuichi Kudo, who has done extensive research in the files of United Alkali.

21. Leslie Hannah, "Strategy and Structure in the Manufacturing Sector," in *Management Strategy,* ed. Hannah; Channon, *Strategy and Structure of British Enterprise.*

22. From data compiled by Peter Grant.

23. Philip S. Florence, *Ownership, Control and Success of Large Companies, 1936–1951* (London, 1961).

24. See, for instance, Theodore C. Barker, *The Glassmakers* (London, 1977); R. A. Church, *Kenricks in Hardware: A Family Business* (Newton Abbot, 1969). See also Kocka, "Modern Industrial Enterprise in Germany," this volume, for a discussion of similar factors in Germany; but compare Channon, *Strategy and Structure of British Enterprise,* p. 248.

25. The interpenetration of finance and manufacturing is a topic worthy of further study. For some illuminating remarks pertinent to the analysis of British business in the twentieth century, see W. D. Rubinstein, "The Victorian Middle Classes: Wealth, Occupation, and Geography," *Economic History Review* 30 (1977):602–623.

26. See B. W. E. Alford, *W. D. & H. O. Wills and the Development of the Tobacco Industry, 1786–1965* (London, 1973).

27. See William J. Reader, *Metal Box: A History* (London, 1976).

28. See Walter E. Minchinton, *The British Tinplate Industry* (London, 1957).

29. For comparative data and alternative definitions of direct investment, see, among others, Donald G. Paterson, *British Direct Investment in Canada, 1890–1914* (Toronto, 1976); Irving Stone, "British Direct and Portfolio Investment in Latin America before 1914," *Journal of Economic History* 37 (1977):690–722. Some of the obscurities in the statistics are unraveled in an unpublished paper by Michael Edelstein of the City University of New York.

30. No study has yet been made of changes in the product ranges of large corporations before 1950. For data after 1950, see Channon, *Strategy and Structure in British Enterprise;* for less systematic information on the period before 1950, see Leslie Hannah, "Strategy and Structure in the Manufacturing Sector," in *Management Strategy,* ed. Hannah.

31. See Hannah, *Rise of the Corporate Economy,* pp. 57, 156–157, 169, 188–189.

32. See Chandler, "United States," this volume; see also idem, *Visible Hand,* pp. 498–500; idem, "Modern Management Structure," pp. 47ff.

33. Walt W. Rostow, *The Stages of Economic Growth,* 2nd ed. (Cambridge, 1971), p. *xx*.

34. See I. C. R. Byatt, *The British Electrical Industry 1875–1914* (Oxford, forthcoming).

35. See, for instance, William P. Kennedy, "Foreign Investment, Trade and Growth in the United Kingdom, 1870–1913," *Explorations in Economic History* 11 (1974):415–444; Donald N. McCloskey and Lars G. Sandberg, "From Damnation to Redemption: Judgments on the Late Victorian Entrepreneur," ibid., 9 (1971):89–108.

36. See J. D. Gribbin, ed., "Board of Trade. Survey of International Cartels, 1944" (London, 1976); William J. Reader, *Imperial Chemical Industries: A History,* 2 vols. (London, 1970–1975).

37. The logic by which the boundaries of market and firm are determined was first clearly enunciated in Ronald H. Coase, "The Nature of the Firm," *Economica,* n.s. 4 (1937):386–405.

38. Many major British firms that bought capital goods—for example, those in the oil and electrical industries—did so through middlemen and other market institutions of this sort rather than directly from the manufacturer. For a less favorable view of the middleman, however, see Peter L. Payne, *British Entrepreneurship in the Nineteenth Century* (London, 1974), pp. 41–45, 53–56.

39. This body of work is summarized in McCloskey and Sandberg, "From Damnation to Redemption."

40. See Alexander Gerschenkron, "Economic Backwardness in Historical Perspective," in *The Progress of Underdeveloped Areas,* ed. Berthold F. Hoselitz (Chicago, 1952); Kocka, "Modern Industrial Enterprise in Germany," this volume.

41. For a general discussion of this issue, see Nathan Rosenberg, ed., *The Economics of Technical Change* (Harmondsworth, 1971); Frederic M. Scherer, *Industrial Market Structure and Economic Performance* (Chicago,

1970), chaps. 15, 16. For an example of contemporary criticism of competition in a technologically developing industry, see British Electrical and Allied Manufacturers' Associations, *Combines and Trusts in the Electrical Industry* (London, 1927).

42. See, for instance, M. Sanderson, "Research and the Firm in British Industry 1919–1939," *Science Studies,* vol. 2 (Harmondsworth, 1972).

43. See especially William P. Kennedy, "Institutional Response to Economic Growth: Capital Markets in Britain to 1914," in *Management Strategy,* ed. Hannah; see also Lance Davis, "The Capital Markets and Industrial Concentration: The US and UK, A Comparative Study," *Economic History Review* 19 (1966):255–272; Chandler, *Visible Hand,* p. 373.

44. See, for instance, I. C. R. Byatt, "Electrical Products," in *The Development of British Industry and Foreign Competition, 1875–1914,* ed. Derek H. Aldcroft (London, 1968), pp. 268–273.

45. See Hannah, *Rise of the Corporate Economy,* pp. 135–137; Neil K. Buxton, "Entrepreneurial Efficiency in the British Coal Industry between the Wars," *Economic History Review* 23 (1970):476–497.

46. See, for instance, Herman Daems, "The Rise of the Modern Industrial Enterprise: A New Perspective," this volume.

47. See Charles Wilson, "Economy and Society in Late Victorian Britain," *Economic History Review* 18 (1965):183–198; Margaret Hall, John Knapp, and Christopher Winsten, *Distribution in Great Britain and North America* (London, 1961); James B. Jefferys, *Retail Trading in Britain 1850–1950* (London, 1954); Derek F. Channon, "Corporate Evolution in the Service Industries," in *Management Strategy,* ed. Hannah.

48. See, for instance, Peter Mathias, *Retailing Revolution* (London, 1967); Patrick Fitzgerald, *Industrial Combination in England* (London, 1927).

49. See Adam G. Whyte, *Forty Years of Electrical Progress* (London, 1930); S. G. Chapman, *Jesse Boot of Boots the Chemists* (London, 1974).

50. In an important sense, however, cartels and mergers also complemented each other. For a fuller consideration of this issue, see Leslie Hannah, "Mergers, Cartels and Concentration: Legal Factors in the US and European Experience, 1880–1914," in *Recht und Entwicklung der Grossunternehmen im 19. und frühen 20. Jahrhundert,* ed. Jürgen Kocha and Norbert Horn, (Göttingen, 1979).

51. See Robert Jones and Oliver Marriott, *Anatomy of a Merger* (London, 1970), p. 124.

52. See Philip Walter Sawford Andrews and Elizabeth Brunner, *Life of Lord Nuffield* (Oxford, 1955); Graham Turner, *The Leyland Papers* (London, 1971); see also R. Church, *Herbert Austin* (London, forthcoming).

53. See, for instance, Peter L. Payne, "Rationality and Personality: A Study of Mergers in the Scottish Iron and Steel Industry, 1916–1936," *Business History* 19 (1977):162–191; idem, *Colvilles and the Scottish Steel Industry* (Oxford, 1979).

54. See Derek H. Aldcroft, "Investment in the Utilisation of Manpower:

Great Britain and Her Rivals," in *Great Britain and Her World,* ed. B. M. Ratcliffe (Manchester, 1975); M. Sanderson, *The Universities and British Industry* (London, 1970).

55. For examples of successful and wide-ranging recruitment of managers by a family, see Barker, *Glassmakers.*

56. See John H. Dunning, *American Investment in British Manufacturing Industry* (London, 1958); idem, *The Role of American Investment in the British Economy* (London, 1969). The high proportion of United States investment resulted in part, of course, from linguistic and cultural affinities, as well as from economic, technical, and managerial factors.

57. Chandler, for instance, makes this argument in *Visible Hand,* pp. 498–499.

58. This is the broader theme of my "Business Development and Economic Structure in Britain since 1880," in *Management Strategy,* ed. Hannah.

59. Hannah and Kay, *Concentration,* chap. 3.

60. For surveys of the literature on Britain, see M. A. Utton, "On Measuring the Effects of Industrial Mergers," *Scottish Journal of Political Economy,* 1974; on the United States, see Thomas F. Hogarty, "Profits from Merger: The Evidence of 50 Years," *St. John's Law Review* (1970). See also Geoffrey Meeks, *Disappointing Marriage: A Study of the Gains from Merger* (Cambridge, 1977).

3/ The Rise of the Modern Industrial Enterprise in Germany

Jürgen Kocka

IN GERMANY, as in the United States, the rise of the modern business enterprise was closely related to the development of modern industrialism. There has been much debate about the chronology of industrialization, which was based on new technology and on the greatly expanded consumption of energy. The consensus seems to be, however, that its first phase began about 1840 and ended with the economic crisis of 1873. During this period the establishment of the railroads and the related acceleration in the development of manufacturing brought the first massive investments to the industrial sphere; the proportion of the gross national product (GNP) represented by net investment increased sharply. Growth became self-sustaining, with only short-term interruptions—a pattern typical of industrializing economies. What made growth possible was an increasingly integrated market that was enlarged through the expansion of transportation (primarily the railroads) and through the attainment of economic and political unity. While national unity was not achieved until 1870–1871, under Prussian leadership, a Custom Union had already been founded in 1834 and soon covered the majority of the then rather indepedent German states. At the same time, the annual output of German coal mines soared from 5 million tons in 1850 to 36.4 million in 1873. The commercial and industrial sectors' share of the GNP increased markedly. Within the industrial sector, the modern factory system was established. Thus Germany began to industrialize about half a century after Britain and perhaps two decades after France, at roughly the same time as the United States.[1]

According to many contemporary observers and most present-day scholars, the depression of the 1870s marked the end of this first, breakthrough, phase of German industrialization. Cyclical downturns were particularly long and deep in the 1870s and 1890s; steady and rapid expansion began again in the mid-1890s and lasted, with short interruptions, until World War I. Between 1873 and 1913, the second phase of German industrialization, the GNP tripled. In 1873 about one-third of the national wealth had come from manufacturing and mining; by 1913 these sectors produced almost half. The annual rate of growth in industrial production during the same period was 3.7 percent. Total output per capita grew faster in Germany than in any other European country; it has been estimated that the annual percentage increase was 1.8 in Germany, 1.3 in Great Britain, 1.4 in France, and 2.2 in the United States from 1870 to 1913. Over these four decades, Germany finally overcame its relative economic backwardness; it overtook all other continental states and, in some important respects, surpassed even Great Britain.[2]

Beginnings and endings are rarely clear-cut in business and economic history; if any period can be identified with the emergence of the modern business enterprise in Germany, however, it is that from the 1870s to World War I. In discussing it, I shall concentrate on developments in manufacturing and mining, both because research has so far been inadequate in other sectors and because transportation and communications have been primarily public rather than private enterprises in Germany. Five major, interrelated factors lay at the center of the rise of the modern firm: the processes of expansion, diversification, and integration; the rise of cartels and associations; changes in the relationship between banks and industry; the rise of managerial capitalism, with its tendencies toward separating ownership and control and the rise of the salaried entrepreneur; and the increasing importance of science and system in production, distribution, and management. After discussing each of these factors, I shall try to place the German case in comparative perspective and examine its relationship to Alfred Chandler's findings and hypotheses.[3]

EXPANSION, DIVERSIFICATION, AND INTEGRATION

The average size of plants *(Betriebe)* and firms grew during the years from the 1870s to World War I, as table 3.1 indicates. While only 23 percent of all manufacturing and crafts workers were in operating units with more than 50 employees in 1882, their proportion had risen to 42 percent by 1907. Mining, engineering (including electrical engineering), chemicals, and textiles led this trend toward concentration. In each of these industrial areas, more than two-thirds of all employees worked in plants with more than 50 others. The least concentrated areas were the manufacture of clothing, food, and wood and leather products. Firms *(Unternchmen)* which often comprised several plants, grew even faster. In order to be counted among the 100 largest firms in 1887, manufacturing or mining corporations had to have at least 3 million marks in share capital; they needed a minimum of 10 million marks twenty years later.

Table 3.1

German manufacturing and mining workers by size of work units,
1882–1907.

WORKERS PER UNIT[a]	% OF ALL WORKERS IN MANUFACTURING AND HANDICRAFTS			% OF ALL WORKERS IN MINING		
	1882	1895	1907	1882	1895	1907
1–5	59.8	41.8	31.2	1.7	0.8	0.7
6–10	4.4	7.4	7.0	0.8	0.6	0.3
11–50	13.0	17.3	19.4	5.9	4.0	2.5
51–200	11.8	17.4	20.8	14.6	11.2	9.6
201–1,000	9.1	12.8	16.7	44.0	36.8	28.7
1,000+	1.9	3.3	4.9	33.0	46.6	58.2

Source: W. G. Hoffmann et al., *Das Wachstum der deutschen Wirtschaft seit der Mitte des 19. Jahrhunderts* (Berlin, 1965), p. 212.

a. Units are defined as locally centralized and integrated operating units *(Betriebe)*.

As in the case of American firms, the expansion of enterprises in Germany involved product diversification and vertical integration. Tables 3.2 through 3.5 present information on the 100 largest manufacturing and mining firms in Germany in 1887 and 1907.[4] These figures have been compiled from stock exchange handbooks and similar sources. Diversification is measured on the basis of the official German census classification, which distinguished roughly 430 different lines of production; these categories resemble the 430 "four-digit industries" used by Chandler, P. Glenn Porter, and others to measure the degree of diversification among large United States firms. Tables 3.2 and 3.3 distinguish four stages of diversification. In category A, one finds nondiversified firms (those active in only one production line). Firms in categories B and C were active in 2 to 4 and 5 to 9 lines, respectively; they can be considered to have adopted a strategy of moderate diversification. In category D one finds fully diversified firms, with 10 or more production lines.

In 1907 only five of the 100 largest firms remained undiversified; twenty years earlier there had been 14 such firms among the 100 largest, mostly in mining and food production. In 1907 there were 32 firms in category C and 19 in category D; in 1887 there had been 25 in category C and 9 in D. Thus diversification increased markedly during these two decades.

Tables 3.4 and 3.5 indicate the degree and direction of integration among mining and manufacturing firms; those that secured their own supplies of raw materials are said to have integrated backward, while those that established their own sales organizations integrated forward. Membership in a tight cartel or syndicate can be regarded as one way for a firm to integrate forward without establishing its own sales organization, since such a cartel sold the products of the member firms collectively. In these tables, c indicates forward integration by the establishment of an individual sales organization; d is forward integration by membership in a tight cartel or syndicate; a is backward integration into raw materials. Even in 1887, only 27 of the 100 largest were pure production firms without any integration of other functions; by 1907, this figure had shrunk to 12. In 1887 more than half had integrated backward, as had three-quarters in 1907. Seventeen had sales organizations of their own in 1887, compared with 33 in 1907; 8 belonged to cartels in 1887, and 61 in 1907 (the sharpest rise in the integration of firms). There were 14 fully integrated firms (firms that had integrated both backward and forward) in 1887 and 62, or nearly two-thirds of the 100 largest, in 1907. The trend toward

Table 3.2

Product diversification in the 100 largest German industrial and mining firms, 1887.[a]

German census category	Industrial category[b]	Number of firms	Range of smallest–largest capital (millions of marks)	Stages of diversification[c] A (1 product line)	B (2–4 product lines)	C (5–9 product lines)	D (10 or more product lines)
III	Mining, petroleum extraction and refining	24	4.0–28.6	7	17	0	0
IV	Stone, clay, and glass products	3	4.0–9.0	0	2	1	0
V, VI	Primary metals products and manufacturing	32	3.8–40+	1	11	16	4
VII	Machinery, instruments, transportation equipment	12	3.8–15.0	0	1	7	4
VIII	Electrical engineering and manufacturing	2	3.0–50	0	1	0	1

Source: Jürgen Kocka and Hannes Siegrist, "Die hundert grössten deutschen Industrieunternehmen im späten 19. und frühen 20. Jahrhundert. Expansion, Diversifikation und Integration im internationalen Vergleich," in *Recht und Entwicklung der Grossunternehmen 1806–1920*, ed. Norbert Horn and Jürgen Kocka (Göttingen, 1979).

(Continued)

Table 3.2—continued.

GERMAN CENSUS CATEGORY	INDUSTRIAL CATEGORY[b]	NUMBER OF FIRMS	RANGE OF SMALLEST–LARGEST CAPITAL (MILLIONS OF MARKS)	STAGES OF DIVERSIFICATION[c]			
				A (1 PRODUCT LINE)	B (2–4 PRODUCT LINES)	C (5–9 PRODUCT LINES)	D (10 OR MORE PRODUCT LINES)
IX	Chemicals	12	3.8–16.5	1	10	1	0
X	Textiles	5	3.8–9.0	1	4	0	0
XIII	Rubber	1	4.5	0	1	0	0
XIV	Wood products	1	4.9	0	1	0	0
XVI	Food and allied products; tobacco	8	3.9–5.9	4	4	0	0
	Total	100	3.8–40+	14	52	25	9

a. Size of firms was determined by the amount of share capital (excluding bonds and reserves). In the case of the few privately owned firms included among the top 100, employment, turnover, and production figures were used instead; these figures were compared with those of the joint-stock companies in the same group.

b. A firm active in more than one industrial category is counted in its major sphere of activity, roughly assessed on the basis of production values.

c. Product diversification is measured by 430 product lines (*Arten*) in the German census of 1925. Examples of such lines are coal-tar dyes, photochemical products, and steam engines.

Table 3.3

Production diversification in the 100 largest German industrial and mining firms, 1907.[a]

German Census Category	Industrial Category[b]	Number of Firms	Range of smallest–largest capital (millions of marks)	Stages of diversification[c]			
				A (1 product line)	B (2–4 product lines)	C (5–9 product lines)	D (10 or more product lines)
III	Mining, petroleum extraction and refining	23	11–72.2	3	17	3	0
IV	Stone, clay, and glass products	3	12–15	0	3	0	0
V, VI	Primary metals products and manufacturing	31	10.1–180	0	1	19	11
VII	Machinery, instruments, transportation equipment	13	10–40+	0	2	7	4
VIII	Electrical engineering and manufacturing	4	14–100	0	0	0	4
IX	Chemicals	17	11.3–25.5	1	13	3	0

Source: Jürgen Kocka and Hannes Siegrist, "Die hundert grössten deutschen Industrieunternehmen," in *Recht und Entwicklung,* ed. Norbert Horn and Jürgen Kocka.

(Continued)

Table 3.3—*continued*.

German census category	Industrial category[b]	Number of firms	Range of smallest–largest capital (millions of marks)	Stages of diversification[c]			
				A (1 product line)	B (2–4 product lines)	C (5–9 product lines)	D (10 or more product lines)
X	Textiles	3	10–22.5	1	2	0	0
XI	Paper products; printing	2	16.3–19	0	2	0	0
XVI	Food and allied products; tobacco	4	10.5–20	0	4	0	0
	Total	100	10–180	5	44	32	19

a. Size of firms was determined by the amount of share capital (excluding bonds and reserves). Employment, turnover, and production figures were used for the few privately owned firms in the top 100.

b. A firm active in more than one industrial category is counted in its major sphere of activity, roughly assessed on the basis of production values.

c. Product diversification is measured by 430 product lines (*Arten*) in the German census of 1925.

Degree of integration in the 100 largest German industrial and mining firms, 1887.[a]

GERMAN CENSUS CATEGORY	INDUSTRIAL CATEGORY[b]	NUMBER OF FIRMS	FUNCTIONS INTEGRATED[c]							
			ab	abc	abcd	abd	b	bc	bcd	bd
III	Mining, petroleum extracting and refining	24	16	2	0	0	6	0	0	0
IV	Stone, clay, and glass products	3	3	0	0	0	0	0	0	0
V, VI	Primary metals products and manufacturing	32	21	2	0	0	3	0	0	0
VII	Machinery, instruments, transportation equipment	12	1	0	0	6	9	2	0	0
VIII	Electrical engineering and manufacturing	2	0	1	0	0	0	1	0	0
IX	Chemicals	12	5	0	0	2	2	3	0	0
X	Textiles	5	0	0	0	0	5	0	0	0
XIII	Rubber	1	0	0	0	0	0	1	0	0
XIV	Wood products	1	0	1	0	0	0	0	0	0
XVI	Food and allied products; tobacco	8	2	0	0	0	2	4	0	0
	Total	100	48	6	0	8	27	11	0	0

Source: Jürgen Kocka and Hannes Siegrist, "Die hundert grössten deutschen Industrieunternehmen," in Recht und Entwicklung, ed. Norbert Horn and Jürgen Kocka.

a. Size of firms was determined by the amount of share capital (excluding bonds and reserves). Employment, turnover, and production figures were used for the few privately owned firms in the top 100.

b. A firm active in more than one industrial category is counted in its major sphere of activity, roughly assessed on the basis of production values.

c. a = raw materials; b = production; c = sales; d = membership in a syndicate.

85

Table 3.5

Degree of integration in the 100 largest German industrial and mining firms, 1907.[a]

German census category	Industrial category[b]	Number of firms	Functions integrated[c]							
			ab	abc	abcd	abd	b	bc	bcd	bd
III	Mining, petroleum extraction and refining	23	3	1	2	14	0	0	0	3
IV	Stone, clay, and glass products	3	0	2	0	1	0	0	0	0
V, VI	Primary metal products and manufacturing	31	1	1	7	20	2	0	0	0
VII	Machinery, instruments, transportation equipment	13	0	0	0	2	6	4	1	0
VIII	Electrical engineering and manufacturing	4	0	0	1	0	0	2	1	0
IX	Chemicals	17	1	3	0	8	2	2	0	1
X	Textiles	3	0	0	0	0	2	1	0	0
XI	Paper products; printing	2	1	0	0	0	0	1	0	0
XVI	Food and allied products; tobacco	4	0	0	0	0	0	4	0	0
	Total	100	6	7	10	45	12	14	2	4

Source: Jürgen Kocka and Hannes Siegrist, "Die hundert grössten deutschen Industrieunternehmen," in *Recht und Entwicklung,* ed. Norbert Horn and Jürgen Kocka.

a. Size of firms was determined by the amount of share capital (excluding bonds and reserves). Employment, turnover, and production figures were used for the few privately owned firms in the top 100.

b. A firm active in more than one industrial category is counted in its major sphere of activity, roughly assessed on the basis of production values.

c. *a* = raw materials; *b* = production; *c* = sales; *d* = membership in a syndicate.

diversification was strongest in primary metals, in electrical engineering, and in the production of machinery. The trend toward integration was strongest in chemicals, primary metals, and mining. Such firms integrated all the various stages of production from the mining of coal and iron ore, via pig iron and steel production, through many stages of working the metal, and sometimes even to heavy engineering; their activities included the utilization of by-products, and they usually took over wholesale marketing.

Technical discoveries added to the impetus for diversification: the discovery of the use of blast-furnace gases as a source of energy induced the foundries to establish or join with steelworks and rolling mills, which could thus be operated more cheaply; at the same time, the incentive for rolling mills to merge with or to establish foundries increased. The aim of exploiting technical advantages through combining various stages of production and thus introducing economies was a frequent motive for diversification. Another was the desire to control several stages of production and thus to ensure their interdependence for the sake of improving quality. Large businesses had a further motive. Since even the slightest upset in production meant massive losses, integration into raw materials and transportation allowed them to minimize this risk. Diversification of this sort made it possible to calculate as fixed costs the charges that had hitherto been dependent on unforeseeable market changes.

Sometimes vertical integration and product diversification were encouraged by the formation of cartels. Membership in a cartel stimulated linkages between mines and foundries, for instance. A firm's production of coal was limited by the rules of the cartel, but coal that the firm planned to use for running its own foundry did not count as part of the fixed quota set by the cartel. Membership might also encourage a firm within the cartel to diversify into another product line that was not (or not yet) subject to cartel regulations, when such regulations restricted the firm's innovations, chances, and profits in its original line of production. In the electrical-engineering and chemicals industries, other stimuli were more effective. The availability of both a pool of highly qualified and expensive technical knowhow that could be put to many uses and relevant methods and machinery called for the widest possible utilization. Here, diversification meant primarily the deployment of technical expertise across the whole technical-industrial field. In the case of the electrical industry, for example, that meant everything from telegraphs to power stations. It also required that the necessary new departments, branches, and subsidiaries be set up. By the mid-1880s, the technical complexity of finished products and services had already led the large electrical-engineering and chemicals concerns, such as Siemens, AEG, and Bayer, to take over retailing through sale to the final customer.

The tendency to diversify remained much more limited in the less capital-intensive industries and in the consumer-goods industries in general. In the labor-intensive industries with highly individualized products and little standardization, the high demands on management created an important barrier to diversification. Highly diversified combinations active in labor-intensive industries other than raw materials and heavy machinery were exceptional before World War I because holding together and effectively running such a heterogeneous concern was regarded as extremely difficult and as requiring more organizational and managerial skills than were then available.[5]

THE RISE OF CARTELS

The leveling off of growth and the fall in prices from 1873 to the mid-1890s led to a rapid increase in the number of enterprises cooperating in cartels or agreements as to output and the price of products, especially in the 1880s. These cartels were based, for the most part, on voluntary agreements among firms that remained largely independent—usually those in the same industry and carrying out the same phase of production; their aim was to establish a common policy in the market. At first, the agreements were a way of setting prices; the cartel gained further stability when it also began to regulate the level of output for each firm and the conditions of its distribution. The most successful cartels also went on to establish joint marketing organizations and were often called syndicates. In 1897, the legality of cartels was confirmed by the highest court of the Reich. German public opinion, which had never very strongly favored laissez-faire ideas, had moved even further away from them after the depression of the 1870s. In general, then, cartels were regarded quite favorably.

According to different scholars' calculations, there were 4 cartels in 1875, 106 in 1890, 205 in 1896, 350 in 1905, 1,500 in 1925, and about 2,100 in 1930.[6] Most were loose regional federations; they were unstable and short-lived because they applied only to specific products. Enterprises that mass produced standardized goods were able to form cartels more easily than firms with widely varying products and short production runs. In 1905 the brick manufacturers had the largest number of cartels—about 130, most of them local; the iron and steel industries followed with 62; chemicals with 32; and the textiles with 31. In 1907 roughly 82 percent of Germany's hard coal was produced by firms that belonged to a cartel, as was 100 percent of its potash, 48 percent of its cement, 50 percent of its crude steel, and 90 percent of its paper. In contrast, only 5 percent of all leather and linoleum, 20 percent of iron and steel manufactured goods, and 2 percent of machines and implements were produced by cartels' member firms. Even before 1914, German firms were involved in about a hundred international cartels as well. Firms that belonged to cartels accounted for roughly 25 percent of Germany's total industrial output in 1907. During World War I and the interwar years this proportion increased; it had doubled by 1938. It was only after 1945, under the influence of the victorious powers, particularly the United States with its strong antitrust tradition, that cartels were banned in West Germany. Exceptions and evasion of the rules remained possible, but other forms of market organization and, above all, cooperation in the form of mergers and integration had by then become more important.[7]

THE ROLE OF THE BANKS

The development of large firms, cartels, and syndicates was closely linked to the changing role of the banks in the industrial system of the German Empire over the past 130 years. The large corporate banks that had mostly appeared in the third quarter of the nineteenth century first played a central role in financing industry during the boom of the 1850s and in the years around 1870; after the early 1890s, banks and industrial enterprises cooperated even more closely. Seven large joint-stock banks, mostly centered in Berlin, came to dominate the Berlin Stock Exchange; they were the Schaaffhausensche Bankverein (established in 1848), the Disconto-Gesellschaft (1851), the Bank für Handel und Industrie (1853), the Berliner Handelsgesellschaft (1856), the Deutsche Bank (1870), the Commerzbank (1870), and the Dresdner Bank (1872). In the two decades before 1914, they brought the older, private, local and provincial banks largely under their influence. By 1904, each had issued between 100 million and 180 million marks of shares, about as much as the largest manufacturing firms. One of their chief functions was financing industrial concerns through long-term credit and by underwriting and marketing industrial securities.

The major banks provided their industrial customers with long- and short-term loans, which constituted three-quarters of their balances in 1913 and were supplied primarily through a large number of small and medium-sized deposits that could be withdrawn on short notice. Thus the German corporate banks acted as mechanisms for the mobilization of scattered savings and channeled them into German industrial enterprises, which depended more heavily on the capital market than their counterparts in Britain and the United States. Gradually, as expansion and merger became more frequent and more significant than the establishment of new enterprises, long-term credit became the main basis of the banks' relationship with industry.[8] Their issues of shares and bonds on behalf of industrial enterprises usually came only after cooperation in long-term credit arrangements had been established. Increasingly, the large corporate banks became more than purely financial intermediaries; they sought to monopolize the financial arrangements of industrial concerns and to serve them with comprehensive policies "from the cradle to the grave." Because of their close ties with industry, the banks began, in contrast to earlier decades, to seek direct influence over manufacturing firms' high-level decisions.[9]

A handful of large banks based in Berlin could not have influenced a much greater number of major industrial enterprises if the firms had not been organized as joint-stock companies (*Aktiengesellschaften*), which, like comparable enterprises in Britain and the United States, were legally incorporated, had charters regulated by law, issued shares, and worked on the principle of limited liability for shareholders. In 1887, 79 of the 100 largest firms were joint-stock companies, as were 77 in 1907; 6 were limited-liability corporations with other legal forms in 1887, and 16 in 1907; only the remainder (15 in 1887;

7 in 1907) were private firms owned by individuals, families, and partnerships. In respect to ownership, the largest firms differed markedly from the bulk of medium-sized and small German enterprises, which did not usually adopt a corporate form.[10] The organization of most large industrial concerns as joint-stock companies gave them an internal structure that allowed the banks to influence their affairs directly.

One of the ways in which the banks could influence corporations directly was through membership on their supervisory boards. In contrast to Britain and the United States, German corporation law after 1870 prescribed a dual board structure. Thus firms had not just one "board of directors" at the top of the corporation, but a supervisory board (*Aufsichtsrat*), on the one hand, and an executive board (*Vorstand*), on the other. The members of the supervisory board were elected by the shareholders or their representatives; they made the most basic decisions, particularly those about investments and top-level appointments. The supervisory board appointed the members of the executive board, who made the day-to-day decisions and actually ran the company. While the executive board members were salaried employees who worked full time as directors, department heads, and executives of the corporation, the members of the supervisory board met only a few times a year. Most of them also held positions in other firms. Before 1914, bank directors made up the largest single group among the supervisory board members of German joint-stock companies and occupied 20 percent of all positions. In 1913–1914, the Deutsche Bank had representatives on 186 other companies' boards. A few leading bank directors had accumulated up to forty-four seats each on supervisory boards before World War I, and by 1930 some held as many as a hundred. Not surprisingly, the supervisory board was the most important channel through which the large banks exercised direct and continuous influence over industrial firms.[11]

As a result of the banks' influence, corporations normally concentrated more on financial and commercial considerations than they would otherwise have done. Bank representatives were concerned with achieving greater efficiency by improving accounting methods and reorganizing individual firms. The banks made the companies they supported less dependent on the short-term fluctuations of the market. Because they preferred large companies to small ones, they accelerated an existing trend toward concentration; they preferred the producer-goods industries, particularly mining, primary metals, and electrical engineering; and they facilitated industrial mergers, the initiative for which normally came from the firms themselves. In general, the banks acted like large flywheels; they did not initiate most changes but, rather, reflected and strengthened existing trends.[12]

The degree of interdependence between banks and industrial enterprises varied from sector to sector, from firm to firm, and from year to year. Broad areas of decision making existed in which conflicts between representatives of the banks and of the manufacturing concerns were not likely to occur and in which, therefore, neither side dominated the other. In general, the banks' influence on industry seems to have reached its peak at the turn of the century and then declined. The trend toward industrial mergers, encouraged by the banks themselves, so increased the power of the large enterprises that their capital needs often outran the capacity of any single bank.

In the early twentieth century, the rate of self-financing— that is, of the use of retained earnings, rather than outside capital, to pay for expansion—in the large manufacturing firms increased. As a result, enterprises became more and more independent of the capital market and thus of the banks. Bank directors on the supervisory boards of large concerns often found themselves in difficult positions. The increasing complexity of the technical and business problems faced by the new, larger enterprises made full-time executives more important than the board members, since they knew more about the day-to-day operations of the firm. Sometimes an inner circle of the supervisory board cooperated closely with the executive board, instead of overseeing its actions. In the long run, the executive board became more influential than the supervisory board, whatever the law; this shift gradually reduced the banks' control of industry and increased the power of the salaried managers.[13]

The Rise of the Salaried Entrepreneur

Both board members of large manufacturing enterprises and directors of large investment banks often performed entrepreneurial functions and wielded entrepreneurial power, despite the fact that they had only a minor stake in the ownership of the firm. In effect, they were salaried entrepreneurs, often called "managers." In describing their emerging role, I shall use the distinction made by Alfred D. Chandler, Jr., among personal, entrepreneurial, and managerial enterprises. According to this scheme, an enterprise is personal when managed by its owners; entrepreneurial when owners hire managers for lower- and middle-management tasks but continue to be responsible for top-level decisions; and managerial when managers who own little or no stock make top-level as well as middle- and lower-level management decisions.[14]

In 1887 and 1907 almost no personal firms were represented among the largest enterprises. Enterprises of the managerial type clearly increased from 1887 to 1907. In mining, firms had often been managerial from their foundation;[15] they were also strong in chemicals and formed a substantial minority in iron and steel. Even as late as 1907, however, most of the 100 largest corporations were still entrepreneurial, and managerial firms were even rarer among the smaller companies.

The new salaried entrepreneur became the object of high expectations and remarkable fears. Some thought him less honest and less ambitious than the owner-entrepreneur; others regarded him as a sign of the bureaucratization of the capitalist economy and thus of its decline. In contrast, many expected the manager to be more socially enlightened and more sensitive to the public good than the owner-entrepreneur and to be less strongly influenced by the hope of private profit; he was expected to resolve traditional class conflicts and to be an agent of moderate social reform. These expectations and fears were not realized. In terms of economic or social behavior and political outlook, the distinction between owner-entrepreneurs and salaried entrepreneurs did not make much relevant difference in Germany. The expansion of firms may have increased rather than diminished with the advent of salaried entrepreneurs, since they were less concerned with such noneconomic motives as family considerations than the founders or owners of firms. Salaried entrepreneurs may also have tended to emphasize long-term planning, to choose future benefits over short-term opportunities, and to consider the continuity of the firm as their primary goal. They generally attempted to ensure the steady development of the company and tended to reject sudden, short-term gains if necessary. They also stressed reinvestment over the distribution of dividends.[16]

The career patterns of top-level salaried entrepreneurs undoubtedly differed from those of owner-entrepreneurs. First of all, they were more likely than owner-entrepreneurs to have received secondary and university-level education. They were also more likely to have been born outside the region in which the firm was located. Most had begun their careers after graduation at low or middle-level salaries and had risen step by step through the company's hierarchy. Many, especially in coal mining, were former civil servants; they were thus able to bring with them an experience of officialdom, special knowledge, certain styles of work, and familiarity with bureaucratic organization when they moved into better-paid positions in corporate management.[17] One of the most important results of the rise of salaried entrepreneurs in terms of economic history was that it helped make specialized technical, business, legal, and organizational skills and knowledge available to corporations through their leaders. In managerial enterprises, achievement could be more important as a criterion for hiring and promotion than it was when ownership and control were inseparable. Thus the increasing importance of salaried entrepreneurs, or managers, reinforced the trends toward professionalism and scientific management in industry.

SCIENCE AND SYSTEM IN MANAGEMENT

Even during the first phase of German industrialization, the academic training of managers already played a substantial role. Among a sample of 400 businessmen from the Rhineland and Westphalia who were active between 1790 and 1870, 66 had received some academic training, primarily of a technical and scientific nature. The large majority were in mining and other extractive industries, largely because state training for mining and foundry officials, initiated during the mercantilist period, had survived the state's withdrawal from entrepreneurial activity in the mines in the 1850s and 1860s.

Moreover, technically trained personnel were becoming increasingly important in firms that depended on engineering and related technology from the middle third of the century on. Graduates of technical schools and colleges were still in the minority but were gaining more positions in engineering and other firms as the Industrial Revolution progressed. Most often they entered business by way of the design and engineering departments that were appearing from the 1850s on. Engineers began to replace managers and foremen with experience but no special training in workshops and factories beginning about 1890. Technical colleges began at about the same time to emphasize practical training; lectures and demonstrations were supplemented by courses in the schools' technical laboratories. In 1899 the technical colleges, all of which were operated by the state, succeeded in gaining the right to grant doctorates and thus achieved equal standing with the universities, which had traditionally been contemptuous of applying science to practical problems.

A third factor in the increasing impact of science on production technology was the activities of the industrial research laboratories, which were established beginning in the 1850s, particularly in the areas of metal production, chemicals, and electrical engineering; they usually maintained close contacts with research and academic departments in the natural sciences and in technological fields at universities and technical institutes.

The more important scientific technology became for the activities of a firm, the more likely it was that some of the technically trained directors of research departments would take over managerial functions and become part of the firm's leadership. The careers of Carl Duisberg at Bayer, a leading chemical firm, Ernst Abbe at Zeiss, (producer of optical tools and the like), and, later, Carl Bosch, at BASF, another chemical firm, demonstrated that this route could lead to the highest levels. Even outside of research departments, however, the proportion of graduates of technical institutes among entrepreneurs increased in these decades, for several reasons. First, industrialists sent their prospective heirs to study at technical colleges, even if their later positions would not have to depend primarily on academic training. Second, it became more common for secondary-level engineering graduates and, after the turn of the century, for engineers with doctoral degrees to rise within a firm and, as salaried entrepreneurs, become members of its executive or supervisory board.

In a sample of 1,300 well-known businessmen active between 1890 and 1930, 52 percent of the salaried entrepreneurs and 37 percent of the owner-entrepreneurs had some academic training. In this respect, Germany was more advanced than Britain or the United States. The German population was 56 million in 1900, and 30,000 engineers graduated from technical colleges in the first decade of the century; during the same period, only 21,000 engineers graduated from colleges and universities in the United States, although its population was 76 million in 1900. That a system of high-level, public technical education grew up quite early in Germany is also indicated by the fact that the number of students in technical colleges reached a peak at the beginning of the twentieth century and then stagnated until after World War I.[18] Academic training remained much less important than on-the-job training and apprenticeship, however, in the recruitment of marketing and financial experts. The German commercial schools developed much more slowly and received much less state support, than the technical schools; academic training in business economics or business administration played hardly any role in the corporations before 1914; later the situation would be different.

While considerable progress was made by the firms in marketing and accounting in the late nineteenth century, it was not necessarily tied to greater academic training. As manufacturing companies took over wholesale and, to some extent, retail functions, new marketing methods had to be developed. By lowering profits, the depression of the 1870s increased the degree of cost-consciousness within enterprises. Literature describing refinements in bookkeeping methods and related techniques rapidly became available; at the same time the increasing frequency with which owner-operated firms were converted to joint-stock corporations made requirements for formal accounting more stringent, as did the increase in firms' participation in cartels. These advances were made not so much by managers with academic business training, however, as by practical men with a middle-level commercial-school education at best.[19]

The greater importance of science in production technology and the development of more systematic methods in marketing and accounting were paralleled by trends toward more systematic management techniques, which supplemented or replaced personal and family-based methods in the large corporations. In this area, as in accounting, academic training played a limited role. "Scientific management" first appeared in the workshops of large enterprises about the turn of the century and was inspired partly by developments in the United States. German managers and engineers visited that country to study its organizational techniques; books and articles describing the shop-floor organization of United States factories appeared in large numbers; by 1907, at the latest, the Taylor system of scientific management was being discussed publicly. Large German companies had developed systematic factory organization on their own, however, and had implemented changes similar to those recommended by Frederick W. Taylor even before his ideas reached Germany. Earlier German bureaucratic traditions, which had emphasized written instructions, precision, and standardization, helped firms in implementing principles of scientific organization within the factory.[20]

At the lower and middle levels of management, the growing staff of an enterprise was organized according to models borrowed from the public bureaucracy; written procedures and regulations and systematic job descriptions were emphasized in the technical and marketing offices as well as in the company's central administration. The division of labor was complex and far-reaching; the hierarchy was carefully defined, and lines of authority and procedures for transmitting information were highly formalized. As a result, private bureaucracies sprang up that differed little from those in the government and in state enterprises.[21]

The case of top-level management was different. While a literature of general business organization and management began to develop after the turn of the century and recommended systematic management procedures and formalized structures for leadership, the application of these ideas seems to have been limited. The officers of the largest companies frequently opposed too systematic a structure at the highest levels of management in order to preserve their own room to maneuver. In spite of their respect for science and technology, for systematic management and regular organization at the lower and middle levels, they regarded personal qualities such as creativity and dynamism, courage and originality, intuition and leadership as decisive at the very top of an enterprise. According to many firms' presidents, too much scientific management would only inhibit those unteachable virtues. Thus the impact of science on the functions of the firm was felt first in production technology and last at the highest levels of management.[22]

At the top levels of large firms before and just after World War I, decision making depended on an intricate mixture of system and improvisation, bureaucratic and personal methods, order and flexibility.[23] As companies grew larger, the number of executive board members increased; they might represent individual functionally defined departments, manage particular areas of production, or oversee single geographic divisions of the enterprise. Even before 1914, these board members were so specialized according to functional areas that a financial director, for instance, might move from one firm to another in a completely different area of industry—perhaps from a powder factory to a firm making electrical machinery—without too much change in his responsibilities. As board members came more and more to specialize in particular areas, the presence of nonspecialized "generalists"—the general directors common on the largest executive boards of the time—became increasingly essential.

Little research has been undertaken so far into the organizational structures and other procedures through which top-level managers administered large integrated and diversified enterprises. Presumably, vertically integrated, centralized, functionally departmentalized organizations were predominant in Germany, as they were in the United States, at the time.[24] Undoubtedly, however, there were many variations and combined structures—well-integrated concerns at the center and loose federations at the periphery. In at least one case—that of the interlocking Siemans' enterprises, Siemens & Halske and Siemans Schuckertwerke, electrical-machinery makers centered in Berlin—the main features of the decentralized multidivisional structure, which typified highly diversified concerns later on, had already developed before World War I. Its structure was an intricate and highly sophisticated mixture of centralization and decentralization, of administrative mechanisms and internal price systems, and of boards, committees, and hierarchies.[25]

The German Case in Perspective

The Broad Outlines Similarities between the development of the modern corporation in Germany and its evolution in the United States are striking. As table 3.6 indicates, the distribution of the largest manufacturing firms among industrial groups was similar in Germany in 1907 and the United States in 1909. In both cases, the large firms clustered in capital-intensive, technologically advanced industries, especially those producing iron, steel, and other metals, on the one hand, and machinery, instruments, and transportation equipment, on the other. These similarities are even more marked when the two economies are contrasted with a third, that of Britain (see table 3.7). In 1905, most of the largest British firms produced consumer goods, especially textiles and food, while firms in the so-called new industries—chemicals, electrical and other machinery, and transportation equipment—were not yet so well represented.[26]

Some differences appear between Germany and the United States, however. Firms in the electrical-engineering and chemicals industries were more prominent in Germany, perhaps as a reflection of the extraordinary importance of scientific research and technology in German industrialization. The two leading electrical manufacturers in the United States—General Electric and Westinghouse—were nonetheless giant enterprises competing successfully with Siemens & Halske and other German manufacturers of electrical equipment in Britain and on the Continent. (The same is true of Western Electric, which does not appear in table 3.7 because it was not an independent company but, rather, a subsidiary of American Telephone and Telegraph.) In the chemicals industry, in contrast, Germany remained supreme until after World War I.

A more significant difference was the market for which firms intended their products. Most of the large United States firms—but not those in Germany—produced goods for the mass or high-volume market; a sizable number of petroleum companies made kerosense and, later, gasoline for the consumer market, for instance, and the rubber companies produced boots, shoes, and then tires for an equally large market. More important, the United States machinery manufacturers, except

Table 3.6

Diversification in the largest manufacturing firms in the United States (1909) and Germany (1907).[a]

GERMAN CENSUS CATEGORY	INDUSTRIAL CATEGORY	U.S. CENSUS CATEGORY[b]	UNITED STATES 1909						GERMANY 1907					
			NUMBER OF FIRMS	STAGES OF DIVERSIFICATION[c]					NUMBER OF FIRMS	STAGES OF DIVERSIFICATION[c]				
				A	B	C	D			A	B	C	D	
IV	Stone, clay, and glass products	32	2	1	1	0	0		3	0	3	0	0	
V, VI	Primary metals products and manufacturing	33, 34	25	2	16	6	1		31	0	1	19	11	
VII	Machinery, instruments, transportation equipment	35, 37, 38	14	7	4	3	0		13	0	2	7	4	
VIII	Electrical engineering and manufacturing	36	2	0	0	0	2		4	0	0	0	4	
IX	Chemicals	28	6	4	2	0	0		17	1	13	3	0	
IX.6	Petroleum refining and related products	29	8	6	1	1	0		3	2	1	0	0	
X	Textiles	22	1	0	1	0	0		3	1	2	0	0	
XI	Paper products; printing	26, 27	3	0	3	0	0		2	0	2	0	0	
XII	Leather	31	2	0	2	0	0		0	0	0	0	0	
XIII	Rubber	30	3	1	2	0	0		0	0	0	0	0	

XVI   Food and allied products; tobacco

20, 21	16	9	5	2	0	4	0	4	0	0
Total	82	30	37	12	3	80	4	28	29	19

Sources: P. G. Porter and H. C. Livesay, "Oligopolists in American Manufacturing and Their Products, 1909–1963," *Business History Review* 43 (1969): 290ff.; Jürgen Kocka and Hannes Siegrist, "Die hundert grössten deutschen Industrieunternehmen," in *Recht und Entwicklung,* ed. Norbert Horn and Jürgen Kocka.

a. Size of firms was determined by the amount of share capital (excluding bonds and reserves). Employment, turnover, and production figures were used for privately owned firms. Note that only 82 American and 80 German firms are represented, since mining and petroleum extracting companies do not appear in the data of Porter and Livesay.

b. Standard Industrial Classifications of the United States Bureau of the Census.

c. $A = 1$ product line; $B = 2$–4 product lines; $C = 5$–9 product lines; $D = 10$ or more product lines.

Table 3.7

Industrial breakdown of the 50 largest mining and manufacturing firms in Great Britain (1905), Germany (1907), and the United States (1917).[a]

GERMAN CENSUS CATEGORY	INDUSTRIAL CATEGORY	U.S. CENSUS CATEGORY[b]	GREAT BRITAIN (1905)	GERMANY (1907)	UNITED STATES (1917)
III	Mining, petroleum extraction and refining, related products	10, 12	1		13
		13, 29	0	13	0
IV	Stone, clay, and glass products	32	1	0	
V	Primary metals products and manufacturing	33			
VI	Metal manufacturing, optical manufacturing, precision tools	34, 36,[c] 38			
VII	Machinery instruments, transportation equipment	35, 37	8	26	20
VIII	Electrical engineering and manufacturing	36	0	3	3
IX	Chemicals	28	5	5	2
X	Textiles	22	10	1	1
XI	Paper products; printing	26, 27	1	1	0
XII	Leather	31	0	0	1
XIII	Rubber	30	1	0	2

XIV	Wood products	24	2	0	1
XVI	Food and allied products; tobacco	20, 21	21	1	7
	Total	—	50	50	50

Sources: Jürgen Kocka and Hannes Siegrist, "Expansion, Diversifikation und Integration," in *Recht und Entwicklung*, ed. Norbert Horn and Jürgen Kocka; Alfred D. Chandler, Jr., *The Visible Hand: The Managerial Revolution in American Business* (Cambridge, Mass., 1977), appendix A; P. L. Payne, "The Emergence of the Large-Scale Company in Great Britain 1870–1914," *Economic History Review*, ser. 2, 20 (1967): 519–542. Because Payne's list of British firms excludes the oil industry and because the size of British food and beverage producers has been inflated by the real-estate holdings of breweries that owned public houses, the British data can be used only for rough comparisons.

a. Size of firms was determined by the amount of share capital (excluding bonds and reserves). Employment, turnover and production figures were used for privately owned firms.

b. Standard Industrial Classifications of the United States Bureau of the Census.

c. Excluding electrical manufacturing.

those who made electrical machinery, concentrated on the mass market by producing hundreds of thousands of office, farm, sewing machines, and, somewhat later, automobiles for domestic and overseas sale each year. Others produced standardized machines—elevators, pumps, boilers, radiators, printing presses, and so on—in considerable volume for world markets. The machinery manufacturers in Germany made heavier equipment, usually to customer specifications. Their competitive strength lay in technical virtuosity; that of the United States firms, in marketing skills and services. Finally, very few food companies appear among the largest German firms in tables 3.6 and 3.7, and many are listed among the largest United States companies. This difference may be related to the larger role agriculture played in the American economy, the larger consumer markets in the United States, and different patterns of consumption, which may have done more to hinder standardization and nationalization of food products in Germany than in the United States.

In both economies, the producers of primary metals, machinery, and electrical-engineering equipment were the most fully diversified, a pattern that seems to confirm Chandler's correlation of diversification with capital-intensive, energy-intensive, and management-intensive industries. Diversification was more advanced in Germany in 1907 than in the United States two years later (see table 3.6). Nineteen of the largest German manufacturers but only three of those in the United States were fully diversified—that is, were active in ten or more of the United States Census Bureau's four-digit industrial categories. A clear majority of the largest German firms, but only fifteen of the United States sample, operated in five or more such "four-digit industries." This result is rather surprising, and it does not square with the notion that the modern business enterprise evolved more slowly in Europe than in the United States. In terms of diversification, the similarity between Germany and the United States was more pronounced in the early twentieth century than that between Britain and Germany. Systematic data for Britain are lacking and ongoing research may modify the picture slightly, but, by and large, the largest British firms were much more specialized and much less diversified than either their German or their United States counterparts.[27] Thus it is dangerous to treat Europe as a single entity for purposes of comparison with the United States, since differences among European economies were often more pronounced than those between any single European country and the United States.

In terms of functional integration as well, the similarity between German and United States firms is notable, and British firms appear generally much less fully integrated.[28] According to Chandler's data, 9 single-function firms remained among the 100 largest United States firms in 1909; 88 were integrated (that is, had taken at least one step backward toward raw materials or forward toward distribution) and 3 cannot be classified.[29] Among the 100 largest German firms in 1907, 12 performed only a single function if membership in a cartel or syndicate is considered a means of forward integration, and 16 if it is not (see table 3.5). The same similarities and differences among Germany, Britain, and the United States would be apparent in an examination of the proportions of managerial, entrepreneurial, and personal firms in the three countries. In this case, however, the differences between Germany and the United States might have been significant, since entrepreneurial corporations in which family members continued to exercise control may well have been more important in Germany before World War I than in the United States at the same time. Although good quantitative evidence for such a comparison is unfortunately lacking, the major growth of the managerial enterprise probably took place after World War I in Germany, and even then many entrepreneurial firms remained among the 100 largest.

As these generalizations suggest, a high degree of diversification and integration can be achieved in corporations of the entrepreneurial type, and the shift to the managerial type may come much later. Furthermore, there is no perfect correlation between size, on the one hand, and diversification and integration, on the other. In terms of mere size, the largest German and British firms were more similar to each other than to those in the United States, and both ranked behind the huge firms on the other side of the Atlantic.[30]

Causes and Conditions   Any explanation of the reasons for these similarities and differences must be tentative, since other countries such as France have not been included because the issue is complex and because available data are still imperfect. Differences in market size do not seem a significant factor; otherwise, Britain and Germany would be more similar and the development of the modern German business enterprise would have lagged behind that of the managerial firm in the United States. The growth rate of markets seems to correlate rather better with the observed patterns if one assumes, as Chandler does, that the rapidly growing markets stimulated diversification, integration, and the development of the modern management structures.[31] More plausible explanations are still needed for this correlation.

Legal differences, another possible causal factor, do not seem to account adequately for the differences among German, British, and United States patterns of corporate growth. It has been argued that some variations between Britain and the United States may have resulted from the fact that British law, unlike United States law, did not strongly restrict the possibility of firms' entering loose federations, agreements, and cartels. Therefore, it is claimed, British firms before the 1930s did not consolidate, integrate, and set up managerial hierarchies when they wanted to dominate a market or control competition; instead, they worked out mutual agreements with other members of a cartel or of a loose holding company in order to maintain their independence. Because United States law made such combinations difficult, the same alternative was less readily available to United States businessmen.[32]

When Germany is included, however, this argument is less convincing. In terms of legal tolerance of cartels, Germany resembled Britain, and attitudes in both countries differed strongly from the hostility United States lawmakers and judges showed toward cartels and similar arrangements.[33] In fact, however, integrated concerns originated in Germany and the United States in much the same way, despite this legal difference. Legal differences do, however, explain another phenomenon. One strategy of forward integration by manufacturing enterprises into distribution was available to German firms but rarely existed in the United States after the passage of the Sherman Antitrust Act in 1890 and was used infrequently in Britain or France. This scheme was collective forward integration, through cartels and syndicates whose managers sold the products of member firms. Thus legal factors seem to explain international differences in strategy, but not in degree of integration.

Several factors were undoubtedly involved in bringing about the differences already described. Organizational and managerial skills seem to have been available earlier in Germany than in Britain, partly because models and tactics developed earlier in the public bureaucracy could be adapted to commercial enterprises.[34] From the 1870s on, protective tariffs made it easier and more attractive for German businessmen, such as those in heavy industry, to diversify and integrate backward into raw materials because customs barriers forced foreign suppliers to sell the same raw materials at a higher price. Thus manufacturers could lower unit costs by securing their own supplies. The tariff situation in Britain clearly differed from that in Germany or the United States; at least until World War I, British businessmen enjoyed less tariff protection.[35] Along with the factors mentioned so far, differences in attitudes and values on the part of businessmen, different educational systems, and different social and cultural traditions probably explain at least some of the evident differences among the nations, but they are notoriously hard to pin down.[36] Certainly the technical education of many German entrepreneurs and their corresponding preference for "organization" and "production" over "market" play a role.

There is a further explanation, however, that may well be the most powerful and comprehensive. Unlike that in Britain, the German situation was characterized by factors that favored very early expansion, diversification, and integration of firms: Germany began to industrialize relatively late and was at first somewhat more backward than Britain and other parts of Western Europe; industrialization then took place more rapidly than in Britain. In most of Germany, industrialization was a less continuous process, and it developed on the basis of a different, older set of commercial and artisans' structures than those that evolved in the most economically developed regions of Western Europe. This difference is particularly evident in the fact that the industries most important in the German Industrial Revolution—railroads, the manufacture of machinery and chemicals, and some raw-materials production—had few if any predecessors, while textiles, the leading area in early British industrialization, had a well-developed tradition dating back to early modern times. Thus when German entrepreneurs, deeply impressed by their example, tried to imitate and catch up to the British industries, they had to found factories almost from scratch.[37] Three consequences of Germany's status as a latecomer to industry are significant for the history of the modern German corporation.

First, German businessmen in important industrial areas could not build on a well-developed industrial and commercial tradition. Specialized merchants and shippers who might provide raw materials and market their products did not exist in sufficient numbers; thus, if industrial firms did not want to give up their plans altogether, they had to fulfill these functions themselves, within their own organizations and with employees. In other words, a low degree of division of labor in the economy as a whole led to a high degree of division of labor within the new enterprises—if they got off the ground at all. This process explains, at least in part, why large-scale, highly integrated, diversified firms existed even in the first phase of German industrialization, during the second third of the nineteenth century and even earlier, especially in the production of raw materials and machinery.[38]

Second, Germany's relative backwardness led to early diversification, since the first industrial enterprises, which necessarily produced goods for rudimentary and unpredictable markets, preferred not to risk their survival on a single product.[39] Relying on several product lines was a particularly rational policy for factories that imitated Western models, often importing equipment and technicians, and that had a large enough capacity to require diversification for full utilization of their physical plants.

Finally, early producers in relatively undeveloped industrial areas had little to fear when they reached out into new markets or introduced new product lines, since they faced virtually no established competitors. As a result, patterns of expansion, diversification, and integration developed that seem to have lacked parallels in Britain or even in the United States. In both countries, small, highly specialized, single-function personal enterprises were more clearly dominant in the first phase of industrialization than in Germany. Furthermore, British and United States manufacturers left the tasks of supplying raw materials and distributing finished goods to independent middlemen; this practice was much less common among early German manufacturers.[40]

Some of the factors that brought about diversification and integration became less powerful as the economy became more developed, as the overall division of labor became more elaborate, and as markets became more transparent or predictable. During the nineteenth century, therefore, certain enterprises became more specialized, and in some industries the proportion of specialized, nonintegrated firms may have increased.[41] As a comparison of tables 3.2 and 3.4 and of tables 3.3 and 3.5 indicates, the high degree of diversification and integration among large-scale German firms in 1907 resulted in part from decisions made in the previous two decades, not from traditions dating back into the early stages of the Industrial Revolution. But by 1887 integration and diversification were already highly advanced. Early experiments in both had survived; their effect was to make large integrated and diversified structures more common and more generally accepted by businessmen in general.

Other consequences of Germany's relative backwardness, which also facilitated early expansion, integration, and diversification, probably gained in force over time. Among them are the increasing importance of joint-stock companies, which generally erected fewer barriers to rapid expansion than did family enterprises, and the related strength of investment banks. Both institutions can be understood as responses to the requirements of industrialization under conditions of relative economic backwardness.[42] Investment banks not only accelerated the expansion, integration, and diversification of manufacturing enterprises, as already described, but their strength was also inversely related to the weakness of the middleman; in Germany the independent merchant was much less important in the process of industrialization than in Britain. While the British middleman participated actively in funding manufacturing firms, in Germany this task was more often undertaken by banks. It seems plausible that a strong tradition of independent middlemen mediating among highly specialized production companies, and between them and consumers, according to the laws of the market posed an obstacle to the rapid diversification and integration of manufacturing firms. This obstacle was much less a factor in Germany than in Britain, because of Germany's comparative backwardness at the start.[43]

In spite of the conclusions that might be based on evidence from Britain and the United States alone, large-scale enterprise and high degrees of functional integration and product diversification do not necessarily indicate advanced or late stages of development. Rather, as the German case and the similar experiences of East Central Europe and Japan suggest, they may well result from the attempt to make up for relative backwardness.[44] There seems to be a reciprocal relationship between the underdevelopment of an economy as a whole and the modernity of the structures and strategies of its largest enterprises, which function as islands of modernity in a sea of traditional small and medium-sized enterprises. At least in the case of single enterprises like Siemens, the early tendencies toward greater size, diversification, and integration were still apparent during later phases of development, when they encouraged the enterprises to respond to new pressures in favor of further growth, diversification, and integration—pressures that resulted from modern technology and other factors already discussed. The mechanisms by which strong traditional factors in a relatively backward economy may facilitate later modernization remain to be fully explored. At least in Germany, enterprises that were apparently at a disadvantage in comparison with those in other economies eventually reaped concrete gains from their very initial backwardness.

NOTES

1. See H. Mottek, "Zum Verlauf und zu einigen Hauptproblemen der industriellen Revolution in Deutschland," in H. Mottek et al., *Studien zur Geschichte der industriellen Revolution in Deutschland* (Berlin, 1960), pp. 11–63; W. G. Hoffmann, "The Take-Off in Germany," in *The Economics of Take-Off into Sustained Growth,* ed. Walt W. Rostow (London, 1964), pp. 95–118; F. W. Henning, *Die Industrialisierung in Deutschland, 1800–1914* (Paderborn, 1973); K. Borchardt, "Wirtschaftliches Wachstum und Wechsellagen 1800–1914," in *Handbuch der deutschen Wirtschafts- und Sozialgeschichte,* ed. H. Aubin and W. Zorn, II (Stuttgart, 1976), 198–275; R. Fremdling, *Eisenbahnen und deutsches Wirtschaftswachstum, 1840–1873* (Dortmund, 1975).

2. See W. G. Hoffmann et al., *Das Wachstum der deutschen Wirtschaft seit der Mitte des 19. Jahrhunderts* (Berlin, 1965), pp. 63, 204ff., 454ff.; R. Wagenführ, *Die Industriewirtschaft* (Berlin, 1933), p. 56ff.; A. Spiethoff, *Die wirtschaftlichen Wechsellagen,* 2 vols. (Tübingen and Zurich, 1955); J. A. Schumpeter, *Business Cycles,* 2 vols. (New York, 1939), I; C. P. Kindleberger, "Germany's Over-Taking of England, 1806–1914," *Weltwirtschaftliches Archiv* 111 (1975): 253–281, 477–504; A. Maddison, *Economic Growth in the West* (New York, 1964), p. 30.

3. As developed in Alfred D. Chandler, Jr., *The Visible Hand: The Managerial Revolution in American Business* (Cambridge, Mass., 1977).

4. Data on the 100 largest German firms, published here for the first time, were collected by Hannes Siegrist as part of a 1976–1978 project at the Bielefeld University Center for Interdisciplinary Research; this project, directed by Norbert Horn and Jürgen Kocka, dealt with the economic and legal factors in the development of the large corporation; for more details, see Jürgen Kocka and Hannes Siegrist, "Die hundert grössten deutschen Industrieunternehmen in späten 19. und frühen 20. Jahrhundert. Expansion, Diversifikation und Integration im internationalen Vergleich," in *Recht und Entwicklung der Grossunternehmen, 1860–1920,* ed. Norbert Horn and Jürgen Kocka (Göttingen, 1979).

5. For a fuller discussion, see Kocka and Siegrist, "Die hundert grössten deutschen industrieunternehmen"; Jürgen Kocka, "Expansion, Integration, Diversifikation. Wachstumsstrategien industrielle Grossunternehmen in Deutschland vor 1914," in *Industrie und Gewerbe im 19./20. Jahrhundert,* ed. H. Winkel (Berlin, 1975), pp. 203–226; data on the top 100 of 1927 will be included in Hannes Siegrist, "Deutsche Grossunternehmen vom späten 19. Jahrhundert bis zur Weimarer Republik," *Geschichte und Gesellschaft* 6, no. 1 (1980).

6. These and the following figures are from W. Wagenführ, *Kartelle in Deutschland* (Nuremberg, 1931), p. *xiii;* H. König, "Kartelle und Konzentration," in *Die Konzentration in der Wirtschaft,* ed. H. Arndt, 2 vols. (Berlin, 1960), I; 310–311.

7. See K. Wiedenfeld, *Kartelle und Konzerne* (Berlin and Leipzig, 1927); H. Levy, *Industrial Germany: A Study of Its Monopoly Organizations and Their Control by the State* (New York, 1966); V. Holzschuher, "Soziale und ökonomische Hintergründe der Kartellbewegung" (Ph.D. diss., Erlangen/Nuremberg, 1937); E. Maschke, *Grundzüge der deutschen Kartellgeschichte bis 1914* (Dortmund, 1964); R. Liefmann, *Kartelle und Trusts und die Weiterbildung der volkswirtschaftlichen Organisation* (Stuttgart, 1910); idem, *Kartelle, Konzerne und Trusts,* 9th ed. (Stuttgart, 1930). Good case studies can be found in H. Lüthgen, *Das Rheinisch-westfälische Kohlensyndikat in der Vorkriegs-, Kriegs- und Wachkriegszeit und seine Probleme* (Leipzig and Erlangen, 1926); A. Klotzbach, *Der Roheisenverband* (Düsseldorf, 1926); W. N. Parker, "Entrepreneurship, Industrial Organization, and Economic Growth," *Journal of Economic History* 14 (1954):26–36.

8. See A. Weber, *Die rheinisch-westfälischen Provinzialbanken und die Krisis* (Leipzig, 1903), p. 337; of 18 joint-stock industrial corporations

founded in the Rhineland and Westphalia in 1896–1900 and listed on the Berlin Stock Exchange in 1901, 16 resulted from conversions of previously existing private companies; only two were entirely new entities.

9. See O. Jeidels, *Das Verhältnis der deutschen Grossbanken zur Industrie mit besonderer Berücksichtigung der Eisenindustrie* (Leipzig, 1905); E. Riesser, *Die deutschen Grossbanken und ihre Konzentration* (Jena, 1910); M. Gehr, *Das Verhältnis zwischen Banken und Industrie in Deutschland seit der Mitte des 19. Jahrhunderts bis zur Bankenkrise von 1931* (Stuttgart, 1959); K. E. Born, *Geld und Banken im 19. und 20. Jahrhundert* (Stuttgart, 1977), pp. 161–167.

10. See R. Passow, *Die Aktiengesellschaft* (Jena, 1922), p. 30.

11. See ibid., pp. 127–211, for an analysis of the legal situation and of the actual makeup of joint-stock companies before 1914; see also F. Eulenburg, "Die Aufsichtsräte der deutschen Aktiengesellschaften," *Jahrbücher für Nationalökonomie und Statistik* 32 (1906): 92–109; W. Sombart, *Der moderne Kapitalismus,* III (Munich and Leipzig, 1927), 740–747; Jeidels, *Verhältnis der deutschen Grossbanken,* pp. 143ff.

12. See Jeidels, *Verhältnis der deutschen Grossbanken,* pp. 162–268. Quantitative analyses of the banks' contributions to German economic growth have so far been inconclusive; see E. Eistert, *Die Beeinflussung des Wirtschaftswachstums in Deutschland von 1888–1913 durch das Bankensystem* (Berlin, 1970); H. Neuburger and H. Stokes, "German Banks and Economic Growth, 1883–1913," *Journal of Economic History* 34 (1974): 710–741; see also the debate in ibid., 36 (1976): 416–427.

13. The pattern described here contradicts the Marxists thesis of "finance capitalism," which stresses the superior role of the banks. See R. Hilferding, *Das Finanzkapital* (Vienna, 1910). See also Jürgen Kocka, *Unternehmensverwaltung und Angestelltenschaft am Beispiel Siemens, 1844–1914* (Stuttgart, 1969), pp. 327, 423–435; Gehr, *Verhältnis zwischen Banken und Industrie,* p. 62; Jeidels, *Verhältnis der deutschen Grossbanken,* pp. 233, 258–272; K. Wiedenfeld, *Das Persönliche in modernen Unternehmertum* (Leipzig, 1911), pp. 104–107; Carl Fürstenberg, *Die Lebensgeschichte eines deutschen Bankiers* (Wiesbaden, 1961), pp. 165–166, 175, 394–395; W. Hagemann, "Des Verhältnis der deutschen Grossbanken zur Industrie" (Ph.D. diss., Berlin, 1931), p. 18. On the rates of self-financing, see W. G. Hoffmann, "Die unverteilten Gewinne der Aktiengesellschaften in Deutschland, 1871–1957," *Zeitschrift für die gesamte Staatswissenschaft* 115 (1959): 271–291, especially pp. 277, 281–282; R. Tilly, "The Growth of the Large-Scale Enterprise in Germany since the Middle of the Nineteenth Century," in *The Rise of Managerial Capitalism,* ed. Herman Daems and H. van der Wee (The Hague, 1974), pp. 145–169.

14. See Alfred D. Chandler, Jr., and Herman Daems, introduction to *Rise of Managerial Capitalism,* ed. Daems and van der Wee, pp. 1–34. The banks' representatives on the supervisory boards of industrial corporations were themselves salaried managers, since the large investment banks were managerial enterprises.

15. For a discussion of the period during which many corporations in the Ruhr were founded, see H. Schacht, "Zur Finanzgeschichte des Ruhrkohlen-Bergbaus," *Schmollers Jahrbuch* 37.3 (1913):147–185.

16. See Jürgen Kocka, "Entrepreneurs and Managers in German Industrialization," in *The Industrial Economies: Capital, Labour, and Enterprise*, Cambridge Economic History of Europe, vol. VII (Cambridge, 1978), pt. 1, pp. 573–580.

17. See H. Sachtler, *Wandlungen des industriellen Unternehmertums in Deutschland seit Beginn des 19. Jahrhunderts* (Halle-Wittenberg, 1937), p. 41; W. Stahl, *Der Elitekreislauf in der Unternehmerschaft* (Frankfort, 1973), pp. 191, 228; T. Pierenkemper, *Die westfälischen Schwerindustriellen 1852–1913. Soziale Merkmale und unternehmerischer Erfolg* (Göttingen, 1979); W. Fischer, *Wirtschaft und Gesellschaft im Zeitalter der Industrialisierung* (Göttingen, 1975), p. 194; Jürgen Kocka, "La nascita del ceto manageriale nell'industria della Germania gugliemina," *Movimento Opereaio e Socialista*, n.s., 1.1–2 (1978): 3–20.

18. See Kocka, "Entrepreneurs and Managers," pp. 534–535, 570–572; K.-H. Manegold, *Universität, Technische Hochschule und Industrie* (Berlin, 1970); P. Borscheid, *Naturwissenschaft, Staat und Industrie in Baden, 1848–1914* (Stuttgart, 1976); U. Troitsch, *Innovation, Organisation und Wissenschaft beim Aufbau von Hüttenwerken im Ruhrgebiet, 1850–1870* (Dortmund, 1977), pp. 35–42, for a discussion of the early laboratories at foundries; H. Sachtler, *Wandlungen des industriellen Unternehmertums*, p. 41, for the investigation of 1,300 businessman listed in the *Reichshandbuch der deutschen Gesellschaft* of 1930–31; see Jürgen Kocka, *Angestellte zwischen Faschismus und Demokratie. Zur politischen Sozialgeschichte der Angestellten: USA, 1890–1940 im internationalen Vergleich* (Göttingen, 1977), pp. 131–132, for comparative figures on engineering graduates in Germany and the United States.

19. See F. Pinner, *Emil Rathenau und das elektrische Zeitalter* (Leipzig, 1918), p. 126; F. Redlich, *Die volkswirtschaftliche Bedeutung der deutschen Teerfarbenindustrie* (Munich and Leipzig, 1914), pp. 8–9; J. J. Beer, *The Emergence of the German Dye Industry* (Urbana, 1959), p. 94; see also F. E. Farrington, *Commercial Education in Germany* (New York, 1914), pp. 23, 144, on the higher commercial schools; F. Redlich, "Academic Education for Business," *Business History Review* 31 (1957): 35–91; A. Isaac, *Die Entstehung der wissenschaftlichen Betriebswirtschaftslehre in Deutschland seit 1898* (Berlin, 1923); W. Böhme, "Ein Vierteljahrhundert Verband Deutscher Diplomkaufleute e.V.," *Der Diplomkaufmann* 10 (1930): 247–259; H. Hartmann, *Education for Business Leadership: The Role of the German "Hochschulen"* (Paris, 1955), p. 18; Jürgen Kocka, "Industrielles Management: Konzeptionen und Modelle vor 1914," *Vierteljahrschrift für Sozial- und Wirtschaftsgeschichte* 56 (1969): 337.

20. See Kocka, "Industrielles Management," pp. 356–360, 365; L. Burchardt, "Technischer Fortschritt und sozialer Wandel. Das Beispiel der Taylorismus-Rezeption," in *Deutsche Technikgeschichte*, ed. W. Treue

(Göttingen, 1977), pp. 52–98; H. Homburg, "Die Anfänge des Taylor-systems in Deutschland vor dem Ersten Weltkrieg," *Geschichte und Gesellschaft* 4 (1978): 170–184.

21. For a description of this process in the firm of Siemens & Halske, see Kocka, *Unternehmensverwaltung*, pp. 363–382, 547; for the interwar period, see O. H. von der Gablentz, "Industriebürokratie," *Schmollers Jahrbuch* 50 (1926): 539–572.

22. See Kocka, "Industrielles Management," pp. 347–356.

23. For a discussion of this complex topic, see Kocka, "Entrepreneurs and Managers," pp. 575–578.

24. See Alfred D. Chandler, Jr., *Strategy and Structure* (Cambridge, Mass., 1962); idem, "The United States: Seedbed of Managerial Capitalism," this volume.

25. See Jürgen Kocka, "Family and Bureaucracy in German Industrial Management," *Business History Review* 45 (1971): 152–155.

26. See P. L. Payne, "The Emergence of the Large-Scale Company in Great Britain 1870–1914," *Economic History Review* 20 (1967): 539–540. This comparison is not without methodological problems, as Payne's list excludes the oil industry, probably on the grounds that the major British oil companies were operating abroad with large amounts of foreign capital. In addition, the size and the relative importance of some breweries may be exaggerated by real-estate holdings such as public houses and hotels. The British picture became more similar to those in Germany and the United States in 1905–1919 and even more so during the 1920s. For more on this subject, see Leslie Hannah, *The Rise of the Corporate Economy: The British Experience* (London, 1976); idem, "Visible and Invisible Hands in Great Britain," this volume.

27. See Levy, *Industrial Germany;* Wiedenfeld, *Das Persönliche,* p. 21; Payne, "Emergence," pp. 527–528; Leslie Hannah, introduction to *Management Strategy and Business Development,* ed. Hannah (London, 1976), pp. 1–19.

28. See Payne, "Emergence," p. 532; further research may qualify this statement.

29. See Chandler, *Visible Hand,* pp. 348, 503–512.

30. On the basis of a preliminary comparison of the data in Payne, "Emergence," p. 539, with those for the total assets (in shares, bonds, and capital reserves) of the largest German firms in 1907.

31. See Chandler, "United States," this volume, for estimates of the annual growth rates of United States, British, and German markets.

32. See Payne, "Emergence," pp. 525–526.

33. See Morton Keller, "Public Policy and the Large Enterprise: Comparative Historical Perspectives," in *Recht und Entwicklung,* ed. Horn and Kocka.

34. See Jürgen Kocka, "Vorindustrielle Faktoren in der deutschen In-(Düs-dustrialisierung," in *Das Kaiserliche Deutschland,* ed. M. Stürmer seldorf, 1970), pp. 265–286.

35. See R. Sonnemann, *Die Auswirkungen des Schutzzolls auf die*

Monopolisierung der deutschen Eisen- und Stahlindustrie, 1879–1892 (Berlin, 1960).

36. See D. C. Coleman, "Gentlemen and Players," *Economic History Review*, ser. 2, 26 (1973): 92–116.

37. See Alexander Gerschenkron, *Economic Backwardness in Historical Perspective* (Cambridge, Mass., 1962), pp. 5–51, 353–364; idem, *Europe in the Russian Mirror* (Cambridge, England, 1970), p. 86; R. Dore, *British Factory—Japanese Factory: The Origins of Diversity in Industrial Relations* (London, 1973).

38. See F. Redlich, "A German Eighteenth-Century Iron Works during Its First Hundred Years," *Bulletin of the Business Historical Society* 27 (1953): 69–96; K. Groba, *Der Unternehmer im Beginn der Industrialisierung Schlesiens* (Breslau, 1936), pp. 6, 12–13; E. Schremmer, *Die Wirtschaft Bayerns* (Munich, 1970), p. 523; H. Rachel and P. Wallich, *Berliner Grosskaufleute und Unternehmer*, 2nd ed., II (Berlin, 1967), 209, 253, 351–352; H. Krüger, *Zur Geschichte der Manufakturarbeiter in Preussen* (Berlin, 1958), pp. 63, 233. For a discussion of the Gutehoffnungshütte, an early integrated and diversified firm producing iron and steel and heavy machinery in 1830, see E. Maschke, *Es entsteht ein Konzern* (Oberhausen, 1969), pp. 19–31; for Harkort's "Mechanische Werkstätte" in Wetter, a diversified producer of machinery and other metal products in 1820, see W. Köllmann, "Frühe Unternehmer," in *Ruhrgebiet und neues Land,* ed. W. Först (Cologne and Berlin, 1968), p. 11; on the diversification at Borsig's early factory (locomotives, machinery, and metal equipment) in 1840, see H. Witt, *Die Triebkräfte des industriellen Unternehmertums vor hundert Jahren und heute* (Hamburg, 1929), p. 93; on the integrated and diversified concerns in Silesia, see K. Fuchs, *Vom Dirigismus zum Liberalismus* (Wiesbaden, 1970), p. 32; see also F. Hellwig, "Unternehmer und Unternehmensform im saarländischen Industriegebiet," *Jahrbücher für Nationalökonomie und Statistik* 158 (1943): 409, 415; W. Herrmann, *Entwicklungslinien montanindustrieller Unternehmen im rheinisch-westfälischen Industriegebiet* (Dortmund, 1954), pp. 10, 22; Troitsch, *Innovation*, pp. 5–12.

39. See E. Dittrich, ed., *Lebensbilder sächsischer Wirtschaftsführer,* I (Leipzig, 1941), 150.

40. See H. J. Habakkuk, *Industrial Organisation since the Industrial Revolution* (Southampton, 1968), p. 4; Chandler, *Visible Hand*, chap. 1; Kindleberger, "Germany's Over-Taking of England," p. 497.

41. Research on these questions does not yet seem to have been undertaken, but see Sombart, *Kapitalismus*, III, 792–793, 796–797.

42. See D. S. Landes, "The Structure of Enterprise in the Nineteenth Century: The Cases of Britain and Germany," *Rapports du XIe Congrès International des Sciences Historiques*, V (Uppsala, 1960), 107–128, especially 117–118; R. Tilly, *Financial Institutions and Industrialization in the Rhineland, 1815–1870* (Madison, Wis., 1966).

43. On these differences between Britain and Germany, see T. Vogelstein, "Die finanzielle Organisation der kapitalistischen Industrie und die

Monopolbildung," in *Grundriss der Sozialökonomik,* 2nd ed., VI (Tübingen, 1923), 390–412; E. Landauer, *Handel und Produktion in der Baumwollindustrie* (Tübingen, 1912); idem, "Über die Stellung des Handels in der modernen industriellen Entwicklung," *Archiv für Sozialwissenschaften und Sozialpolitik* 34 (1912): 879–892. On some of the social and psychological aspects of this difference, see Kocka, "Expansion," pp. 217–218n29.

44. See I. Berend, "Investment Strategy in East-Central Europe in the 19th–20th Centuries," *Proceedings of the Sixth International Congress of the International Economic History Association* (Copenhagen, 1974), p. 49; J. Hirschmeier, *The Origins of Entrepreneurship in Meiji Japan* (Cambridge, Mass., 1966), p. 211.

4/ The Large Corporation in Modern France

Maurice Lévy-Leboyer

TODAY, for the first time, the corporate sector in France seems to conform to the general pattern of economic structure and hierarchical organization that is evident in other major industrial countries. The large corporations cluster in the industrial sectors that supply extensive markets with mass-produced goods ranging from food and beverages to chemicals, machinery, and electrical equipment.[1] Many have entered new markets unrelated to their original activities, and in managing their multiproduct lines and multinational activities, they have often given a large measure of autonomy to their operating units. These firms are managed by means of some variation of the divisional structure; in each, a general office is responsible for measuring performance, for planning and allocating resources, and for coordinating and controlling the work of the operating units. By 1970, 54 of the 100 largest companies in France had adopted this type of organization, compared with 50 in Germany, 57 in the United Kingdom, and 80 in the United States (see table 4.1).[2]

Furthermore, concentration of industrial production and distribution emphasizes the extent of institutional change. Although France has long been looked on as a country of petty entrepreneurs, one finds there, by the early 1970s, a total of 18 giant industrial groups, including subsidiaries in which the parent firms held 30 percent or more of the shares of stock outstanding; they were responsible for 11 percent of the total value added in manufacturing, 11 percent of the work force, 15 percent of net domestic capital formation, and 23 percent

Table 4.1

Distribution of the 100 largest corporations in France, 1950–1970.[a]

TYPE	1950	1960	1970
	Product lines		
Single	42	28	16
Dominant	21	27	32
Diversified (related)	33	40	42
Diversified (unrelated)	4	5	10
	Organizational structure		
Functional	50	32	14
Functional-holding company	24	29	12
Pure-holding company	20	18	12
Multidivisional	6	21	54

Sources: G. P. Dyas and H. T. Thanheiser, *The Emerging European Enterprise: Strategy and Structure in French and German Industry* (London, 1976); F. Roure, *Etude typologique financière des holdings pures françaises. Analyse des holdings américaines* (Paris, 1975), vol. IV.

a. Size of corporations measured by sales values.

of French exports.[3] Such a degree of concentration reflects, in part, the adoption of modern organizational and managerial techniques, which have created new sources of efficiency. First, they have made possible the rationalization and integration of operations that were formerly left to market mechanisms and thus have lowered unit costs; second, they have allowed planning processes to stabilize the use of productive facilities and to expand market demand.

But the transformation is a recent one. Previous studies have established that earlier in this century industrial integration was lacking in France, so firm size, measured by total assets, was smaller than in other industrial economies. In the 1920s, for example, Alsthom (the leading electrical-equipment manufacturer) and Saint-Gobain (the glassmaker and chemical producer), the two largest French corporations in terms of share capital issued, were only 5 to 7 percent as large as Imperial Chemical Industries or the German giant I. G. Farben. Similarly, industrial firms were slow to use their experience, whether technical or commercial, to diversify into new products or processes. Of course, there were some exceptions; Saint-Gobain and Schneider (metal maker and producer of armaments) began to promote new technologies and moved into new markets when demand for some of their earlier products dried up.[4] At the same time, a few leading firms in the more modern sectors added complementary activities. Louis Renault, in particular, integrated his enterprises vertically from steel to the manufacturing of automobiles and diversified horizontally to producing aircraft engines, tanks, and military equipment and even to operating air, bus, taxi, trucking, and freight-delivery companies; the latter were adjuncts to his activities in marketing and after-sales service. By and large, however, only a small minority of leading firms made such moves before World War II. Indeed, as a general rule, large industrial corporations failed actively to take up such policies of integration and diversification.

Large French firms were slow not only in adopting a strategy of diversification but also in taking up the new organizational forms. The multidivisional structure pioneered by Saint-Gobain as early as 1905, which was adopted in the 1920s by Kuhlmann, Péchiney, and other chemical companies, as well as by some in the engineering and iron and steel industries, could have given more flexibility and closer control over the activities of an industrial group and thus contributed to its integration.[5] Yet the use of this new structure was not expanded in the interwar years and in many cases was even discontinued. In 1950, as table 4.1 indicates, far more of the largest firms were organized as loose-knit groups in which one firm had large shareholdings, or *participations*, to use the French term, in the others. For managerial purposes, they did not offer an efficiency comparable to that of the multidivisional organization; their predominance indicates a continuing preference, voluntary or not, for indirect rather than direct control over operations.

This attitude is reflected in the high proportion of funds invested by the major firms in financial assets. Table 4.2 shows the ratio of portfolio investment (stocks and bonds) to fixed capital assets (buildings, machinery, and other equipment) from 1912 through 1937, calculated sector by sector on the basis of data taken from balance sheets of the leading corporations. The overall ratio for industry was, of course, highest in 1912, because it was weighted heavily by firms with both financial and industrial activities in the production of coal, petroleum, tex-

Table 4.2

Asset structure of large French corporations, 1912–1937.[a]

SECTOR OR INDUSTRY	1912			1927			1937		
	PORTFOLIO INVESTMENT (% OF TOTAL ASSETS)	FIXED CAPITAL EQUIPMENT (% OF TOTAL ASSETS)	PORT-FOLIO: EQUIP-MENT (RATIO)	PORTFOLIO INVESTMENT (% OF TOTAL ASSETS)	FIXED CAPITAL EQUIPMENT (% OF TOTAL ASSETS)	PORT-FOLIO: EQUIP-MENT (RATIO)	PORTFOLIO INVESTMENT (% OF TOTAL ASSETS)	FIXED CAPITAL EQUIPMENT (% OF TOTAL ASSETS)	PORTFOLIO: EQUIPMENT (RATIO)
Public utilities	11.5	69.8	0.2	11.3	66.5	0.2	26.3	53.0	0.5
Coal	27.6	11.3	2.4	11.0	45.8	0.2	17.5	61.4	0.3
Petroleum	27.1	18.2	1.5	35.1	26.2	1.3	24.0	34.3	0.7
Chemicals	10.7	36.2	0.3	12.5	27.6	0.5	21.6	26.1	0.8
Electrical industries	47.1	15.8	3.0	22.6	25.5	0.9	31.1	23.0	1.4
Metals	12.2	38.3	0.3	13.1	31.7	0.4	15.6	35.5	0.4
Machinery	6.7	35.1	0.2	6.9	26.1	0.3	10.3	34.8	0.3
Automobiles	1.6	35.1	0.1	2.6	47.7	0.1	5.8	31.2	0.2
Textiles (including man-made fibers)	7.8	28.7	0.3	6.1	22.4	0.3	15.4	26.1	0.6
Food	4.5	47.7	0.3	–	–	–	8.5	29.9	0.5
Industry (total)	17.4	31.4	0.6	10.6	32.8	0.3	34.4	34.4	0.5

Sources: Annuaire Desfossés and financial press.

a. Although the samples used have been restricted to the larger firms (about thirty corporations at each date) by setting a limit in terms of total assets, the data indicate only broad trends, since many firms amortized their fixed capital assets fully; examples are the coal mines before World War I and Pont-à-Mousson. In 1932 the ratio of portfolio to fixed capital assets was already increasing in the public-utility sector and in industry, particularly in chemicals and rubber.

tiles, including man-made fibers, and electrical equipment. It was lower after World War I but still rose in the 1930s, particularly in the industries producing chemicals and electric machinery and equipment. This shift to portfolio investment suggests that firms were losing direct managerial control over a number of enterprises they had promoted and financed, a development at variance with the pattern of tight control that has been observed in the United States in the same two sectors. American firms that had been managed in the 1880s and 1890s under a trust or some other form of holding company were centralized and integrated at the turn of the century and later reorganized on a multidivisional basis after they diversified into new markets. That the reverse process was evident in France once again suggests that managers there had deprived themselves of the benefit of the best administrative practices and that they could be held responsible for the apparent immaturity of the corporate sector.

This negative appraisal of the French experience adds a new dimension to some of the comments that have often been made in the past about the nation's poor industrial performance, since it differentiates between two types of potential weaknesses: a "technological gap" and a "managerial gap." The technological gap may have been temporary, since the failure of the large corporations to develop and invest in new technology resulted primarily from the depression of the 1930s and the war. It was speedily overcome, in fact, once capital and economic growth regained their previous levels. In contrast, the managerial gap, which was exemplified during the interwar years by the corporations' neglect of the multidivisional form of organization, may have been more permanent. It is often ascribed to two fundamental factors: first, a cultural bias that restricted the recruitment of business managers and limited their motivations; second, imperfect capital markets that encouraged the survival and continuing importance in policymaking of financial and family holding companies (in 1971 such institutions were still said to control 125 of the 200 leading corporations).[6] But many scholars have remained skeptical of these views. Like those of the interwar years, various recent studies call attention not to the potential growth resulting from an increase in concentration and from structural change, which resulted from overcoming the technological gap, but instead, to the ability of large corporations to set prices by adjusting output level, to enter market-sharing agreements and cartels, and (on the assumption that they believe in Malthusian practices) to slow down technical progress and retard its positive effects on the economy as a whole.

In short, although the corporate sector has been technologically modernized, some critics thus continue to challenge its efficiency on the grounds that social values and financial power, which were decisive in the past, may still limit business expansion and economic growth.[7] Most of the interpretations prevalent today rest on this conventional hypothesis. Their theories, however, have not yet been tested in their true historical perspective and they should be revised if the overall picture of the past is at variance with the one they suggest. Three questions, then, remain to be answered. First, have economic constraints hampered the development of large corporations and, if so, can we explain the slow rise of the corporate sector without resorting to sociocultural factors? Second, were managers, because of their social background, indifferent to (or eager for) greater productivity and expanded markets? And, finally, why did the group or holding-company structure evolve and become so widespread during the interwar period? The remainder of this chapter will address these questions.

THE GROWTH OF THE CORPORATE SECTOR

The two underlying conditions that encouraged the growth of the large corporation in the United States and, to a lesser extent, in Britain and Germany were lacking in France: urban and industrial markets were smaller; and capital markets and banking facilities were not so fully developed. By the 1880s, when a well-planned railroad system was completed, France had an effective all-weather transportation network, but the anticipated expansion of the market did not materialize. The demand for both modern consumer goods and industrial equipment grew more slowly, in part because the size of the population was stagnant and in part because the agricultural sector remained so large, compared with that of other industrial economies. Two-thirds of the total population was still living in small villages in the 1880s, and the rural population figure was still as high as 56 percent by 1911. As a result, moreover, the market was more strongly affected in France than elsewhere by the severe agricultural depression of the 1880s. Thus when time was the critical factor in taking up new initiatives, the failure of urban market to expand could only stifle incentives to develop large-scale production methods and to integrate industrial production with high-volume distribution within a single enterprise in a way that was tried out at the time in the United States and Germany.

Further, this lack of integration, particularly in the new, technologically advanced industries such as chemicals and electrical and light machinery, permitted the large United States and German firms to extend their marketing organizations into France. By providing essential technical and after-sales services, as well as credit for consumers, and by adjusting production and research to changing market demands, these foreign firms were soon able to provide technologically complex products at lower prices and with better services than their competitors; they thus created formidable barriers against entry into these markets by French firms.

In the more traditional sectors, such as food, textiles, and metals, competition increased at the production level as improved plants and transportation facilities permitted supply to surpass demand. And in the ensuing depression, which lasted for some twenty years in the last part of the century, merchants as a group appear to have strengthened their hold on distribution. Perhaps because they had better credit and sales organizations, they were able to forestall many attempts at forward integration on the part of the manufacturers. In the metal trade, for instance, wholesalers organized as a syndicate induced eight metal-fabricating and light machinery-making companies, including Peugeot, Japy, Labbé freres, and Saut du Tarn, to sign an agreement in 1909 pledging not to sell their products directly to retailers or consumers. Thus, apart from some products, including bicycles, small arms, sewing machines, and, after 1907, automobiles, which were not covered by the traditional merchants' network, large French manufacturers had only begun to move into marketing and distribution by World War I.[8] Very few among them had had the chance to expand as so many did in the United States, by integrating forward into wholesaling.

A second method of growth has been through merger. In the United States and Britain, a mature capital market permitted companies to merge and then, at least in the case of the United States, to rationalize the facilities of the constituent enterprises. When there had been a buoyant demand for securities, as had been the case at the turn of the century and again during the 1920s, American industrialists, financiers, promoters, and speculators had had little difficulty in carrying out mergers that increased the size of firms and often brought about concentration within industries.[9] In France, also, with the improvement of industrial prospects early in the twentieth century and in the 1920s, economic expansion was accompanied by increasing activity on the stock market (this pattern recurred in the 1950s); rising stock prices at that time were correlated with merger activity (see figure 4.1). Nevertheless, compared with the United States and Britain, the contribution of the capital markets to the growth of the corporate sector remained quite limited.

Before 1913 and during World War I, the volume of security issues and the number of mergers remained rather low—probably because of widespread prejudice against industrial shares and the lack of experience in marketing these securities on the part of banks and brokerage houses, which had previously dealt primarily in railroad bonds, public utilities, and foreign securities. Various instances of backward integration through merger nonetheless occurred during the period in chemicals, aluminum, and steel, as well as in the automobile and light-machinery industries; most were undertaken in response to rising prices, which compelled firms, from the 1890s on, to seek protection against short supplies by controlling their sources of energy and raw materials and eventually by moving into the manufacture of parts and components.[10] On the whole, however, these steps were taken by strong companies that could have acted without external financing and thus without resorting to the stock market. A review of the financial journals indicates that only 9 or 10 mergers took place annually before the end of the war, and only 65 in the entire period between 1900 and 1919. Still, a few of them led to the creation of large corporations. Thomson-Houston, for example, in which General Electric Company of the United States long held a minority interest, began as a holding company in the public-utilities sector; it

Figure 4.1. Security issues and mergers in the Paris Stock Exchange, 1900–1965

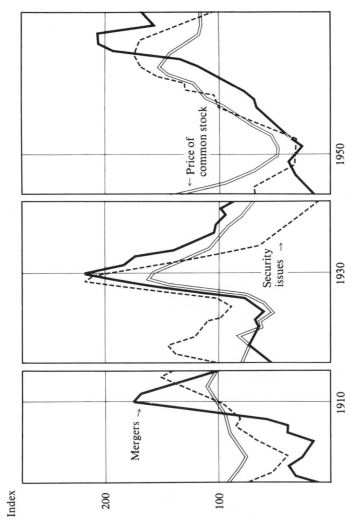

Sources: Annuaire statistique de la France (1966), pp. 532 (stock issues) and 541 (stock prices); J. Houssiaux, *Pouvoir des monopoles*, table 8, p. 340 (number of mergers, 1900–1950); B. Guibert, *La mutation industrielle de la France* (1975), vol. I, table I.7, p. 98 (mergers, 1950–1970), vol. II, table VII.2, p. 119 (security issues, 1950–1970).

All the series are index numbers, computed with the average of each series as a base for each of the three periods; the price of stocks and the value of the stock issues have been deflated with the price series published in *Bulletin mensuel de statistique*, no. 3 (March 1978); the series plotted on the table are three-year-moving averages.

moved into manufacturing by taking over 10 factories through mergers in 1909 and 1917, a move duplicated by other firms in the electrical-manufacturing industry. It thus became the seventh largest firm listed on the Paris Stock Exchange at that time.

After World War I, the scope for expansion through merger widened, partly because the difficulties encountered in placing and delivering large military orders had made both officials and manufacturers conscious of the importance of the economies of scale. If technological innovations prompted firms to build large plants, however, overproduction and falling prices threatened those enterprises, particularly chemical and metals firms, which were saddled with excessive capacity developed during the war. During this period, many firms made use of devices ranging from interlocking stock holdings to full amalgamation with other firms in an attempt to control their markets. Some resorted to forward integration, thus linking producers and customers, in order to assure steady deliveries; this tactic was chosen in heavy industries, with steel companies and foundries beginning to produce fabricated metal products after the war.[11] Others adopted a policy of amalgamation with firms whose products were complementary to their own as a means to diversify, divide risks, and improve their financial positions. On the average, 18 mergers occurred each year from 1920 through 1926—twice the prewar figure; even though there were more mergers, however, inflation and disappointing market performance restricted the number of firms that participated. Most of those that did so were companies that had accumulated war profits and were eager to broaden their product ranges, as in the case of the chemicals and electrical-machinery industries in southeastern France; Progil and Péchiney in chemicals and Ugine in alloys were founded along these lines in 1919 and 1920. Others were firms that had lost part of their productive capacities in northern France and could reinvest war indemnities to build larger and sometimes more diversified product lines by merging companies that had been independent before the war.[12]

These adverse circumstances, which were commercial and industrial in nature during the late nineteenth century and financial after 1900, explain why the growth of the modern corporate sector was slower in France than in other leading industrial nations. It was not, in fact, until Premier Raymond Poincaré stabilized the franc in 1926 that the nation experienced a stock-market boom comparable in scale to those that had occurred about a quarter of a century earlier in New York and London (see figure 4.1). For a while, then, the situation improved markedly. In the five years from 1928 to 1932, no fewer than 244 firms took part in mergers, according to a study by J. Houssiaux. A steep rise in the price of industrial shares brought the value of the 100 largest companies listed on the Paris Stock Exchange to a total of 65 billion francs, or 11 billion in prewar francs; this is three times the figure reached in 1919 and twice that of 1912. The boom, however, was short-lived; furthermore, it did not modify the ranking of the largest firms nor the industries in which they clustered. Of the new corporations in the modern, rapid-growing industries, only a few joined the 25 largest firms; they were Péchiney, Air liquide, and Rhône-Poulenc, all three among the top 25 in 1929 and 1937; André Citroën in 1929; Compagnie française des Pétroles, Standard française, and Gillet-Thaon, all in 1937. In other words, nearly four-fifths of the top-ranking firms at each date were old, established enterprises dating back to the nineteenth century. The coefficients of variation shown in table 4.3 provide further evidence that, apart from short periods of prosperity, industrial expansion and stock-market booms did not affect the relative ranking of firms, the range of their market values, or the composition of the 25 and even the 100 largest firms. These coefficients, calculated in order to measure the entry of new firms into the leader group, increased only twice, in the period from 1900 through 1913 and, later, in the 1950s and 1960s. As stressed earlier, basic changes in the corporate sectors, though perceptible in 1900–1913, did not fully come about until after World War II.

It was not simply the pace at which the French corporate sector developed that contributed to its uniqueness but also its structure. Table 4.4 shows the industries in which the modern business enterprise first appeared in France and those in which it clustered; as the data suggest, the pattern differed in each of the three major chronological periods. For the half-century before 1919, firms in the coal and metal industries were typical

Table 4.3

Market value of the 25 and 100 largest French industrial firms, 1881–1969.

	25 LARGEST FIRMS			100 LARGEST FIRMS		
YEAR	AVERAGE VALUE (IN MILLIONS OF FRANCS)	STANDARD DEVIATION (IN MILLIONS OF FRANCS)	COEFFICIENT OF VARIATION (STANDARD DEVIATION: AVERAGE VALUE, AS %)	AVERAGE VALUE (IN MILLIONS OF FRANCS)	STANDARD DEVIATION (IN MILLIONS OF FRANCS)	COEFFICIENT OF VARIATION (STANDARD DEVIATION: AVERAGE VALUE, AS %)
1881	41.6	32.7	78.7	–	–	–
1912	135.8	112.3	82.3	52.1	74.4	142.5
1919	211.3	93.9	44.4	94.4	83.2	88.2
1929	1,527.3	686.1	44.9	658.8	615.3	93.4
1937	862.2	284.4	33.0	368.3	318.2	86.4
1959	1,753.8	882.7	50.3	652.4	774.2	118.7
1969	1,883.3	985.3	52.2	737.3	839.3	113.8

Sources: Data for 1881 from B. Gille, La sidérurgie française au XIXème siècle (Paris, 1968), p. 295; J. Bouvier, F. Furet, and M. Gillet, Le mouvement du profit au XIXème siècle (Paris, 1965), pp. 296ff. Other data from J. Houssiaux, Le pouvoir des monopoles (Paris, 1958); G. P. Dyas, "The Strategy and Structure of French Industrial Enterprise" (Ph.D. diss., Harvard University, 1972).

of the large corporation; they made up 44 percent of the sample and 58 percent of its market value. Their importance may explain why their status as private companies was often a subject for debate; like those of other property-owning companies, their assets included large amounts of land and physical facilities; at the same time, however, the coal producers and many metal companies enjoyed state mining concessions and were operated by state-trained personnel, under the supervision of state engineers. The question of their transfer back to public ownership therefore remained controversial during the whole period, until the 1947 nationalizations.

In the interwar period, a new group came into prominence. It was made up of producers of intermediate goods and capital equipment, companies that were to suffer the most from the instability of the period. In fact, among these new firms, those in the chemical sector managed to improve their positions; they increased in number (from 11 to 17 of the 100 largest firms between 1919 and 1937), in capitalization (from 13 percent to 26 percent of total market value), and in ranking (the largest corporations listed on the stock market at the end of the 1930s were, in order: Saint-Gobain, Péchiney, Air liquide, and Rhône-Poulenc). Conversely, firms that supplied the market with machinery, ships, automobiles, and electrical equipment offered the least resistance to the depression of the 1930s; they were reduced by half in number among the 100 largest (from 31 to 15), and they receded in rank (Thomson-Houston fell from 7th to 64th; Fives-Lille, from 17th to 92nd; Alsthom, from 32nd to 104th). Just as they benefited from the upsurge in demand during wartime and reconstruction, they were undoubtedly suffering from manufacturing overcapacity well before the recession set in during the 1930s.

The most significant changes in the corporate sector in the third, or postwar, period—that is, since 1945—were the continuing growth in the number of firms in technologically advanced industries, the increasing diversification of product lines, and the growing number of companies producing goods for mass markets. First, the companies producing intermediate goods became more numerous during this period than those in heavy industry; in 1961, after the nationalization of the coal industry and the amalgamation movement in steel, there were

Table 4.4

Industrial breakdown of the 100 largest firms listed on the Paris Stock Exchange, 1912–1969.

Industry	1912 Number	1912 Average Market Value (in millions of francs)	1919 Number	1919 Average Market Value (in millions of francs)	1929 Number	1929 Average Market Value (in millions of francs)	1937 Number	1937 Average Market Value (in millions of francs)	1959 Number	1959 Average Market Value (in millions of francs)	1969 Number	1969 Average Market Value (in millions of francs)
Coal[a]	17	119.0	15	159.4	15	1,102.5	16	324	0	0	0	0
Petroleum	2	15.1	3	42.7	6	302.3	5	466	11	1,143	11	1,226
Chemicals	9	36.5	11	111.6	13	1,170.3	17	573	17	1,129	15	1,302
Cement	3	34.7	1	45.8	3	399.0	4	190	6	332	7	375
Glass	0	0.0	0	0.0	1	151.8	1	395	1	318	1	1,561
Metals	25	55.8	29	111.8	24	549.0	20	377	32	532	17	573
Machinery	9	34.4	12	68.5	5	413.2	7	229	6	314	6	403
Electrical industries	11	40.1	6	115.8	11	516.9	4	337	9	490	13	573
Shipbuilding	6	25.5	7	48.1	0	0.0	1	129	1	88	0	0
Automobiles	2	27.4	6	50.2	3	873.7	3	445	4	884	6	649
Rubber	2	32.2	2	89.5	3	759.7	4	373	3	577	2	2,249
Paper and printing	2	7.6	0	0.0	1	311.0	3	166	1	280	3	461
Food and beverages	7	24.9	6	49.8	4	447.0	10	323	7	275	15	380
Textiles	5	23.9	2	42.4	11	366.2	5	408	2	146	4	304
Total	100	52.1	100	97.3	100	668.7	100	376	100	652	100	737

Sources: Annuaire Desfossés; Compagnie des Agents de Change, Receuil complet des Sociétés par actions.

a. After the 1947 nationalizations, no collieries were present among the 100 leading firms, a fact that helped modify the structure of the group, since the market value of coal companies was '2.0 billion francs and 2.3 billion francs, or 38.8 percent of the group's total market value in 1912 and 2.3 billion francs, or 24.6 percent of the total market value, in 1919.

41 firms in intermediate goods and 17 in heavy industry among the 100 largest corporations. Second, the firms in these sectors entered new markets by broadening their product ranges to include goods such as electronic equipment, computers, and consumer durables; 2 automobile manufacturers and 2 makers of electrical machinery and equipment were back among the 25 major enterprises. Third, the 100 largest firms came to include some from industries not previously represented. The new members of the groups were firms that processed or produced petroleum (6, including Aquitaine, Compagnie française des Pétroles, and Esso, were among the top 25), pharmaceuticals and toilet articles (including l'Oréal and Roussel-Uclaf), and building materials (Boussois and Ciments Lafarge); all these firms were selling to a great number of customers. Finally, companies in other industries using large-batch and continuous-process mass-production methods to supply unsophisticated, often branded, goods to large consumer markets—those listed under industrial categories of rubber, paper, printing, food, beverages, and textiles—improved their positions; they increased in number from 10 to 24 of the top 100 between 1919 and 1969 (see table 4.4), and their share of the 100 leaders' total market value grew from 6 percent to 18 percent during the same period.

In addition to the factors already discussed—foreign competition from within and wholesale trade barriers in the late nineteenth century, inflation and structural disequilibrium in the capital-equipment industries in the 1920s—this three-stage pattern of evolution highlights another reason for the slow development of the corporate sector in France, namely, the delayed growth of the consumer market and of the companies ready to serve it. Indeed, it has only been in the third period, that is, since World War II, that large corporations have been in a position to supply the market with mass-produced articles. In the United States, on the contrary, large firms producing petroleum, rubber, food, tobacco, and other consumer goods were among the first modern business enterprises that began in the 1880s. More specifically, 38 of the 100 largest French companies in 1968 were clustered in these "new" industries, where 46 of the 100 largest United States firms had been some 40 years earlier.[13] One might well ask whether this peculiar development was not responsible for the long-standing public prejudice against big business in France, as it was apparently not able to prove its usefulness to the French consumers until after World War II. Only then did the public begin to recognize the autonomous functions of large corporations, to differentiate them from those of the older firms that had supplied the needs of the government in the past, and to accept the idea that they could respond effectively to market demand with production growth.

MANAGERS AND MANAGERIAL ATTITUDES

It was not simply the economic setting that delayed the rise of modern business enterprise in France; other factors, such as the lack of social mobility and the élitist recruitment of business executives, have also been held responsible for the slow growth of the corporate sector. It has been asserted that, as a consequence, managers lacked what is called "achievement motivation." Case studies present a different view of the problem, however; they indicate that, with the advent of complex technology and of large-scale organizations, the social origins and objectives of managers changed, although these changes did not necessarily encourage the growth of the modern firm.

Managers continued to come from the privileged classes. In one sample of 396 company directors collected for the years 1893 through 1973 in the electrotechnical industries, 84 percent still belonged to the upper social strata. The total is thus quite close to the 86 percent with privileged family backgrounds found in the French public administration, and much higher than the 63 to 65 percent for students and professionals.[14] Nevertheless, procedures for the selection and promotion of managers changed in two ways. First, instead of using kinship as a criterion, as in the past, firms laid greater emphasis on the technical education of managers and executives. Beginning in the 1890s, as a matter of fact, state engineers moved into key areas of the private sector, in part because the civil service and the army were saturated and in part because the large corporations offered job opportunities equivalent in status to those of the public sector but much superior in terms of promotions and rewards. Among the 396 directors already described, 243, or 64.5 percent of the total, had been trained at one of the *grandes écoles,* 100 of them at the

Ecole Polytechnique, and the same pattern was repeated in other industries. Second, as long as the modern industries were financially dependent on the capital market, as in the prewar period, bankers, civil servants, and even political leaders quite frequently became senior executives; in the electrical sector they made up 40 percent of the total number of presidents and vice presidents up to 1913. In the interwar years, however, when the balance between capital and management had changed, 62 percent of the presidencies were held by founders of firms, compared with 28 percent before the war. Men who had made their careers in a single firm more easily reached the top executive office; the proportion of such career men among managing directors increased after 1910–1920 from 17 percent to 66 percent. In short, education and work experience introduced a measure of flexibility into the recruitment of top-level business executives.

Management practices, however, appear to have been less flexible than recruitment procedures. In both France and the United States, management techniques rested on past experience. In the United States, nearly all managers were trained for or worked in profit-making enterprises, and the railroads, the first large corporations, provided the models for patterns of organization and methods of capital and cost accounting.[15] In France, experience and value systems were of a different sort. Most managers were trained as engineers to enter such non-profit bureaucratic organizations as the army and the civil service or to manage the state-supervised railroads and coal companies, which used a large labor force and stable technology. Their primary concern was with hierarchy and work discipline, leadership, and division of authority. To illustrate, Henri Fayol, who was the first continental writer on the science and practice of management and who epitomizes the ideas of his generation, believed that the number of subordinates any person in a responsible position could supervise was limited. Consequently, in the years immediately following World War I, when his influence was at its peak, he argued for the creation of carefully defined, multilevel business hierarchies within enterprises in order to ensure that orders would be smoothly transmitted and effectively executed. The key was the substitution of status authority for personal authority.[16]

Another significant element that guided management in the early part of the century, when the new generation assumed business responsibilities, was its reverence for technology and specifically for the continuous-process and assembly-line techniques that had been perfected overseas. There was genuine admiration among French industrialists for the achievements of industrial enterprises in the United States, most conspicuously those in mechanical engineering and electrical-machinery. The ideas of Louis Renault and André Citroën, for example, were deeply influenced by the visit they made to the United States in 1912, at the time when Frederick W. Taylor's methods of scientific management had gone beyond the experimental stage and Henry Ford's factories were producing 800 cars a day, or 30 to 35 times their own combined output. Renault took over and helped popularize time and motion studies, and Citroën was converted to the necessity of "intensive production, in large batches, which could be planned ahead with mathematical precision."[17] He was responsible for introducing the assembly line into the munitions trade in 1915 and into the automobile industry by 1919; later on he continued to make use of United States patents and machine tools, maintaining teams of engineers to study new techniques from the United States until the end of his career. The ideal of that generation, with its bureaucratic and engineering interests, was not so much the development of a market, which would have been more in line with United States merchandising traditions, but the establishment of functional organizations, logically built, where a staff made up of highly trained engineers would set the rules in the expectation that the rank and file of the labor force would carry them out docilely and that middle management would not have to interfere.

These principles were acceptable so long as markets were expanding. In the automobile industry, where internal financing was made easier by low capital-output ratios (many of the firms were primarily assembling firms at that time), profits were very high. Gross profits were in the range of 20 to 27 percent of annual turnover before 1913 and were still at about 11 to 13 percent for some of the leading firms up to the end of the 1920s. Financial autonomy was therefore preserved, and family entrepreneurs kept their original share in the concerns, often in spite of new capital issues.[18] Even though they had proved to be successful, however, the firms' organizational principles could not resist the impact of the depression of the 1930s on profits.

Citroën provides a striking example. Because of his emphasis on the assembly line and on economizing on intermediary inventories and labor costs, he overlooked a series of problems that ruined the enterprise. The financial failure of his firm resulted from three different factors. First, the company had no formal pricing policy, nor were there systematic methods to adjust production and inventory to short-term fluctuations in demand. After their appointment to the board in 1927, representatives of banks and the steel industry tried to organize the firm's system of internal controls; they introduced three sets of controls— one for production prices and inventory, another for financial accounts, and a third for capital spending. But they were asked to resign in December 1930 by Citroën himself, who still controlled the voting stock in his company; as he explained at a shareholders' meeting, he believed there could not be "une dualité de direction dans une affaire d'automobiles."[19] In order to restore authority and save on administrative costs, he transferred all control officers who had been appointed at intermediate levels back to his own office as president and thus reestablished personal centralization. The second reason for the firm's failure was that the threat of business fluctuations was not fully perceived. Manufacturers had benefited from exceptional circumstances—from thirty years of steady growth between 1900 and 1930, from government purchases during the war, and from a depreciating currency that helped push up foreign sales in every sector of French industry until the mid-1920s (overseas sales accounted for 30 to 35 percent of automobile production, for instance). When the downturn came, Citroën and others could not believe it would last; as he explained in public hearings held in Paris and New York in July and October 1931, he was convinced that replacement demand and reduction in prices through further modernization of equipment were bound to draw back customers at home and to obtain new ones "in 107 countries abroad."[20] If, in fact, the manufacturers had reduced their expenditures and waited for demand to revive, the situation might have righted itself, but a third factor leading to failure, their faith in technology and capital investment, induced them to do just the opposite. Sales at Citroën had been slashed by 53 percent between 1929 and 1932 —from 103,000 to 48,000 cars per year; so the manufacturers met this decrease in demand by designing new models and by rebuilding factories. In two years Citroën spent 230 million francs, or one-third of the value of his existing plants, to increase their capacity from 500 to 600 units a day and to build a totally new car that he hoped would recapture foreign markets from United States competitors. Late in 1934 he found himself unable to meet more than 900 million francs of accumulated liabilities—the equivalent of that year's sales—and went into bankruptcy.

The fate of this firm and of the automobile industry as a whole was in no way unique. The short period of prosperity from 1927 to 1931 had led to excessive expectations and erroneous investment decisions by many entrepreneurs who, because they had similar training and business attitudes, reacted in much the same way. Consequently, profits were low or disappeared altogether in the ensuing depression, and many companies had to reduce production or liquidate some activities— not deliberately, in order to conform to some Malthusian design, but to salvage the ailing concerns.

The 1930s were more than just years of retrenchment, however. Attempts were made at the time to adjust managerial structures and revise market policies. First of all, production methods were rationalized. New advisory boards working independently of the existing finance and planning departments were instituted, often at the level of the main office. They began to revise organizational procedures, reduce costs and duplications, reallocate production among plants and departments, close shops and even set up new ones; many industries experimented with various indicators in order to forecast prices and potential markets for new products in terms of annual sales volume. A major overhauling of the industry began as more flexible organizational and control structures were introduced, and flows of information between the central office and operating units were improved, as they had been in United States industry in 1920– 1921, one cyclical downturn earlier. As early as the winter of 1935–36 the new management of Citroën, which had conformed to these trends, undertook a nationwide market study that led to the determination of a potential demand, among city dwellers and young people, for small utility cars; they were being produced as early as September 1939, on the very eve of the war.[21] So, in spite of the depression, business organizations were becoming more receptive and adaptable.

Second, as sales began to fall, first in the export trade and later at home, large corporations began to concern themselves with marketing. Steel and metalworking industries were operating at one-third of capacity during most of the 1930s. Yet some attempts to expand sales met with positive results. For instance, Propex—a company that had been founded in 1929 by Pont-à-Mousson (a producer of foundry pipes) by the Compagnie Générale des Eaux, a long-established supplier of water to French cities, and by representatives of the soap industry—was quite successful in its drive to develop water systems in rural areas with the financial assistance of local authorities. Similarly, Vallourec, a marketing company formed in 1930 by two industrial groups that accounted for 45 percent of steel-pipe production, opened up a new market when it signed its first contract with Iraq Petroleum Company.[22] Other obstacles quite apart from the impact of the depression, however, frustrated business firms when they tried to expand markets. As Saint-Gobain discovered in 1932, Alsthom in 1935, and many other firms during the same period, the market did not respond to their sales efforts. For example, farmers would not generally use fertilizers as long as their technical education was neglected, and consumption of electricity for home heating and other purposes could not increase if the construction of new buildings and the modernization of existing ones were held down. Public utilities and public services had not caught up with the advances made in the productive branches of the economy, and, unfortunately, this imbalance was to last for almost a generation.

Nonetheless, business firms had become aware by the 1930s of consumers' responses to price and income changes and of the potential of the growing urban markets. Their recognition of these factors helped prepare the way for the major changes that occurred in the corporate sector after World War II. Production and technology had been the main concern of executives and managers during the 1920s; organization and marketing were to become those of the next generation.

Cartels and Holding Companies

Institutional as well as economic and social factors may also have impeded the growth of the modern business enterprise in France. As mentioned earlier, many scholars still argue that large-scale business organizations would have developed earlier if it had not been for the interlocking financial interests and the open or secret agreements that bound industrial corporations together.[23] Two types of manufacturers' associations—cartels and financial holding companies—were the most important of these institutional barriers.

The first and oldest were the cartels, mutual agreements entered into by independent firms. Their goal was either to adjust the utilization of capacity to demand and to stabilize prices, as was generally the case in the 1880s and even earlier, or to divide domestic markets and fix prices and production quotas in order to maintain a steady stream of investment in the new industrial sectors, which were unprotected by tariffs against foreign competition and dumping (that is, selling below cost) by foreign firms.[24] The second sort of cartel came into general use after 1900–1905 and proved quite beneficial to the participants; they acted as selling agencies and often stimulated exports by setting domestic prices at a higher level than those offered on the international markets—thus helping the leaders, which had lower costs but the same selling prices as the other cartel members, increase their output and improve productivity.

The second type of business association, the holding and trust companies, had broader functions. In some cases, they were created to control the activities of a number of industrial subsidiaries, to set their prices and volume of output, and to allocate capital among them. Normally they issued debt instruments to buy outright or to be exchanged for the shares of the companies that were to come under their control; in 1912, for example, the Société Générale de Dynamite had a portfolio worth 20 million francs, or 87 percent of its total assets, allocated among 10 chemical firms that operated under its supervision and that were later amalgamated into Nobel-Bozel. In other cases, holding companies were instituted by large corporations or financially related groups of firms to provide them with financial services such as raising capital and procuring credit. The Société

Parisienne d'Electricité, one of the very first, acted from 1900 on as the equivalent of a finance department for a group of three large electrical-utility companies, including the Paris subway, and, at a later date, for manufacturing plants at Jeumont; the Union Européenne was founded in 1920, along the same lines, to operate on behalf of the Schneider group; the Union des Mines, in 1923, to act on behalf of the leading collieries and a few other companies, of which Denain-Anzin and Asturienne des Mines were the most important.

In short, these institutions fell into two categories. On the one hand, cartels and the holding companies, when they had been set up to control industrial operations were transitional forms: most of the cartels prepared the way for later mergers in such sectors as aluminum, electrochemicals, and metals, usually because one member became strong enough to lead the field and eventually to absorb the other member firms; industrial holding companies and their subsidiaries, like their United States counterparts, were normally consolidated into large enterprises. On the other hand, holding companies that had been formed to provide financial services to a group of firms proved more stable; once established, they remained and often built sizable investment portfolios, perhaps because financial concentration protected their creators against cyclical and technological change.[25] For example, by 1912 the Société parisienne pour l'Industrie electrique and two other holding companies in the same field already controlled a total of 61 million francs in securities, and the accompanying voting power, in a number of operating utilities; this was equivalent to the total amount held by the Banque de l'Union Parisienne, and half of the financial assets belonging to the Banque de Paris et des Pays-Bas.[26] As a matter of fact, with the passage of time, these financial holding companies became very powerful indeed. The total value of *participations* (shareholdings taken to permit control or active interest in an enterprise) and securities (held as portfolio assets for financial purposes) owned by the leading industrial and financial corporations are shown in table 4.5. The percent of *participations* and securities held by these financial holding companies rose from 5.9 to 15.5 percent between 1919 and 1932, then fell back slightly to 14.0 percent in 1937, while, during the same period, the proportion held by investment banks decreased from

Table 4.5

Participations and security holdings of large French corporations, 1919–1937.[a]

CORPORATE TYPE	1919			1932			1937		
	NUMBER	VALUE (IN MILLIONS OF FRANCS)	% OF TOTAL	NUMBER	VALUE (IN MILLIONS OF FRANCS)	% OF TOTAL	NUMBER	VALUE (IN MILLIONS OF FRANCS)	% OF TOTAL
Banque de Paris et des Pays-Bas	1	231.5	–	1	549	–	1	569	–
Union Parisienne	1	97.1	–	1	482	–	1	215	–
Other banks	18	360.3	–	20	653	–	18	403	–
All investment banks	*20*	*688.9*	*27.6*	*22*	*1,683*	*12.7*	*20*	*1,187*	*8.6*
Lyonnaise des Eaux	1	76.8	–	1	1,178	–	1	1,746	–
Other public utilities	37	139.9	–	53	2,307	–	47	2,713	–
All public utilities	*38*	*216.7*	*8.7*	*54*	*3,485*	*26.3*	*48*	*4,460*	*32.3*
Coal producers	11	140.5	–	16	1,389	–	16	1,599	–
Petroleum producers	2	12.7	–	7	734	–	6	922	–
Chemicals producers	9	133.0	–	7	1,191	–	7	1,185	–
Steel producers	24	839.0	–	16	1,403	–	20	1,476	–
Machinery and electrical-equipment producers	18	315.4	–	17	1,299	–	18	1,026	–
5-industry total	*64*	*1,440.6*	*57.8*	*63*	*6,015*	*45.4*	*67*	*6,208*	*45.0*
Electrical holding companies	8	129.0	–	17	1,537	–	17	1,490	–

Industrial holding companies	3	18.4	—	6	517	—	8	445	—
All holding companies	11	147.4	5.9	23	2,053	15.5	25	1,935	14.0
Total of large corporations	133	2,493.6	100.0	162	13,236	100.0	160	13,790	100.0

a. *Participations* are holdings in a firm for purposes of control, rather than purely for investment purposes.

27.6 to 8.6 percent (the share of the largest, the Banque de Paris et des Pays-Bas, fell from 9.3 to 4.1 percent).

The impressive growth of the financial holding companies, compared with other institutions, and their apparent stability raise the problem of the ambiguity of their role. Large corporations were normally impelled to increase their share of a market and diversify into new ones, thus contributing to the growth of industrial output. The holding companies, in contrast, because they had the power to allocate capital within an industrial group and thus to substitute their own decisions for those that would have been made by autonomous firms, could prevent or at least slow down integration within sectors and delay gains in productivity. In other words, even if capital was not misallocated in the long run, as is implied by the superior growth performance of the sectors in which the holding companies or some substitutes were dominant (see table 4.6), they may still

Table 4.6

Indexes of production in major French industries, 1900–1960
(1913 = 100).

Industry	1900	1913	1919	1929	1939	1950	1960
All industries	72	100	62	138	111	142	269
Chemicals	54	100	81	192	169	228	604
Automobiles	9	100	40	564	509	795	2,998
Steel pipes	–	100	23	325	269	513	1,313
Electricity	19	100	161	861	1,221	1,835	4,007

Sources: R. Richeux, *L'industrie chimique en France. Structure et production, 1850–1957* (Paris, 1959); Patrick Fridenson, *Histoire des Usines Renault, 1898–1939* (Paris, 1972); C. Omnes, *Histoire de la métallurgie française de première transformation, 1880–1970* (Paris, 1979); *Annuaire statistique de la France* (Paris, 1966).

have inhibited the growth and modernization of the corporate sector. It is therefore necessary to explain, first, why the holding companies were created and, second, why they were maintained, taking the place of more traditional industrial and financial institutions.

The Origin and Development of Holding Companies

One key to understanding the development of the financial holding companies that tied industrial groups together was the

need for external finance in the early part of the twentieth
century. Among its causes was the desire to achieve economies
of scale in emulation of United States industry and to obtain
the heavy capital investment required by much of the new technology. Some of the leading industries had moderate capital-
output ratios; around 1931 they were between 0.9 in the electrical-equipment industries, with a sales average of 4 billion
francs a year, and 1.25 in chemicals, where annual turnover averaged 12 billion francs. Nonetheless, research costs and the carry-
over of large inventories, accumulated because of seasonality of
demand (particularly for fertilizers) and of power supplies
(whenever hydroelectricity was used), made firms there sensitive
to changes in price and to the availability of credit. Capital requirements were particularly massive in the production and
distribution of electricity, which soon occupied a central position similar to that of the railroads in the nineteenth century.
In this sector, capital-output ratios reached 9 to 12 (10 times
what they were in the electrical-equipment and chemical industries), while annual sales averaged 20 billion to 23 billion
francs.

To make matters more difficult, financing from sources that
had supplied funds in the past was now less readily available.
World War I brought destruction and dismantling of factories,
which had to be repaired out of current income. Furthermore,
inflation during and after the war wiped out past savings and
prevented new funds from being accumulated in the capital
market and in the banking system in 1913, deposits in the
four leading banks had amounted to 5.83 billion francs; when
calculated in constant 1913 francs, deposits with the same banks
averaged only 3.8 billion francs in 1920–1926 and 6.0 billion
francs in 1927–1931—that is, only 66 percent and 103 percent
of the prewar level. Given the imbalance between the need for
and the availability of funds, industrial firms had to devise practical solutions for their credit requirements. In the early postwar years, when purchasing raw materials and supplies was a
problem, at least for the recently formed companies, they used
ordinary banks associated with their groups; later, in the 1920s,
they found ways for their sales to be financed by setting up their
own consumer credit agencies.[27] Because of investment requirements, however, they soon turned to entirely new institutions,

either as a means of providing funds for new industrial ventures or to guarantee their current debts in the capital market.

One device that brought about economies of scale and bargaining power in negotiating for supplies and financing was to establish a new enterprise as a joint venture by several going firms, thus making these large operating companies also into holding companies. This method was used in the early 1920s by the leaders in the chemical industries: they had the financial and technical means to experiment with new processes as a part of their policy of diversification, and they found ready partners, especially among the collieries, which were then eager to bring more elaborate products, such as carbonized coal and its derivatives, into the market. Of course, the legal devices used in these joint ventures varied: Kuhlmann, in association with such important coal companies as Anzin, Marles, and Courrières, set up a series of independent firms; Saint-Gobain and Air Liquide followed a similar policy through a common subsidiary, La Grande Paroisse, founded in 1919, and its subenterprises; after 1923 Péchiney and Mines de Lens developed a large cooperative organization open to all the collieries willing to join it.[28] But in all these cases the principle involved was identical. The parent firm brought in patents, raw materials, plants, even some initial financing, and the subsidiaries were given the opportunity to expand their operations in an independent fashion; their autonomy—legal, technical, and, most conspicuously, financial—was sometimes explicitly stated as the objective.[29]

In the electrical-machinery industries, where various forms of association had been tried out, some firms were able to consolidate their positions through merger; that was the case with, among others, Fives-Lille, the leader in machinery and railroad equipment, and Schneider, which amalgamated one of its subsidiaries in the 1920s with two electrical equipment producers, Grammont and a licensee of Westinghouse Electric, the American manufacturer. More often, however, the major companies, which had means accumulated from the war and access to United States licenses, resorted to setting up jointly owned subsidiaries. They launched a number of such firms by bringing together their own divisions with smaller, but growing, enterprises that offered markets, research teams, or some organizational assets. Thomson-Houston, which had continuing ties with

General Electric, started industrial subenterprises in the early 1920s in the various branches of the electrical industry (lighting, radio, X rays, telephone, and so on); in October 1928, it gave a 25-year lease on its engineering department to Alsthom, a large corporation it had founded, on an equal basis, with an Alsatian firm, which was to supply about 60 percent of the French demand for generators and heavy equipment.[30] The economic advantages for the parent firm of this process of divisionalization were many: because of the high levels of production of the subsidiaries compared to that of their competitors, it contributed to lowering unit costs; it increased stability, since any slackening in activity was expected to fall on the marginal firms; and it facilitated the process of raising outside funds. The two founders of Alsthom, for example, were able to abstain from subscribing to the further issues of the company, so that their common share in its capital stock fell from an initial 84 percent to 56 percent in September 1928 and to 50 percent by April 1931.

But the increase in borrowing capacity made possible by joint ventures was inadequate when an industry required special facilities, particularly long-term financing for the production and utilization of electricity. As already noted, groups that combined firms manufacturing equipment with enterprises that used it—such as transportation, light, and power companies—had earlier in the century set up financial branches to pool the surplus resources of member firms and to raise extra capital by issuing stocks with their mutual guarantee. After World War I, although firms tended to specialize in one of the two sectors, this type of organization became general, with the objective of financing individual concerns when they had heavy financial commitments.

The large firms manufacturing machinery and equipment are a good example of this development. They had always assisted their customers by providing long-term credit or by taking capital shares in part payment; they used to sell them at a later date to finance further work. Thomson-Houston had parted in such a way with its portfolio of tramway companies during the 1907 recession, and it repeated the operation in 1926 after it had transferred its participation in Matériel Téléphonique to the recently formed, United States-based International Telephone and Telegraph Company. Similarly, Swiss companies that owned and operated factories producing electric cables and motors in eastern France liquidated them after World War I and handed them over to Compagnie Générale d'Electricité (CGE). In the 1920s, however, as the formation of groups was being completed and, as it became more difficult to sell *participations* (the securities of utilities that had been received in payment for equipment), new financial resources had to be tapped and new financial forms devised. The holding of securities was left with the parent firm, but the financing of their issue became a separate function carried on by different institutions: from 1924 to 1926, for example, the Société Financière Electrique, which had connections in New York, was created to handle the accounts of the Thomson group, and the Union Financière et Electrique was set up to do the same for CGE.

Public utilities had similar problems. Preliminary studies, construction, and commercial operations, which were carried on by 1,200 to 1,300 firms, required a great deal of capital. As a result, companies naturally tended to coalesce into new group structures, this time loosely organized and led either by old firms bringing in capital and experience from other public services or by more recently established companies that had assumed dominant positions by successfully undertaking and financing major projects. Once again, both old and new firms, because of overcommitments, shifted part of the responsibility for planning and financing to subcompanies set up for that purpose. For instance, two of the eight or ten group leaders of the period—Energie Industrielle, founded in 1906, and the Union d'Electricité, founded in 1919—established a series of subenterprises in the 1929 boom; among them were two holding companies, Hydro-Energie and Union Financière pour l'Industrie Electrique, that had specific financial purposes.[31] In short, the creation of chains of holding and subholding companies was a continuous process; they had been set up on the initiative of industry and were to answer its needs in a period of abnormally rapid industrial development. Thus the classical relationship between business and financial intermediaries, in which the latter are described as controlling the former, had been reversed; industry had taken the lead in building financial structures to make up for the impoverishment of the country and the deficiencies in the banking system.

GROUP ORGANIZATION AND THE INSTABILITY OF PROFITS

As these cases indicate, the managerial structures that resulted from the establishment of holding companies in France may have been inefficient and costly, at least in comparison to the multidivisional firm then being developed overseas. Two general types of group organization, in fact, emerged during those years. One form, found in the chemical industries as well as in the coal, iron and steel, and metal-fabricating industries, comprised a corporation with a core of traditional activities, which were modernized throughout the 1920s, and a series of subenterprises financed by the parent firm. Saint-Gobain, the largest French corporation in 1929, with 1.3 billion francs in assets and a market value of 3.7 billion francs, is typical of this category: according to its balance sheets, the firm had 250 million francs in factories producing glass, fertilizers, and chemicals —and twice that amount in inventory and commercial credits; it also had financial assets—industrial *participations* and loans of various length—valued at 605 million francs, which were invested in 150 domestic and foreign subsidiaries operating in a wide variety of new industries, including petroleum drilling and refining and the manufacture of cellulose, man-made fibers, and other products. Saint-Gobain therefore tended to act as a holding company with 45 percent of its gross revenues derived from its own industrial activities, 25 percent from its subsidiaries, and 30 percent from purely financial operations. Nor was this a unique case; many companies' accounts show the same shift in resources from their own activities to those of subsidiaries, probably because of the parent firm's ability to issue new stock (strict rules of amortization had been maintained by the older companies, so that their position looked safer) and because managers' high expectations led many to resort freely to external financing. On the average, five to seven increases in capital stock were registered per firm during the 1920s; in the case of Kuhlmann, the number went as high as thirteen.

The second organizational structure used by French business groups was more disjointed. It resulted from the creation of holding and subholding companies, a process already described in the case of public utilities. In their case, risks were more evenly divided, so that the various firms' revenues were more autonomous and secure. Even though *participations* and security holdings could reach high levels (they were entered in 1937 for 2.2 billion francs in the balance sheets of the Lyonnaise des Eaux and four other companies working in a group as distributors of water, gas, and electricity), their share remained modest compared with the firms' combined assets: the ratio of security holdings to total fixed assets in the electricity-producing sector was 1:2 in 1929 for the leading companies, against 4:5 in the machinery and electrical-equipment industries and 2:3 in petroleum. In this case, however, the organizational structure was still defective: public-utility companies had financial interests in common, but they lacked a stable central office to allocate resources and to monitor and coordinate the activities of the many subsidiaries. Of course, executives of these companies usually sat on the board of several member firms within the same group; they held an average of nineteen directorships, and a few among them held as many as fifty or sixty, in the electricity-producing industry. Nevertheless, such interlocking directorates were, at best, a poor substitute for a more rational organization. French business seems to have been in a transitional stage: when the parent firm had direct control, as in the first case, it suffered from excessive centralization and overinvestment; where the control was financial, as in the second case, managerial and operating costs were probably much too high.

Why, then, was there no attempt made to reform the corporate sector and, more specifically, the holding-company structure? Why did it survive the depression? The usual explanation is based on the assumption that stability of profit is a function of size: because of their control over the market, the argument states, the large corporations were spared the impact of the depression and the need to adjust their organizations to meet new demands. This assumption, however, does not fit contemporary evidence; instead, companies' annual reports complained about hard times and gave several reasons for the severity of their situation. First, they blamed the depression for the reduction in export trade. The decrease in foreign sales was significant because, apart from the electricity-producing industries and a few others, new manufacturing industries had sold an average of 35 to 40 percent of their products abroad until the mid-1920s. Second, the firms' difficulties were attributed to the collapse of agricultural prices in 1932 and 1934, years when other costs, taxes, and freight rates were either stable or increasing; the farmers' distress was a severe blow for the community at large. A third factor was identified as the general reduction in public expenditures for transportation systems and hydroelectricity after 1932; deflationary policies closed essential markets for the machinery and electrical-equipment industries. A study of 50,000 medium-sized companies indicates that, even though depreciation had been deferred, net profits were cut by 50 to 60 percent and external financing by 80 percent between 1930 and 1935.[32] Large corporations did not fare any better, however. In the few accounts summarized in table 4.7, net profit fell by 80 percent during the same period, while the collapse of the stock market made further security issues impossible. In the closing months of 1934, the market value of the 25 largest firms had been reduced to 39 percent of their total assets; Thomson-Houston was valued at 13 percent and Citroën at 1.4 percent. The depression was probably hardest on the large corporations, since they produced intermediate and capital goods, which were the most sensitive to the business cycle.

Few bankruptcies occurred, though, among the large French corporations and members of industrial groups. This fact suggests that the financial structure created in the 1920s acted as a shelter. For the majority of business concerns, in fact, the inflation brought about by World War I and that of the early 1920s had contributed to reducing the burden of past debts and had prevented the issue of new debentures on a large scale. In 1929, the bonded debt of the 100 largest corporations (some 3.8 billion francs) amounted to only 9.4 percent of their book assets and 6.3 percent of their capital stock, measured by market value. Their position was therefore not endangered by fixed interest charges when the slide began. Moreover, firms received assistance from other member of their groups. Many of the ventures that had been launched during the boom were in jeopardy. Price cutting brought losses on inventories; in 1932–1934, for example, during the first two years of the operation of a refinery on the Gulf of Berre, a joint venture of Saint-Gobain and Shell Oil, petroleum prices fell by 70 percent. Other firms had orders canceled; Alsthom, for instance, was working at less than 3 percent of capacity in 1935. In addition, inaccurate forecasts of re-

Table 4.7

Average annual profits of four large French corporations, 1882–1939.[a]

PERIOD	PROFIT OR LOSS (% OF ASSETS) A	CASH FLOW (IN MILLIONS OF FRANCS) B	NET PROFIT B	GROSS INVESTMENT (IN MILLIONS OF FRANCS) C	NET INVESTMENT (IN MILLIONS OF FRANCS) C	RATIO B:C
Forges du Nord et de l'Est						
1882–1899	6.6	2.3	–	0.8	–	2.9
1900–1913	15.1	6.4	–	4.1	–	1.6
1914–1926	3.1	12.7	–	42.7	–	0.3
1927–1931	10.7	55.6	–	29.6	–	1.9
1932–1936	2.9	15.5	–	4.6	–	3.4
1937–1939	7.4	30.7	–	17.4	–	1.8
Saint-Gobain						
1900–1913	6.8	–	7.9	–	2.9	2.7
1914–1926	7.8	–	20.1	–	14.5	1.4
1927–1931	7.6	–	59.8	–	146.4	0.4
1932–1936	2.1	–	22.8	–	–30.6	–
1937–1939	3.7	–	44.3	–	–7.4	–
Alsthom						
1927–1931	2.3	20.8	–	43.4	–	0.48
1932–1934	1.2	6.0	–	14.6	–	0.41
1935–1936	–2.9	–31.3	–	2.7	–	–
1937–1939	3.9	13.6	–	–4.9	–	–

					Pont-à-Mousson			
1922–1926	—	—	—	—	57.7	—	41.1	1.40
1927–1931	—	—	—	—	75.8	—	61.4	1.24
1932–1934	—	—	—	—	67.9	—	49.4	1.37
1935–1936	—	—	—	—	20.9	—	-5.5	—
1937–1939	—	—	—	—	85.2	—	51.8	1.64

a. Data from the various balance sheets of the companies are not strictly comparable, since accounting procedures were not standardized. Practices are in conformity with modern rules at Forges du Nord et de l'Est (in the steel industry) and at Alsthom (in the electrical-engineering industry), but not at Pont-à-Mousson (which operated foundries) and Saint-Gobain (a glass and chemical manufacturer) because of their policies of amortization. For every firm, the profit or loss is the percentage of the balance (*solde net*) in the profit and loss account to the company's financial resources (capital, reserves, and provisions). The cash flow is the profit plus the amortization provisions set aside in order to replace equipment or to reduce the value of the portfolio. Gross or net investments (that is, including or excluding amortization charges) may be negative, like profit and cash flow, because the firms had to make allowances for bad debts, for writing off poor investments, and for the fall in prices that depreciated the value of their inventories and equipment.

turns from investment outlays and future income had been made, particularly in the electricity-producing sector, where prices were reduced by government order in 1935–1937. Even firms that had been able to withstand the crisis because they had previously maintained a strict policy of depreciation or had diversified at home and abroad suffered from a sharp decrease in revenue. At Saint-Gobain, for example, net profits from 1932 to 1939 averaged out at 65 percent of the 1930 level and dividends at 11 percent.[33] Inventories, equipment, and accounts receivable were consequently readjusted downward and, on the other side of the balance sheet, losses were deducted from the firms' financial reserves. In the cases of Alsthom and the Berre refinery, equity was reduced by 50 percent and 75 percent, respectively. Downward readjustments were costly, however. In some cases they were made up by new credit lines from the parent firm and by converting short-term debts within the group into equities. At Saint-Gobain, for instance, short-term credits were reduced from 230 million to 105 million francs between 1933 and 1939, even though investments in subsidiaries remained at 550 million to 600 million francs. In other cases, the difference was made up by mergers with the debts (and assets) being taken over by the parent or absorbing firm in order to save companies from default. By means of such transfers, the impact of the depression was spread throughout an industrial group. Blocks of shares were sold and capital was scaled down by many corporations. Even with the assistance provided by the holding companies, the corporate sector was in a state of financial near-exhaustion until the upturn in prices and rearmament orders, together with the passage of new laws regulating depreciation allowances for tax purposes in May 1938 and February 1939, contributed to the revival of French industry on the very eve of World War II.

THE FRENCH EXPERIENCE IN SUMMARY

To conclude, the evolution of the corporate sector in France differed markedly from the experience that may be observed in other industrializing economies. Large-scale organizations to distribute large volumes of standardized consumer goods, sold under brand names, were not built during the system's formative years. Similarly, managerial enterprises—those in which policy decisions are made by salaried managers themselves, with relatively little external supervision—were tried out in the 1920s and could have succeeded because of the appearance of a new generation of engineers and because the ideologies of the period were oriented toward growth, if it had not been for the impact of the depression and of deflationary policies that were pursued too long. Thus the modernization of the large corporation after World War II came as a break with the past, a "historical discontinuity," in Alexander Gerschenkron's terminology, and not as the duplication of foreign or past institutions.

Broadly speaking, the French experience presents five significant elements. First, the building of large firms was overdue; they emerged at least twenty years later than those in the United States and Germany, and they did not develop a solid base in the prewar years as they had in Britain. Second, the large firms were slow to diversify out of heavy industry; typical products of the modern business enterprise were, first, capital equipment, then intermediary products including energy, and finally, automobiles and consumer durables. This three-stage development resulted from the imbalance between the potential output of large-scale enterprises, which could provide the facilities and coordination essential for large-batch, continuous-flow production, and the growth of consumer demand. Third, the market for such volume-produced goods expanded discontinuously. It grew before World War I, when the recovery from the great depression of the late nineteenth century brought a high level of domestic capital formation; next, during World War I and during reconstruction; and finally, in the 1920s, when rising exports (the result of inflation and exchange depreciation) and then a strong home demand (after the stabilization of the currency) kept production and capital investment rising steeply.[34] Fourth, the attitudes and training of managers, which led them to concentrate on improved engineering and to develop science-based technology, also induced them to prefer quality production to the making of unsophisticated articles suited for mass markets. Fifth, financial constraints, particularly the inability of the banks and the capital markets to cope with businesses' new requirements, finally brought into being large industrial groups tied together by financial holding companies.

The logic and efficiency of this system has often been questioned, apparently on the assumption that French managers and executives could have matched the success of their counterparts in the United States. But this view must be held to be unrealistic. Large enterprises in the two countries had altogether different organizational forms and marketing policies. The United States multidivisional and the French holding-company structures resulted from totally different environments. Each was created for a distinct purpose. The goal of the multidivisional enterprise was to control economic performance, allocate resources, and open up new activities, while the holding company functioned as a central financial unit providing capital for the development and expansion of industrial groups. The multidivisional structure was normally established to reallocate surplus funds within more mature institutions, often with forty years of experience and accumulated reserves; the holding company, on the contrary, was set up to procure capital and to finance investment in new risk-taking business ventures.

In the United States, marketing was of cardinal importance from the start; in France it was neglected until after World War II. One reason for the difference may have been that French industrialists had benefited from an expanding market, during the key period from the 1890s through the 1930s; similarly, they had the advantages of the cooperation of the state in such strategic sectors as transportation and energy during the war and reconstruction. Furthermore, the potential of the new technologies and their achievements in the United States may have led the French firms to overestimate the capacity of the domestic market; immediately after the war, for instance, there were a third as many telephones in France as in New York City and one-twentieth as many cars per capita as in the United States. Only after 1932 did the negative attitude of the government and the reduction in consumer demand because of the depression force manufacturers to change their attitudes and to experiment with new marketing and management techniques as part of a policy of industrial rationalization.

The development of managerial structures in France thus appears both more complex and more discontinuous than in the other industrial countries. It occurred in two major stages: first, technological change and financial experimentation; then, during the 1930s, the beginning of concentration on marketing and organization. It was therefore only after World War II that methods of organizing and operating big business in France became similar to those of the United States and other technologically advanced market economies.

NOTES

1. See Gareth P. Dyas, "The Strategy and Structure of French Industrial Enterprise" (Ph.D. diss., Harvard University, 1972), p. 19; see also A. P. Weber and F. Jenny, *Concentration et politique des structures industrielles* (Paris, 1974); M. Hannoun, "Les nouvelles unités de production des grandes firmes industrielles" (Ph.D. diss., Université de Paris-X, 1976); Gareth P. Dyas and Heinz T. Thanheiser, *The Emerging European Enterprise. Strategy and Structure in French and German Industry* (London, 1976), appendix 3, pp. 269ff.

2. Ranking large corporations raises methodological problems that are not easily solved. The simplest way is to rely on accounting data provided by the firms themselves. J. Houssiaux, in his *Pouvoir des monopoles* (Paris, 1958), has based his rankings on net and gross assets; this procedure offers additional advantages, since it can also be used for nationalized companies such as Renault and Houillères de France, which are not listed on the stock exchange. Gareth P. Dyas, in his "Strategy and Structure," has taken gross sales turnover in current francs as his criterion. Unfortunately, because balance-sheet data cannot accurately be compared for different periods, it was not possible to use either of these methods here. Firms do not depreciate equipment and inventories according to any standardized rule; coal and other mining companies, in particular, used to depreciate their capital assets until their accounting value was one franc. Similarly, Pont-à-Mousson, among others, depreciated its assets systematically; the fixed equipment was valued at 13.2 million francs in the 1932 accounts, although it was valued at 230 million francs on the basis of fiscal returns (760 million francs had been invested since the firm's establishment, of which 530 million francs had been depreciated). In addition, portfolio securities valued at 282 million francs by the fiscal authorities were valued at 11.5 million francs on the firm's books. Inaccuracies of a different sort are present when firms are classified according to turnover. Because prices are sensitive to market changes, they do not allow the real strength of a firm to be assessed. Stock-market values have therefore been used as a measure of firm size in this chapter; values have been obtained by adding the value of shares and that of bonds. Share values have been calculated on the basis of the number of shares outstanding and their average price during the year; the value of the bonds was calculated in the same way. The policy of product diversification (from a single product to related and unrelated diversified products) and that of structural adaptation (from a functional to a multidivisional organization), on which table 4.1 is based, have been described in Alfred D. Chandler, Jr., *Strategy and Structure* (New York, 1966).

3. R. de Vannoise, "Etude économique et financière de 18 groupes

industriels français en 1972," *Economie et Statistique* 87 (March 1977): 11–28; M. Hannoun, "L'appareil de production des groupes industriels en 1972," ibid., pp. 29–52. In 1969, the 20 leading French firms had an annual turnover equivalent to 15.6 percent of the gross national product, compared with 14.5 percent in the United States, 17.0 percent in Japan, 19.4 percent in Germany, and 27.5 percent in Great Britain; see B. Guibert, *La mutation industrielle de la France* (Paris, 1975), p. 106.

4. See A. de la Bouillerie, *La société des Forges et Ateliers du Creusot* (Paris, 1957); Manufactures des Glaces et Produits chimiques de Saint-Gobain, Chauny et Cirey, *Compte-rendus aux Assemblées générales des actionnaires* (Paris, 1933–1939).

5. See M. Lévy-Leboyer, "Hierarchical Structures, Rewards and Incentives in a Large Corporation: The Early Managerial Experience of Saint-Gobain, 1872–1912," in *Recht und Entwicklung des Grossunternehmen im 19. und frühen 20. Jahrhundert,* ed. Norbert Horn and Jürgen Kocka (Göttingen, 1979); *Les Establissements Kuhlmann, 1825–1925* (n.p. n.d.), p. 51–52.

6. In *Strategy and Structure,* Dyas has emphasized cultural attitudes among French managers, including their reluctance to share responsibility and the prestige attached to the chairman's status, even in small firms. On the distribution of wealth and its implications for the large corporation, see Herman Daems, *The Holding Company and Corporate Control* (Leyden, 1977); A. Babeau and D. Strauss-Kahn, *La richesse des français* (Paris, 1977), pp. 166–167, in which no significant differences in inequality are found among industrial countries. See also F. Morin, *La structure financière du capitalisme français* (Paris, 1974), pp. 68–71; Morin finds that families and banks have majority control (more than 50 percent of the capital) in 38 and 5 cases, respectively, and minority control (5 percent to 50 percent) in 62 and 20 cases out of a sample of 200 firms, but his results are partially due to the method used.

7. See, for instance, Houssiaux, *Pouvoir des monopoles.*

8. Relationships between industry and trade are described in P. Passama, *L'intégration du travail. Formes nouvelles de la concentration industrielle* (Paris, 1910).

9. See R. A. Nelson, *Merger Movements in American Industry, 1859–1956* (New York, 1959); Leslie Hannah, "Mergers in British Manufacturing Industry 1880–1918," *Oxford Economic Papers* 26 (1974); idem, *The Rise of the Corporate Economy: The British Experience* (London, 1976).

10. See Passama, *Intégration du travail;* see also Comité des forges, *La sidérurgie française, 1864–1914* (Paris, 1920); J. Boudet, *Le monde des affaires en France de 1830 à nos jours* (Paris, 1952); C. Omnes, *Histoire économique et financière de la métallurgie française de première transformation: L'industrie du tube d'acier, 1880–1970* (Paris, 1977). The pattern is the same in the electrochemical industries; waterfalls were annexed by Forges in 1889, by Alais et Camargue in 1897, and by Saint-Gobain in 1913, and so on.

11. Among these associations were those between Vicoigne and Pompey,

Anzin and Marine-Homécourt, and Lens and Forges du Nord et de l'Est. Among metal producers that integrated forward were Saulnes, Pont-à-Mousson, and Longwy, which took over 30 percent of Louvroil-Recquignies and thus prepared for the integration of the steel-pipe industry in 1919–1920. Les Forges due Nord et de l'Est followed the same pattern; it invested in coal and iron mines in 1909–1911, combined six companies in 1920 (including Pont-à-Vendin, the largest French steel plant, which was being sold by Lens and Commentry), and amalgamated four steel-rolling mills including Montataire and Hautmont in 1933–1934. See Boudet, *Monde des affaires en France;* Omnes, *Métallurgie française;* Houssiaux, *Pouvoir des monopoles,* p. 371.

12. See H. Morsel, *Histoire d'une grande entreprise: La société d'Ugine, 1889–1922* (Paris, n.d.); idem, "Les industries électro-techniques dans les Alpes du Nord de 1869 à 1929," in P. Léon, *L'industrialisation en Europe au XIXème siècle* (Paris, 1973), which gives an account of Péchiney; see also C. J. Gignoux, *Histoire d'une enterprise française* (Paris, 1937); P. Cayez, "Une explosion du capitalisme urbain: La naissance de la société Progil, 1918–25," in *Colloque franco-suisse d'histoire économique* (Lyons, 1977).

13. See Alfred D. Chandler, Jr., "The Structure of American Industry in the Twentieth Century: An Historical Overview," *Business History Review* 43 (Autumn 1969): 292–293.

14. P. Lanthier, "Les dirigeants de l'industrie électrique en France, 1893–1973," in Maurice Lévy-Leboyer, ed., *Le patronat de la seconde industrialisation* (Paris, 1979). See also A. Girard, *La réussite sociale* (Paris, 1961), pp. 337ff.; Maurice Lévy-Leboyer, "Le patronat français a-t-il été malthusien? *Le mouvement social* 88 (1974): 25; P. Birnbaum, *La classe dirigeante française* (Paris, 1978).

15. The impact of the railroad on the structure of modern business firms has not been studied in France. Large department stores, however, were actually collections of more or less independent stores under a common administration that supplied collective services, controlled performance, and therefore had to devise internal structures and set rules, as in the case of Bon Marché in the 1870s. See M. B. Miller, "The Department Store and Social Change in Modern France. The Case of the Bon Marché, 1860–1920" (Ph.D. diss., University of Pennsylvania, 1976), pp. 68–69,

16. Henri Fayol, *General and Industrial Management* (1916; reprint ed., New York, 1949); M. B. Brodie, *Fayol on Administration* (London, 1967).

17. André Citroën, "L'avenir de la construction automobile," *Revue parlementaire et politique* (May 1929), p. 236. See also P. Fridenson, *Histoire des usines Renault: Naissance de la grande entreprise, 1898–1939* (Paris, 1972); J. P. Bardou et al., *Le révolution automobile* (Paris, 1977); J. L. Loubet, "Une entreprise automobile française: Citroën, 1929–1939" (M.A. thesis, Université de Paris-X, 1977).

18. René Panhard held 18 percent of the 5 million francs in capital of Panhard et Levassor in 1898; there was no change until 1929, when its capital reached 50 million francs. Louis Renault had bought back his

brothers' shares in Renault, so that he held 100 percent of the firm at the time of the war; in 1922, when it was incorporated into a limited-liability company, 19 percent of the capital was left to a group under the Mirabaud Bank; as early as 1928, when the capital was raised from 80 million to 120 million francs, Renault took over the whole issue and held 96.6 percent in 1944. In 1924, at the time of the foundation of the *société anonyme,* André Citroën held 25 percent of the capital in his firm; he still had 19 percent in 1927–1928, when it was increased from the original 100 million to 400 million francs; since shares with plural votes were allowed until 1933, he still had 22 percent of the votes.

19. André Citroën, "Compte-rendu à l'Assemblée des actionnaires," December 4, 1930; see also Loubet, *Citroën,* pp. 87–88.

20. André Citroën, "La fabrication en grande série dans les usines Citroën," hearing of Société des Ingenieurs de France, July 3, 1931; idem, *L'industrie automobile* (Paris, 1931).

21. See Loubet, *Citroën,* pp. 168–172.

22. See A. Baudant, "Pont-à-Mousson. Stratégies industrielles d'une dynastie lorraine" (doctoral diss., Université de Paris-I, 1979); Omnes, *Métallurgie française,* pp. 206ff.

23. See, for instance, Houssiaux, *Pouvoir des monopoles,* pp. 3, 268–270; Morin, *Capitalisme français,* p. 14.

24. See H. W. Ehrmann, *Organized Business in France* (Princeton, 1957); A. Hirsch, "Cartels et Ententes," in *Histoire économique de la France entre les deux guerres,* ed. A. Sauvy, IV (Paris, 1974); see also T. Mallet, *Etude sur le développement d'une société industrielle à la fin du XIXème siècle: la Cie de Saint-Gobain* (Paris, 1972); L. F. Haber, *The Chemical Industry, 1900–1930* (London, 1971); H. Morsel, "Contribution à l'histoire des ententes industrielles (à partir de l'exemple des chlorates)," *Revue d'histoire économique et sociale* 54 (1976): 118–129; Omnes, *Métallurgie française;* Baudant, *Pont-à-Mousson.*

25. The transitory nature of holding companies is noted in Alfred D. Chandler, Jr., *The Visible Hand: The Managerial Revolution in American Business* (Cambridge, Mass., 1977), chap. 10; see also Haber, *Chemical Industry.* On the renegotiation of cartels in the 1930s, see A. Piettre, *L'evolution des ententes industrielles en France depuis la crise* (Paris, 1936). The distinction between holding companies set up to control industrial firms and those used as financial subsidiaries by industrial groups or firms is made in J. Tchernoff, *Ententes économiques et financières: Cartels, Syndicats, Trusts, Holdings devant les lois* (Paris, 1933); it is taken up again in B. Marois and O. Pastré, "Les groupes financiers à dominante industrielle," *Banque* 367 (November 1977):1173–78.

26. The securities held by the Société parisienne pour l'Industrie électrique (under Louis Empain) in 1912 amounted to 44 million francs (out of 57 million francs in total assets); those of the Société d'Applications industrielles (the Giros-Loucheur group), to 11 million francs; and those of the Société centrale pour l'Industrie électrique, to 6 million francs. The total for the three firms is thus 61.2 million francs, compared with 54.6

million francs in industrial *participations* (plus 106.3 million francs in portfolio assets) for the Banque de Paris et des Pays-Bas and 17.5 million francs (plus 45.5 million francs in financial assets) for the Banque de l'Union parisienne.

27. Firms depended on banking services before the war, even though they might have set up their own financial departments, as Saint-Gobain did in 1905. After the war, their relationship was reversed, and firms or groups of firms founded or absorbed financial institutions. Among the general banks founded were the Banque parisienne pour l'industrie, founded by the Empain group in 1929, and the Banque des Pays du Nord, founded by the Schneider group in 1919, after the Union Européenne industrielle et financière had been established by Schneider, Empain, and the Banque de l'Union parisienne in 1920. A number of middle-sized credit institutions were also controlled by enterprises; from the mid-1920s on, for instance, Pont-à-Mousson controlled Eaux et Assainissement, which provided credit for public-works projects, the Société Mosellane Industrielle et Financière, and the Compagnie Générale des Services Urbains. After the war, automobile companies created financial companies to supply short-term credit; among these was the Société auxiliaire pour développement de l'industrie française, which acted as an intermediary between Citroën and the Crédit Français in 1922 through 1924. The same company was bought by Citroën and became a credit institution—the Société pour le Développement de la Vente à Crédit (SOVAC)—operating in 1926 through 1929, while Renault opened DIAC in 1924 and Peugeot made use of DIN, established in 1928. During the 1930s, the same type of credit industry was established to finance the purchase of other consumer durables; some examples were the Crédit Electrique and the Matériel Domestique, set up by Alsthom.

28. See Haber, *Chemical Industry;* Gignoux, *Entreprise française;* Cayez, *Capitalisme urbain; Etablissements Kuhlmann;* see also Compagnie de Saint-Gobain, *Livre du tricentenaire, 1665–1965* (Paris, 1965); R. Richeux, "L'industrie chimique en France: Structure et production, 1850–1957" (doctoral diss., Université de Paris, 1959).

29. Edmond Gillet, a senior member of Gillet et Fils, a family holding company with interests in chemicals and textiles, wrote in 1925, "Le but commun que nous poursuivons—judiciaire, comptable, technique—est de faire de Progil [a subcompany they had founded in 1919] une affaire sachant où elle va, au lieu de la maintenir dans l'état d'un fils de famille, ne se préoccupant pas d'établir un budget parce que comptant sur son pére." Quoted in Cayez, "Capitalisme urbain."

30. See M. Battestini, *L'industrie française de gros matériel mécanique et électrique* (Paris, 1935); M. Lafarrère, *Lyon, ville industrielle* (Paris, 1960); M. Brumeaux, "La Télémécanique électrique" (M.A. thesis, Université de Paris-X, 1977); P. Lanthier, "Les groupes industriels internationaux et le développement de l'industrie électrique en France, 1880–1940 (doctoral diss., University of Paris-X, 1979).

31. P. Pézenat, *Naissance et développement de quelques entreprises de production et de distribution d'électricité, 1880–1939* (Paris, 1972); H.

Morsel, *Les groupes dans les industries électriques en France avant la nationalisation* (Paris, 1977); R. Kuisel, Ernest Mercier: French Technocrat (Berkeley, 1967).

32. According to a survey by M. Malissen, the rate of retained profits was 51.2 percent of gross profits in 1922–1926 (that is, during the period of inflation), 35.2 percent in 1927–1931 (the years of high investment), and 31.0 percent in 1931–1939, although gross profits in current francs had receded to 11.3 million francs after a mild increase from 12.3 million to 15.9 million francs. See *L'autofinancement des sociétés en France et aux Etats-Unis* (Paris, 1953).

33. Saint-Gobain had depreciated 60 of its 150 *participations* in subsidiaries to one franc by 1933. This procedure helped the firm absorb losses; for instance, it agreed to the lowering of the capital of the Société de Berre, the oil refinery that had just been opened, from 200 million to 50 million francs, although it held 60 percent of the company, and then to subscribing alone to a new increase of 100 million francs in 1934. In the same way, Saint-Gobain took over the Usines Dior; it let Grande Paroisse, its subsidiary, absorb Ammoniaque Synthétique and took upon itself the rescue of many firms in distress (as is described in detail in the annual reports to the general assembly). Because the accounts are presented in net terms, however, with the gross results remaining undisclosed, it is difficult to measure the real impact of the crisis during most of the 1930s.

34. The growth rate of the gross national product per active person was in the range of 4.6 percent per annum in the 1920s, compared with 1.7 percent in 1900 to 1913. Capital investment was rising at an annual rate of 5.8 percent in the 1920s and 3.3 percent from 1900 to 1913. See A. Vincent, "Les comptes nationaux," in *Histoire économique,* ed. A. Sauvy, III (Paris, 1972); J. J. Carré, P. Dubois, and E. Malinvaud, *French Economic Growth* (Berkeley, 1975).

5/ Regulation of Large Enterprise: The United States Experience in Comparative Perspective

Morton Keller

REGULATION OF THE MARKET is as old as the market itself. For as long as society has enjoyed the benefits of enterprise, it has sought to check its excesses. Medieval authorities sought to enforce a just price and forbade usury; early modern times saw extensive mercantilist efforts to bend economic activity to the interests of the state. English common law gradually developed constraints on monopolies and contracts in restraint of trade and on objectionable trade practices such as forestalling, engrossing, and regrating. Regulation has been as much a part of the history of Western capitalism as trade, investment, entrepreneurship, and technology.

During the late nineteenth and early twentieth centuries, that history took a new turn. The large business enterprise emerged as the primary instrument of production and distribution. The merger of firms into large-scale combinations, the integration of production and distribution within firms, and the steady accretion of company control in the hands of salaried managers were widespread and consequential developments. In recent years emergence of big business has been the subject of a rich and revealing historical literature.

The regulatory response to this development, however, has not been the beneficiary of comparable historical analysis. Substantial work has been done, of course, on the judicial and administrative regulation of the large enterprise, particularly in the United States, but this literature tends to dwell on the impact (or lack of impact) of regulation on the enterprises it is regulating. It has less to say about the development of public policy toward big business as a historical phenomenon with its own form and character. Nor has there been comparative analysis of the strategy and structure of regulation to match the recent literature on the managerial revolution in a number of Western countries.

What follows is a tentative attempt at such an overview. This essay examines the regulatory response to the rise of big business as a distinctive historical development, passing through discernible phases of evolution through the nineteenth and early twentieth centuries. In it I try to see that process in comparative perspective (though with special attention to the United States). My underlying assumption is that both the growth of large enterprise and the regulatory response were parts of a more general theme: the effort of the private and public institutions of the West to come to terms with the awesome new economic power unleashed by industrial development and technological change.[1]

THE NINETEENTH CENTURY

The large enterprises that appeared in a number of Western countries during the nineteenth century had a number of things in common. The needs of investment capital, production, management, and marketing transcended national boundaries, and everywhere public policy was called on to respond to the rise of industrial capitalism. It did so, however, in ways that were profoundly affected by the character of each country's history and culture.

Statutory and legal frameworks of business regulation differed among Western nations in timing and character. The French structure of business regulation arose in response not to the coming of large enterprise but to the French Revolution. The law of March 2, 1791, proclaimed the freedom of industry and commerce from state restrictions; the Civil Code of 1804 stripped fraudulent or unlawful contracts of their legal force and defined commercial illegality as acts "contrary to good morals or to public order"; the Commercial Code of 1807 regulated a variety of business practices; and the Penal Code of 1810 imposed penalties on those who "effect or attempt to effect an artificial increase or reduction in the price of a product." These acts were designed to underpin the Revolution's break with the restrictive, merchantilist economic policies of the *ancien régime*.[2]

Nineteenth-century French commercial law and legislation —typified by the Companies Act of 1867, which minimized government restraints on the creation of firms—reflected the primacy of small, often family-sized units in the nation's economic life. Trade associations came under legal restraint when they threatened local market relations (as in an influential 1851 case involving Calais lumber merchants). Businessmen's agreements restricting competition for a specific period of time were upheld by the courts, but not when they imposed an unlimited prohibition on competition in a particular locale as well.[3] Toward the end of the nineteenth century, the competitive threat of German cartels loomed larger, and domestic pressure to allow business combines grew. Prerevolutionary mercantilist and guild traditions reappeared in a new guise. An 1884 law legitimated professional societies, labor unions, and trade associations. But what one legal expert has called "the ghost" haunting French regulatory law continued to be "the suppression of freedom" in commercial affairs. In this area, as elsewhere in French life during the nineteenth and early twentieth centuries, individualism and corporatism engaged in never-ending conflict with one another. Big business in France made its way in a society with strong commitments both to laissez-faire and family-sized enterprises and to state-supported, large-unit consolidation.[4]

German commercial law closely resembled the French model. The Prussian Trade Regulation Act of September 7, 1811, which restricted the powers of guilds and abolished the price-fixing authority of the police, echoed the French statute of 1791. The German Civil Code of 1896 followed the French Civil Code of 1804 in declaring that "a transaction in violation of good morals is void" and that someone "who designedly injures another in a manner violating good morals" is liable to indemnification. The 1896 Statute against Unfair Competition was based on several articles of the French Code.[5]

The language of French economic liberalism thus entered into German law, but there was no equivalent of the French Revolution to foster a liberal alternative to Germany's corporative past. In the 1870s United States ambassador Andrew White called the ever more numerous German cartels "some new form of guilds." German courts readily legitimated cartels and their practices. The Bavarian Landgericht held in 1888 that "it was not *contra bonos mores* for business men belonging to a branch of industry which is suffering from a depression to get together and enter into agreements regulating the ways and means of operating their industry with a view to promoting recovery. On the contrary such course of action would seem incumbent upon prudent business men." The Reichsgericht in the Saxon Wood Pulp Cartel case of 1897 affirmed that cartels were often in the interest of the public as well as of their members, for if prices fell too far then society itself would suffer.[6] These decisions displayed the strong German inclination to accept tightly organized forms of economic activity, without the French disposition to support a market system dominated by freely competing family-sized firms. For all the similarity of language in the two nations' laws, *pro bono publico* had a very different meaning for each of them.

The British regulatory response was no less idiosyncratic. As in the case of France, economic liberalism secured a strong foothold in nineteenth-century English public policy. The Companies Act of 1862 was as much a bulwark of entrepreneurial freedom as the French law of 1867, and the Board of Trade did little to impede an orgy of railroad incorporation in the 1840s. Cartels at first met with opposition from courts steeped in the antimonopoly attitudes of nineteenth-century English common law. *Hilton* v. *Eckersley* (1856) held a mill-owners' cartel to be against the public interest: "They agree to carry on their trade not freely as they ought to do, but in conformity with the will of others; and this not being for a good consideration is contrary to public policy."[7]

By the end of the century, however, the British tradition of economic liberalism and free trade had to come to terms with the fact that cartels were an important part of the nation's economic life. In two major cases, *Mogul* v. *McGregor* (1889) and *Maxim* v. *Nordenfelt* (1894), modern British cartel policy emerged. The court in the *Mogul* case upheld a rebate granted by a cartel of steamship lines to its exclusive customers. *Maxim* enforced the ancillary covenant of an armaments cartel in which the defendant had agreed not to sell munitions anywhere for twenty-five years. Major elements of modern British regulatory policy are evident in these decisions. In sharp contrast to the United States experience, judges were inclined to exercise self-restraint in economic controversies: "To draw a line between fair and unfair competition, between what is reasonable and unreasonable, passes the power of the Courts" (*Mogul*); "In England, at least, it is beyond the jurisdiction of her tribunals to mould and stereo-type national policy" (*Maxim*). A relatively cohesive and homogeneous business community made arbitration rather than litigation the preferred mode of conflict resolution. (A major British arbitration act was passed in 1889; no significant arbitration law was passed in the Uinted States until the 1920s.)[8]

While it may seem that the British acceptance of cartel practices was similar to that of the Germans, its underlying rationale was very different. British policy rested on a belief in enterpreneurial freedom and the sanctity of contracts that overrode any distinction between the cartel and the individual businessman, or even between fair and unfair competition, which, as one of the *Mogul* judges said, "would impose a novel fetter upon trade." Another spoke of "the injustice of not allowing an association of traders to do those things which could be done by an amalgamation of the same persons."[9] German cartel policy, in contrast, assumed that the public good was best served by restraints on competition. These are quite dissimilar conceptions of the public good, and the difference in part explains why German public policy was so much more positively helpful to cartelization than was its British counterpart.[10]

The United States regulatory response to the rise of large enterprise differed sharply from the European experience. On the face of things, it was a policy suffused with paradox. The nation with the strongest traditions of individualism, voluntarism, localism, and hostility to the active state nevertheless developed the most elaborate, extensive system of legal and statutory regulation. The seedbed of integrated big business produced a regulatory system that more than any other was committed to fostering small-unit competition; the land of the trust became the land of antitrust.

For much of the nineteenth century, United States economic policy was not unlike that of France and England. It, too, was dedicated to the precepts of liberalism and laissez-faire. General-incorporation laws made chartering little more than an administrative formality; few constraints were placed on corporations' internal affairs. Indeed, the states heartily competed to see which could be most attractive to chartered companies. The already permissive New Jersey corporation law was further liberalized in 1899, so that "the conduct and conditions of [a corporation's] . . . business are treated as private and not public affairs." The external impact of corporations—on customers, competitors, and society at large—was another matter, however. Conflicting economic interests, public opinion, and party politics fostered a steady growth of legislative and judicial supervision, based on the states' chartering authority and on their police power to protect the public health, safety, and welfare.[11]

The conflict between the internal pressure on corporations to pursue autonomy and the external pressure on them for accountability attained a scale and intensity in the United States that had no European analogue. Why was this so? Surely in part because of the rapidity with which big business came to the country and the scale it attained. The sense of a sudden change in economic life, and thus in the life of the society at large, was far more intense in the United States than in Europe. What was more, this corporate-managerial revolution occurred in a society with no older tradition of feudalism, corporatism, or social and political hierarchy. Nowhere were nineteenth-century individualism and laissez-faire less challenged by opposing social values; nowhere did big business develop faster or further. The result was a politics of regulation—and a regulatory system—unique in character.

The railroads were the United States' first big business, and railroad supervision was the first great regulatory battleground.

From the 1820s to the 1870s, states, counties, and towns oscillated between providing freedom and subsidies for railroads to expand and seeking to mitigate or regulate the effects of that expansion. As consolidation in the late nineteenth century made the railroads truly national enterprises, regulation became a national issue as well. E. L. Godkin of the *Nation* presciently warned in 1873: "The locomotive is coming in contact with the framework of our institutions. In this country of simple government, the most powerful centralizing force which civilization has yet produced must, within the next score years, assume its relations to that political machinery which is to control and regulate it."[12]

In 1887 Congress responded to more than a decade of agitation for federal railroad regulation by enacting the Interstate Commerce Act. This law defined and laid down the penalties for rate discrimination and created an Interstate Commerce Commission (ICC) with the power to investigate and prosecute violators. In the years that followed, railroads continued to expand and consolidate, and new regulatory laws were added. These included the Elkins Act of 1903, designed to end rebates to favored customers; the Hepburn Act of 1906, granting rate-making power to the ICC; the Mann-Elkins Act of 1910, which set up a Commerce Court to review rate and other disputes; the Adamson Act of 1916, prescribing an eight-hour day for railroad workers; and the Esch-Cummins Act of 1920, which returned the railroads to private ownership after a wartime hiatus of government operation.

This record cannot be characterized either as one of subservience to the railroads or as a coherent national railroad policy. The interests involved were too varied, conflicting, and effervescent for either tendency to prevail. Some larger railroads wanted federal regulation to serve as a substitute for rate pooling, which consistently failed because the courts refused to enforce it. Other lines favored state supervision; still others opposed all regulation, state or federal. The interests of small railroads often conflicted with those of the larger lines. Commercial, agricultural, and industrial shippers were no less varied; their attitudes toward regulation differed according to their size and location and the extent of the rail service currently available to them. Railroad labor unions and public opinion in general were also factors to be reckoned with. So too were the regulators themselves: state railroad commissions, state legislators, Congress and the President, the ICC, and, not least, the state and federal courts. It is not surprising that the United States system of railroad regulation was conspicuous for its scale and extent— and for its inability to promote the development of a stable, rationalized, and efficient national railroad system.[13]

The performance of the ICC reveals how difficult it was to have a viable form of national administrative supervision in a federalist, pluralistic polity. During the first ten years of its existence, the commission handed down rulings on more than 800 rate controversies, but the size, complexity, and intensely competitive character of the railroad business and the limits on the ICC's power (its decisions could be reviewed by the courts) severely limited its impact. The commission adopted a judicial rather than an administrative model from the first. Its initial chairman, the former judge and legal treatise writer Thomas M. Cooley, announced, "The Commissioners realize that they are a new court, . . . and that they are to lay the foundations of a new body of American law." The major achievements of the ICC by 1900 were to bring about greater uniformity in railroad accounting and the classification of operating costs and greater publicity about the conduct of the railroad business. Closer control was not possible; nor, thought Chairman Cooley, was it desirable: "The perpetuity of free institutions in this country requires that the political machine called the United States Government be kept from being overloaded beyond its strength. The more cumbrous it is the greater power and intrigue and corruption under it."[14]

Similar conditions attended the creation and early application of the Sherman Antitrust Act. The use of the trust and later the holding company to evade state laws forbidding one corporation from holding the stock of another unloosed strong public fears of corporate power. The corporate trust—"a perfectly new device in the law"—had a disturbing ambiguity about it. One commentator wrote in 1887, "The Standard Oil has grown to be a more powerful—corporation, shall we call it? or what? for this is one of the questions—than any other below the national government itself."[15] The trust in the generic sense of a "huge, irresponsible, indeterminate" corporation became the object of widespread public, legislative, and judicial concern. By 1890 ten states had passed antitrust laws, and six state supreme courts had found trust agreements to be illegal as monopolies, conspiracies in restraint of trade, or against public policy. The Sherman Act, adopted by a virtually unanimous congressional vote in 1890, outlawed "every contract, combination in the form of trust or otherwise, or conspiracy, in restraint of trade or commerce." The sweep and vagueness of this formulation, and the law's reliance on the courts rather than on an administrative agency to determine when it had been violated, avoided the risk that the Supreme Court would declare it unconstitutional. Beyond that, the language of the Sherman Act reflected the prevailing uncertainty as to just what form regulation should take—and just what should be regulated.[16]

Not surprisingly, the Sherman Act at first proved to be no more effective as a regulatory device than the ICC. In the 1890s the Department of Justice lacked the personnel, the money, and the inclination to prosecute offenders vigorously. The courts, too, severely limited the utility of the act. They held that a firm might well dominate its sector of the economy without doing anything illegal, and they developed a distinction between legitimate business practices and "illegal commercial piracy." In its *E. C. Knight* decision of 1895, the Supreme Court held that even though the American Sugar Refining Company controlled over 90 percent of the nation's sugar-refining capacity, it did not violate the Sherman Act because it was engaged in manufacturing, not in interstate commerce. In a series of decisions from 1897 to 1899, however, the Court made it clear that the Sherman Act would be applied—and applied vigorously—against trading and pricing cartels.[17]

By the end of the nineteenth century a distinctive public policy toward the large enterprise had emerged in the United States. In contrast with the European situation, pools, trusts, and cartels had little or no legal standing, but holding companies (particularly of manufacturing firms) were acceptable combinations. Furthermore, despite the creation of the ICC, regulation was being handled primarily through litigation and court decisions, not through administrative decrees. The *form* of regulation—a mass of state laws, the Interstate Commerce and Sherman Acts, and constant and heavy litigation—indicated the widespread popular distrust of big business; the regulatory *function* reflected the diversity of interests at play, the political power of large enterprise, and the weakness of the administrative state.

THE EARLY TWENTIETH CENTURY

In the years after 1900, large enterprises throughout the West tended more and more to resemble one another. By 1930 the 100 largest firms in the United States and in Great Britain each accounted for about 25 percent of the net manufactured output of their countries. They were no less alike in their managerial, marketing, and financial structures. In 1901 the English observer Henry Macrosty commented that "after a century of competition we find that a new motive is gripping the industrial world, the desire to put an end to competition, while maintaining the private ownership and direction of industry."[18]

Might the same be said of public policy? Did regulatory structures, particularly those of Germany, Great Britain, and the United States, respond in similar ways to the emergence of mature systems of big business? Certainly there are grounds for arguing that such a convergence of policy did in fact take place. The administrative state—regulatory agencies, administrative law, and the like—grew in all countries. The goals of rationalization and efficiency appealed to political as well as corporate leaders. One study of British political thought from 1890 to 1914 is aptly titled *The Quest for National Efficiency;* an interpretation of American politics and society during this period is called *The Search for Order.*[19]

The regulatory policies of leading industrial nations appeared to converge during the course of the early twentieth century, in pace with the increasing uniformity of large enterprises. "By the time the [First World] War came," said A. H. Feller, "corporation law throughout Europe had reached a certain level of stability." By the 1920s courts in the United States had come closer to the European willingness to accept cartel practices. At the same time, Germany, which established its Cartel Court in 1923; Great Britain, which conducted its first trust investigation in 1919; and France, which passed a law penalizing excessive company profits in 1926, began to echo the American policy of paying heed to the dangers as well as celebrating the advantages of bigness and combination. In the late nineteenth century, regulatory policy everywhere established the ground rules that accompanied the emergence of big business; in the early twentieth century the emphasis shifted to accommodating regulation to mature systems of large enterprise.[20]

Nevertheless, a closer look at the record suggests that underlying national differences continued to leave their mark on regulatory policy. Each country had its own mode of supervision, its own politics of regulation, its own way of dealing with specific issues such as boycotts, tying contracts, price cutting, and resale-price maintenance. Public policy continued to reflect the fact that large enterprise functioned in distinct and distinctive national milieus.[21]

Big business in Germany had a much closer relationship to the policies of the state than was the case in Great Britain or the United States. The atavistic character of the Kaiser and his court had a heavy and often oppressive weight on the career of a leading businessman like Albert Ballin of the Hamburg-Amerika Line. At the same time, the freedom of firms to form cartels remained secure and uncontested. It was, said one commentator, "a right somewhat akin to the right to make use of a highway, and only subject to correction of abuses of power." As Ballin observed, the United States government could require the dissolution of a syndicate, while under German law its dissolution could be a punishable offense.[22] German courts repeatedly ruled that cartels protected the interests of the nation against the selfishness of individuals. A Reichstag committee investigating cartels in the early 1900s was critical of numerous practices—particularly those of the steel cartel—but recommended no restrictive legislation; nor was any enacted. The courts treated cartel cases in terms of the law of industrial property rights, patents, trade regulations, copyrights, and the like. In contrast to the United States' emphasis on antitrust law, there was no cartel law as such in Germany until after World War I.[23]

The German Cartel Law of 1923, the first statute to refer specifically to cartels, created a Cartel Court with the power to adjudicate charges of abuses by these associations. On the face of things this was a regulatory device comparable to the American Federation Trade Commission. The Cartel Court heard

more than 2,000 complaints during the 1920s, but the relief
that it granted rarely went beyond allowing the aggrieved party
to withdraw from the cartel. For the most part, the court sustained cartel boycotts (*Sperre*) of nonmembers and "loyalty rebates" to exclusive customers. It exercised little or no restraint
on the pace of cartelization; one estimate is that there were 1,500
cartels in 1923 and 2,500 in 1925. Although the Company Act of
1930 (which copied the British Companies Act of 1928) brought
German company law into closer accord with that of other
countries, only organized labor and the Socialists challenged the
structure of cartelization that had become so prevalent in German enterprise. No organized counterforce of competing business interests, no countertradition of free-market competition
left its mark on early twentieth-century German public policy
toward the large enterprise.[24]

Though there were many similarities between the reform
politics of Edwardian British Liberalism and early twentieth-
century progressivism in the United States, antitrust was not
one of them. The major British concern in the years after 1900
was not the power of big business but its efficiency—that is, its
capacity to compete with its German and American rivals.

The consolidation and integration of British firms, always
slower than that of their overseas counterparts, quickened during World War I and after. A number of businessmen, poli-
ticians, and publicists in the 1920s called for the "rationalization" of industry. Some hoped that the Board of Trade might
play a role in this regard comparable to that of Herbert Hoover's
Department of Commerce. Moreover, British regulatory policy
increasingly concerned itself with the internal management of
firms. The Companies Department of the Board of Trade won
independent status in 1904, a year after the creation of the
Bureau of Corporations in the United States Department of
Commerce and Labor. Successive Companies Acts—those of
1900, 1908, and especially 1928—tightened government supervision of the formation and management of firms and the is-
suance of securities, in much the same way as the United States'
Federal Trade Commission Act of 1914 and Securities Exchange
Act of 1934.[25]

Yet the major thrust of British public policy toward large

enterprises—in dramatic contrast with the German pattern—was to keep state involvement at a minimum. Arbitration rather than litigation remained the preferred mode of resolving conflicts among firms; "arrangements and understandings and gentlemen's agreements" more extensive "than the average man ever dreamed of" continued to be the norm.[26] Far less big-business litigation came before the British than before the United States courts. Eleven of the 50 largest industrial corporations in the United States faced government-initiated lawsuits in the appellate courts during the early twentieth century; none of the 50 leading British firms were so involved. The major United States firms were parties to about 300 appellate cases through 1906, and about 350 from 1907 to 1916. The comparable British firms figured in only 22 reported cases between 1895 and 1935.[27]

Nor was there a pronounced and vigorous judicial response to combination as such. One observer concluded in 1925 that "speaking broadly, and as a practical matter, the law does not forbid monopoly at all." He found, however, that only 11 cases involving the power of cartels came before the courts between 1829 and 1925 (8 of these from 1898 on). Six involved challenges to contractual arrangements between cartels and outside parties; given the courts' respect for sanctity of contract, it is not surprising that all were decided in favor of the cartels. When the cartel sought to enforce its provisions against its own members in 4 other cases, however, the decision in 3 went against the combine.[28] A 1937 review of British legal obstacles to industrial integration concluded that "the progress of industrial integration by means of contractual association proceeds without assistance from the legislature and in face of considerable opposition from the common law; but this opposition varies in its intensity and success."[29] Perhaps the fairest judgment is that public policy both reflected and sustained the halting, uncertain progress of British business consolidation during the early twentieth century.

The ostensible goal of regulation in the United States after 1900 was clear enough. "The policy of the law looks to competition," observed a federal court in 1900; "the fundamental purpose of the Sherman Act was to secure equality of opportunity and to protect the public against the evils commonly incident to the destruction of competition," the Supreme Court concluded in 1923.[30] Yet this was the period during which big business in the United States took its modern form. How, in fact, did regulatory law and legislation cope with the growing disparity between public-policy theory and economic reality?

During the years before World War I, concern over the size, structure, practices, and power of the large enterprise had a central place in American public life. James Bryce observed in 1905 that the dominant issue in American politics "was the one least discussed in Europe: I mean the propriety of restricting industrial or mercantile combinations of capitalists."[31] This was a direct response to the rapidity and scale of corporate consolidation in the United States. It was also part of a broader, pervasive fear of social change that expressed itself in a variety of forms: prohibition, restriction of immigration, legalized racial segregation, the conservation movement. This larger context helps explain why the regulatory goals of antitrust were so much stronger in the early twentieth-century United States than in any other Western society.

The vast literature on the trusts, that appeared in the years after 1900 was divided between two schools of thought. The first saw corporate consolidation as a sinister social development and called for policies designed to maintain a system of free competition among roughly comparable business units. The other saw large enterprise as a progressive force that held out the promise of greater efficiency, lower costs, and labor peace. These attitudes stemmed not from traditional class divisions but rather from particular individual or group interests. Samuel Gompers of the American Federation of Labor welcomed the rise of big business; small businessmen were among the most ardent supporters of antitrust policies.[32] Given this range of views, it is not surprising that American regulatory policy, in sum, was neither sharply adverse toward nor warmly protective of large enterprise. Rather, it may best be seen as a complex, varied response to an equally complex and varied economic system.

Early twentieth-century national regulation developed in a kind of counterpoint to state corporation law. Wiley B. Rutledge, Jr., concluded in 1937, "During the half-century in which the Federal Government has been extending its control over corporate enterprise, the states have been engaged simultaneously in abrogating their control." During the decade from 1915 to 1925, a deluge of state laws legitimated no-par stock offerings. In the late 1920s a number of commonwealths—among them California, Illinois, Michigan, Ohio, and Pennsylvania—made their corporation laws still more liberal than they had been before. As Rutledge observed, "In general, they are designed to give the maximum freedom to the incorporators, and to adjust statutory provisions to the requirements of the large scale mass production enterprise."[33]

Federal policies followed a more tortuous path. By the end of the nineteenth century it seemed clear that, while the courts would not uphold trusts or cartels, they were ready to allow manufacturing firms to combine into holding companies. This trend was a helpful prelude to the great burst of industrial mergers around 1900. Alfred D. Chandler, Jr., has noted that "after 1899 lawyers were advising their corporate clients to abandon all agreements or alliances carried out through cartels or trade associations and to consolidate into single, legally defined enterprises."[34]

If judicial policy helped set the stage for the turn-of-the-century merger movement, it also contributed to its end. The slowdown of mergers after 1902 coincided not only with the satiation of the market for industrial securities but also with the Supreme Court's 1904 *Northern Securities* decision, the first to suggest that a holding company might be vulnerable to the Sherman Act. Thereafter (with an occasional spectacular exception, such as the public utilities combines of the 1920s) corporate growth occurred more often through managerial investment in production, marketing, research, and other facilities than through consolidations fostered by promoters and investment bankers. Meanwhile, Sherman Act antitrust actions multiplied. The new Bureau of Corporations provided the government with better fact-gathering facilities; the Expediting Act of 1903 gave priority in the federal courts to Sherman Act and ICC cases; and the Department of Justice was strengthened by larger appropriations and the creation of an Antitrust Division.

During Theodore Roosevelt's presidency (1901–1909), 44 Sherman Act suits were filed; under William Howard Taft (1909–1913) the number rose to 90.[35]

The Supreme Court's *Standard Oil* and *American Tobacco* decisions were the most important in pre–World War I antitrust law. They forced two of the largest corporate holding companies to break up into separate (and theoretically competing) firms. More significantly, the Court's adoption of the "rule of reason" in applying the Sherman Act meant that the character and practices of large enterprises, not their size or the percentage of the industry that they controlled, would determine their liability. Flexible (and highly complex and technical) considerations would henceforward characterize United States antitrust law.[36]

The *American Tobacco* case nicely demonstrates how the character of regulation had changed in accord with the new technology, managerial structure, and marketing conditions of big business. The complexity of the American Tobacco Company's corporate structure (there were several layers of holding companies) and the intermixture of production and marketing functions made its dissolution very difficult. Each of the numerous component companies of the American Tobacco combine had to be dealt with as an individual conspirator in restraint of trade: "Every concern made brands owned by some other concern, or had made for it by some one of the other companies a brand or brands which it owned." The several kinds of American Tobacco equities also had to be treated separately; the interests of bondholders, preferred stockholders, and common stockholders often conflicted with one another. The complex dissolution plan that followed on the Court's decision was worked out in a series of conferences by American Tobacco officials, company lawyers, federal circuit-court judges, and the Attorney General and his staff. The settlement created new, supposedly independent firms—Liggett and Myers, P. Lorillard, and others—out of the original American Tobacco combine. Efforts were made to assure these new companies the brand names, factories, distribution facilities, and earning power necessary to compete on reasonable terms with the mother firm. At the same time, it was recognized that "the business itself offers insuperable obstacles to the creation of perfect competitive conditions under any method of distribution." In fact, the tobacco industry retained an essentially oligopolistic character. Here was regulation far more complex in its character and ambiguous in its results than simple antitrust.[37]

The Clayton and Federal Reserve Acts of 1914 were passed at the end of the formative period of big business in the United States, just as the Interstate Commerce and Sherman Acts marked its beginning. As might be expected, the later laws had much in common with the complex and articulated mode of legal regulation that had emerged in step with large enterprise. The Clayton Act exempted labor unions and agricultural marketing associations from the Sherman Act and forbade specific business practices such as price discrimination, tying contracts, and interlocking directorates that "substantially lessen competition or tend to create a monopoly." In sum, it adapted the Sherman Act to new economic conditions by specifying what sorts of associations were permissible and what sorts of behavior were not.

The Federal Trade Commission Act made "unfair methods of competition in commerce" as illegal as conspiracies in restraint of trade. More important, it was the charter of administrative (as distinct from judicial) oversight of the modern business enterprise. For the first time, a government agency—the Federal Trade Commission–was given a broad grant of power (in the words of the act) to investigate corporations' "organization, business, conduct, practices, and management . . . and relation to other corporations and to individuals" and to issue legally enforceable cease and desist orders. As with the Clayton Act, the emphasis now was more on the practices than on the structure of big business.[38]

By 1914 the framework of regulation, like the structure of big business that it regulated, was largely in place. Public policy had not necessarily become more straightforward, however. It is true that trade associations were fostered by the Republican administrations of the 1920s and that a series of Supreme Court decisions stretching from *United States* v. *United States Steel* (1920) to *Appalachian Coals* v. *United States* (1933) upheld combinations and cartel practices. Other decisions, however, such as *American Column and Lumber* v. *United States* (1921), held otherwise. And although tying contracts and resale-price maintenance won wide support in British and German law, American courts in the 1920s dealt severely with these anti-competitive devices. The legal historian James Willard Hurst has concluded after a review of three generations of United States antitrust law, "What stands out as most basic in the record is the lack of well-defined, comprehensive, sustained planning of public action affecting concentration of private economic control."[39]

This indeterminacy was due not only to the political and economic power of big business but also to the variety and range of the interests at play. As Hurst observes, "Growing diversity of the economy produced growing diversity of competing special interests." Thus the American Newspaper Publishers' Association, anxious to lower the price of newsprint, was a prime mover in the antitrust suit against the International Paper Company. Similarly, Kansas oil producers, reacting to a price cut imposed on them by Standard Oil, put pressure on Congress to order the investigation that led to antitrust actions against that firm.[40] Technological change brought its own, new forms of business competition and regulatory pressure: between railroads and trucks, between coal and oil producers, among the producers of new products competing for the same consumer dollars. The result, in Hurst's words, was that "the regulatory situation might well be too cloudy on the merits to make possible dogmatic judgments of where the public interest lay."[41]

Similar conflicts of interest doubtless existed in other nations, but the size and scale of the United States economy and the decentralized character of the political and legal process made this pluralistic war of all against all a uniquely important part of the American regulatory system.

NOTES

1. See Alfred D. Chandler, Jr., *The Visible Hand: The Managerial Revolution in American Business* (Cambridge, Mass., 1977); Leslie Hannah, ed., *Management Strategy and Business Development: An Historical and Comparative Study* (London, 1976); Herman Daems and Herman van der Wee, eds., *The Rise of Managerial Capitalism* (The Hague, 1974); David S. Landes, *The Unbound Prometheus: Technological Change and Industrial Development in Western Europe from 1750 to the Present* (Cambridge, 1969).

2. Francis Déak, "Contracts and Combinations in Restraint of Trade

in French Law: A Comparative Study," *Iowa Law Review* 21 (1935–1936): 397–454, especially pp. 417–419.

3. See Theodore Zeldin, *France 1848–1945: Ambition, Love and Politics* (Oxford, 1973), pt. 1, secs. 5–7; Déak, "Contracts and Combinations," p. 402.

4. John Wolff, "Business Monopolies: Three European Systems in their Bearing on American Law," *Tulane Law Review* 9 (1935):325–377, especially pp. 333–334; see also Francis Walker, "The Law Concerning Monopolistic Combinations in Continental Europe," *Political Science Quarterly* 20 (1905):27–36; V. G. Venturini, *Monopolies and Restrictive Trade Practices in France* (Leyden, 1971), chap. 1.

5. Reinhold Wolff, "Social Control through the Device of Defining Unfair Trade Practices: The German Experience," *Iowa Law Review* 21 (1935–1936):355–396, especially p. 357.

6. White is quoted in Heinrich Kronstein, "The Dynamics of German Cartels and Patents. I," *University of Chicago Law Review* 9 (1941–1942): 646; for these cases, see J. Wolff, "Business Monopolies," pp. 328–333; see also Walker, "Monopolistic Combinations," pp. 14–21.

7. Hilton v. Eckersley, 119 Eng. Rep. 781, 793 (6 El. & Bl. 47 (1856)). See also Richard Brown, "The Genesis of Company Law in England and Scotland," *Juridical Review* 13 (1901):185–204; Henry Parris, *Government and the Railways in Nineteenth Century Britain* (Toronto, 1965).

8. Mogul v. McGregor, L.R. 23 Q.B.D. 598, 617 (1889), [1892] A.C. 25; Maxim v. Nordenfelt [1894] A.C. 535, 553–554.

9. Mogul v. McGregor, L.R. 23 Q.B.D. at 617.

10. See J. Robertson Christie, "Contracts in Restraint of Trade," *Juridical Review* 12 (1900):283–303; Felix H. Levy, "The Sherman Law and the English Doctrine," *Cornell Law Quarterly* 6 (1920–1921):45ff.

11. Edward Q. Keasbey, "New Jersey and the Great Corporations," *Harvard Law Review* 13 (1899):210–211; Morton Keller, *Affairs of State: Public Life in Late Nineteenth Century America* (Cambridge, Mass., 1977), pp. 409–422.

12. Quoted in James A. Garfield, *The Future of the Republic: Its Dangers and Its Hopes* (Cleveland, 1873), p. 20.

13. Ari and Olive Hoogenboom, *A History of the ICC: From Panacea to Palliative* (New York, 1976), is a good survey of the subject and its literature.

14. Quoted in Keller, *Affairs of State,* pp. 429–430; see also Henry C. Adams, "A Decade of Federal Railway Regulation," *Atlantic Monthly* 81 (1898):433–443.

15. Charles B. Elliott, "The Consolidation of Corporations Existing under the Laws of Different States," *Central Law Journal* 17 (1883):383; F. J. Stimson, "Trusts," *Harvard Law Review* 1 (1887):133–134.

16. Stimson, "Trusts," p. 143; Keller, *Affairs of State,* pp. 434–438.

17. See Hans B. Thorelli, *The Federal Antitrust Policy: Origination of an American Tradition* (Baltimore, 1955), chaps. 7–8; United States v. E. C. Knight Co., 156 U.S. 1 (1895); United States v. Trans-Missouri Freight

Ass'n, 166 U.S. 290 (1897); United States v. Joint Traffic Ass'n, 171 U.S. 505 (1898); Addystone Pipe and Steel Co. v. United States, 175 U.S. 211 (1899).

18. Leslie Hannah, *The Rise of the Corporate Economy: The British Experience* (Baltimore, 1976), pp. *ix–x;* Henry Macrosty, *Trusts and the State* (London, 1901), p. 12.

19. G. R. Searle, *The Quest for National Efficiency: A Study in British Politics and British Political Thought, 1899–1914* (Berkeley, 1971); Robert H. Wiebe, *The Search for Order, 1877–1920* (New York, 1967).

20. A. H. Feller, "The Movement for Corporate Reform: A World-Wide Phenomenon," *American Bar Association Journal* 20 (1934):347–348; see also Robert Liefmann, *Cartels, Concerns and Trusts* (New York, 1932), pp. 175ff.

21. See Fritz E. Koch, "Methods of Regulating Unfair Competition in Germany, England, and the United States," *University of Pennsylvania Law Review* 78 (1930):693–712, 854–878.

22. See U.S. Congress, Senate, Committee on Interstate Commerce, *Trusts in Foreign Countries* (Washington, D.C., 1912), pp. 115–116. See also Lamar Cecil, *Business and Politics in Imperial Germany, 1888–1918* (Princeton, 1967), especially pp. 114ff.

23. See William Notz, "Recent Developments in Foreign Anti-Trust Legislation," *Yale Law Journal* 34 (1924–1925):163; R. Wolff, "Social Control," pp. 358–359.

24. Liefmann, *Cartels,* pp. 168–170; R. Wolff, "Social Control," pp. 376–381; National Industrial Conference Board, *Rationalization of German Industry* (New York, 1931), pp. 39, 45. See also William C. Kessler, "German Cartel Regulation under the Decree of 1923," *Quarterly Journal of Economics* 50 (1935–1936):680–693.

25. Hannah, *Rise of the Corporate Economy,* pp. 29ff.; Conservative Party, *Industry and the State: A Conservative View* (London, 1927), p. 24; Bishop C. Hunt, "Recent English Company Law Reform," *Harvard Business Review* 8 (1930):183.

26. P. L. Payne, "The Emergence of the Large-Scale Company in Great Britain, 1870–1914," *Economic History Review,* 2nd ser. 20 (1967):526.

27. Case figures from *American Digest, 1658–1896* (Saint Paul, 1897–1904); *Decennial Edition of the American Digest, 1897–1906* (Saint Paul, 1908–1912); *All England Law Reports Annotated Index and Table of Cases, 1895–1935* (London, 1936). Company lists from Payne, "Emergence," pp. 539–541.

28. F. D. Simpson, "How Far Does the Law of England Forbid Monopoly?" *Law Quarterly Review* 41 (1925):393–394ff.

29. Geoffrey Vickers, "Legal Obstacles to Industrial Integration," *Law Journal* 84 (1937):237.

30. United States v. Chesapeake & Ohio R.R., 105 F. 93 (C.C.S.D. Ohio, 1900); Ramsey Co. v. Bill Posters' Ass'n, 260 U.S. 501, 512 (1923).

31. James Bryce, "America Revisited: The Changes of a Quarter-Century," *Outlook* 79 (1905):847.

32. See Thorelli, *Antitrust Policy,* chap. 6; Paul T. Homan, "Industrial Combination as Surveyed in Recent Literature," *Quarterly Journal of Economics* 44 (1929–1930):345–375.

33. Wiley B. Rutledge, Jr., "Significant Trends in Modern Incorporation Statutes," *Washington University Law Quarterly* 22 (1937):309, 337.

34. Chandler, *Visible Hand,* pp. 333–334.

35. Thorelli, *Antirust Policy,* pp. 534–537; Oswald W. Knauth, *The Policy of the United States toward Industrial Monopoly* (New York, 1914), pp. 86, 92.

36. Standard Oil Co. of New Jersey v. United States, 221 U.S. 1 (1911); United States v. American Tobacco Co., 221 U.S. 106 (1911). See also Henry Seager and Charles A. Gulick, Jr., *Trust and Corporation Problems* (New York, 1929), chaps. 8, 11, 19.

37. Albert C. Muhse, "The Disintegration of the Tobacco Combination," *Political Science Quarterly* 28 (1913):249–278, especially pp. 254, 276. See also William Z. Ripley, ed., *Trusts, Pools and Corporations,* rev. ed. (Boston, 1916), chap. 8; Revis Cox, *Competition in the American Tobacco Industry, 1911–1932* (New York, 1933).

38. James W. Hurst, *Law and Social Order in the United* (Ithaca, 1977), pp. 246–247; Gregory Hankin, "Functions of the Federal Trade Commission," *Illinois Law Quarterly* 6 (1923–1924):188.

39. Hurst, *Law and Social Order,* p. 266. See also Ellis W. Hawley, "Herbert Hoover: The Commerce Secretariat and the Vision of an 'Associative State,' 1921–1928," *Journal of American History* 62 (1974):116–140; United States v. United States Steel, 251 U.S. 407 (1920); Appalachian Coals, Inc., v. United States, 288 U.S. 377 (1921); on tying contracts, see United Shoe Machinery Co. v. United States, 258 U.S. 433 (1922); Edwin R. A. Seligman and Robert A. Love, *Price Cutting and Price Maintenance: A Study in Economics* (New York, 1932).

40. Hurst, *Law and Social Order,* p. 217. On the paper trust suit, see Morton Keller, *In Defense of Yesterday: James M. Beck and the Politics of Conservatism* (New York, 1958), pp. 68–69; on the Kansas oil producers, see Francis Walker, "The Oil Trust and the Government," *Political Science Quarterly* 23 (1908):18–46.

41. Hurst, *Law and Social Order,* p. 218.

6/ Emergence of the Visible Hand: Implications for Industrial Organization

Oliver E. Williamson

SPECIALISTS in the study of industrial organization and historians of the modern business enterprise have much to learn from each other. Indeed, current efforts to combine the contributions of business historians and economists concerned with the emerging theory of firms and markets appear highly promising. This essay focuses primarily on *The Visible Hand: The Managerial Revolution in American Business* by Alfred D. Chandler, Jr. In discussing this and other works, I shall concentrate on the theoretical and public policy issues that are of interest in the study of industrial organization. Like Chandler's earlier *Strategy and Structure, The Visible Hand* provides insights into the organizational innovations that led to the development of the modern corporation. Partly because it relies very little on recent literature exploring market failures and industrial organization, however, Chandler's interpretation of visible hand developments is sometimes troublesome. These matters are discussed in a later section of the chapter, after an overview of the book's argument and importance.[1]

Note: Research for this chapter was supported by the Center for the Study of Organizational Innovation and by a grant from the National Science Foundation; it was revised during a fellowship at the Center for Advanced Study in the Behavioral Sciences. The revision benefited from comments by Alfred D. Chandler, Jr., and David Teece.

Significant Contributions

Among the most significant contributions of *The Visible Hand* are, first, that it affirms that organizational innovation is an important though neglected factor in economic development and, second, that it reveals the modern business enterprise as a complex institution that can be fully understood only from a combined historical and organizational perspective. It also demonstrates that technology is important but not decisive in shaping the organization of industry and provides insight into a series of other issues related to industrial organization.

Organizational Innovation Organizational innovation is used here to describe not only new hierarchical methods of organzing economic activity (organizational structure) but also the incentive, control, and planning instruments that are associated with new organizational forms. Specialists in business history have long been aware that organizational innovations have had profound efficiency (productivity) consequences. This message is repeated and reasons for believing it to be correct are further developed in Chandler's *Visible Hand*.

Arthur H. Cole has called attention to the importance of organizational innovation and has asserted that "if changes in business procedures and practices were patentable, the contributions of business change to the economic growth of the nation would be as widely recognized as the influence of mechanical inventions or the inflow of capital from abroad." And Thomas Cochran has conjectured that "business organization rather than technology or capital [was] the leading sector in bringing about economic growth." A few other economists appear to be sympathetic to such views; for example, Kenneth J. Arrow has observed, "Truly among man's innovations, the use of organization to accomplish his ends is among both his greatest and his earliest." In general, however, this message appears to have been ignored or lost.[2]

Chandler argues in *The Visible Hand* that the rise of the modern business enterprise between 1840 and World War I is not to be explained by entrepreneurial talents,[3] capital markets,[4] or public policy (tariffs, patents, antitrust) but was "the organizational response to fundamental changes in processes of production and distribution made possible by the availability of new sources of energy and by the increasing application of scientific knowledge to industrial technology."[5] He furthermore asserts that organizational economies are more significant than conventional scale economies: "Far more economies result from the careful coordination of flow through the processes of production and distribution than from increasing the size of producing or distributing units" in simple plant scale or employment respects.[6]

In examining the development of the railroads during the latter part of the nineteenth century, for instance, Chandler notes that the "swift victory of the railway over the waterway resulted from organizational as well as technological innovation." These organizational developments involved the creation of a hierarchical apparatus to "monitor, evaluate, and coordinate" a complex system. Indeed, but for organizational innovations that gave the managers of large systems greater knowledge and control, larger rail systems experienced diseconomies of scale. So significant were the organizational innovations introduced by the railroads during this period that Chandler finds it fitting to declare them "the first modern business enterprises." He furthermore observes that while Albert Fishlow credits half of the substantial increase in railroad productivity between 1870 and 1910 to technological developments, the other half remains unexplained; organizational innovations account for much of this.[7]

No serious student of business history can read Chandler's discussion of organizational innovation without granting that a prima facie case for the importance of organizational innovation has been made. It is hoped that the book will help direct more concentrated research attention to this relatively neglected topic. Among the issues that warrant investigation is the difference between what Cochran has referred to as the business revolution and the managerial revolution that concerns Chandler. Thus whereas Cochran argues that the business revolution was complete by 1840, in that the nation then "had a commercial structure capable of adopting machine technology . . . as fast as it could be developed," Chandler contends that the managerial revolution did not get under way until 1840. Inasmuch as the "mercantile experience" that Cochran emphasizes is distinguishable from the internal organization of the multifunction enterprise that concerns Chandler, no necessary contradiction exists.[8] Nevertheless, the tension between these two views of United States business history needs to be sorted out.

Organizational Complexity Although simple models of organization have obvious appeal, they can sometimes be misleading. Chandler's book makes clear that the evolution of the modern business firm in the United States occurred over a long period, and successive improvements did not occur in a single industry but were distributed across several. This is not to say that the study of simple tasks—pinmaking, sandal making—is uninstructive or that studies of organization that rely primarily on events associated with the industrial revolution in England and Europe are not useful. But such studies are incomplete and can, by emphasizing technological simplicity or ideological class tensions characteristic of other cultures, impair an accurate understanding of organizational innovation in the United States. Textile manufacture, for instance, is the most frequently discussed example of the organization of industry during the industrial revolution in Europe; Chandler, however, establishes that, although the "integrated textile mills were the first large factories in [the United States], the new textile industry had little impact on the development of modern industrial management."[9] Preoccupation with textiles is accordingly unrewarding if the aim is to discover the origins of the modern business enterprise and to evaluate their significance. Factory organization, with its emphasis on the technology of production, simply falls well short of business organization, which deals with the organization of the firm.

Indeed, insofar as factory organization is concerned, the Springfield Armory was a more significant innovator than were the textile mills. Not only did the armory precede textile mills in specializing and subdividing the task, but significant accounting and quality control procedures were first devised there. Chandler concludes that modern factory management, which he distinguishes from business management, "had its genesis in the United States in the Springfield Armory."[10] The railroads, however, were the first modern business enterprises. Among other things,

They were the first to require a large number of salaried managers; the first to have a central office operated by middle managers and commanded by top managers who reported to a board of directors. They were the first American business enterprise to build a large internal organizational structure with carefully defined lines of responsibility, authority, and communication between the central office, departmental headquarters, and field units; and they were the first to develop financial and statistical flows to control and evaluate the work of the many managers.

In all this they were the first because they had to be. No other business enterprise up to that time had had to govern a large number of men and offices scattered over wide geographical areas.[11]

It was firms that produced food, tobacco, and machinery, however, that brought modern industrial enterprise to fruition; the functional structure associated with modern industrial enterprise, with departments specialized in sales, production, finance, and so on, first appeared here. (This is what I have referred to elsewhere as the traditional or unitary [U-form] structure.)[12] This structure evolved in conjunction with the simultaneous development of mass production and mass distribution. Important early contributors included James Duke's American Tobacco, Swift & Company, Singer Sewing Machine Company, Cyrus McCormick's agricultural-machinery company (subsequently International Harvester), and Remington Typewriter.[13] Somewhat later but nonetheless important contributors to the refinement of the integrated, functionally organized enterprise were General Electric and Du Pont. Indeed, Du Pont was so advanced in its staffing and capital appropriations procedures that Chandler reports that "nearly all of the basic offices and methods used today in the general management of modern industrial enterprise" were in place in Du Pont prior to World War I.[14]

Curiously, Chandler assigns relatively little space and uncertain significance to the development of the multidivisional (M-form) enterprise. Indeed, at some points he appears to suggest that the U-form really is the modern form. Thus he observes that by 1917 "leading American industries and the economy as a whole had taken on their modern form" and that the "centralized, functionally departmentalized structure became the basic organizational form used by modern American enterprises." He nevertheless acknowledges that the U-form enterprise had "structural weaknesses" and discusses the appearance during the 1920s of the multidivisional structure, as a remedy for these shortcomings, at Du Pont and General Motors.[15] Inasmuch as Chandler has documented and discussed the M-form innovation at length elsewhere,[16] and inasmuch as I have offered an interpretation of its remarkable control properties,[17] I will not examine these further here. Possibly, however, the importance of the M-form may have been unintentionally slighted in *The Visible Hand.* Also, it is probably worthwhile observing, for purposes of perspective, that whereas integration in the unitary form enterprise represented a shift of transactions out of intermediate goods markets (at both manufacture and distribution stages) into the firm, the multidivisional structure involves the substitution of internal incentive, control, and resource-allocation devices for functions that are traditionally associated with capital markets. Transactions that could have been and at one time were executed across markets have thus been relocated within the firm, where they are executed under common ownership—with all of the incentive and control advantages (and limitations) attendant thereon.

The upshot is that the modern business enterprise is a remarkable but complex institution. Those who aspire to understand it and would venture public policy recommendations that appertain thereto are well advised to read *The Visible Hand* and *Strategy and Structure* with care.

Technology and Organization The substitution of internal organization for market exchange is attractive less on account of technological economies associated with production than because of what may be referred to broadly as "transactional failures" in the operation of markets for intermediate goods.[18] *The Visible Hand* makes clear, however, that technology is an important factor in the evolution of the modern business enterprise. Absent certain technological preconditions, the incentives to shift transactions out of markets and into firms are sharply attenuated.

The importance of energy, in particular steam power, is especially important in this connection. The effects were both direct, in terms of which industries were immediately affected, and indirect, in terms of infrastructure (mainly the railroads). Chandler observes with respect to the former that

> As long as the processes of production and distribution depended on the *traditional sources of energy*—on man, animal, and wind power—there was *little pressure to innovate*. Such sources of energy simply could not generate a volume of output in production and number of transactions in distribution large enough to require the creation of a large managerial enterprise or to call for the development of new business forms and practices. The low speed of production and the slow movement of goods through the economy meant that the maximum daily activity at each point of production and distribution could be easily handled by small personally owned and managed enterprises.[19]

My interpretation of this is the following: access to a steady source of energy introduced an incentive to explore new forms of organization, which, though feasible, had previously been (implicitly or explicitly) rejected. If steam engines involved nontrivial capital outlays, if there were economies of scale in moving to larger-size engines, and if there were large start-up costs associated with the noncontinuous usage thereof, efficient utilization of the steam engine required that work be regularized in ways that had previously been unnecessary. The question then was whether entrepreneurial, flexible, small-group modes of organization, which arguably have distinctive attractions of their own, could be reorganized in a way that permitted *net* gains to be realized. In order for this to occur, the potential economies that steam power and the regularization of work afforded had to more than offset the preferences of workers for nonregularized modes of organization. That is, inasmuch as work could have been but was not regularized before a steady source of energy was available, harnessing thermal energy had to yield economies that, together with such benefits as regularization by itself afforded, more than compensated for the sacrifice of autonomous work habits.[20]

But cheap, reliable thermal energy had more than energy-substitution effects. Coal and later petroleum provided reliable heat sources that were used directly in metalmaking, metalworking, refining, and distilling. Indivisibilities were frequently associated with the design of vessels that could utilize this heat efficiently. Also, flow-process (or expedited batch-process) economies now became available that had been unimportant in the earlier small-scale modes. Special organizational problems were thereby posed, problems that had not appeared in the "mechanical industries"—which involved the fabrication and assembly of products made of wood, leather, and cloth—where the "coordination of operations and supervision of workers required little more attention to plant design and organizational procedures than in the textile factories at Lowell during the 1830's."[21] The reason, presumably, was that decomposability between successive stages was easier to accomplish economically (in the sense that buffer stocks afforded temporary separability between successive stages) in batch-process mechanical manufacture than it was in flow-process (and, later, assembly-line process) manufacture.

Coal was thus central to the evolution of industry in the United States. In Chandler's words, "Of all the technological constraints, the lack of coal was probably the most significant in holding back the spread of the factory in the United States. The opening of the anthracite coal fields in eastern Pennsylvania lifted this constraint. Anthracite first became available in quantity for industrial purposes in the 1830's."[22]

The use of thermal energy for electricity to power electric motors also warrants mention. Although the assembly line could be made to operate with gravity slides, rollways, and other non-electric mechanisms, the *moving* assembly line relied on motor-driven conveyors. In addition to regularizing work, its most obvious consequence, the assembly line also served to reduce work-in-process inventories in what had previously been a batch-process manufacturing arrangement, thereby realizing inventory economies. Whereas previously buffer inventories effected temporary separability between successive work stations, thereby permitting each to proceed in a quasi-independent manner, autonomy was no longer feasible. Instead, the processes of mass production with fabricated metal became almost as continuous as those in flow-process industries.[23] More generally, the appearance of what are thought of as mass-production techniques varies directly with the ease with which flow processes or quasi-flow processes are effected.[24]

Other Organizational Issues   Of special significance to industrial organization is the role of infrastructure and the importance of distribution. Both of these have been seriously neglected previously. The importance that Chandler attaches to these makes this less likely in the future. Also of interest to industrial organization specialists are Chandler's discussions of cartel formation (and breakdown) and what I have referred to elsewhere as "first mover advantages."[25]

By infrastructure I mean transportation, mainly rail, and communications, initially telegraph but later telephone. Once again, coal plays a significant role. Also, as noted earlier, the railroads played a distinctive role as organizational innovators in developing the modern industrial enterprise. What I wish to emphasize here, however, and what Chandler calls repeated attention to, is that the spread of the factory system depended on the "reliability and speed of the new transportation and communication. Without a steady, all-weather flow of goods into and out of their establishments, manufacturers would have had difficulty in maintaining a permanent working force and in keeping their expensive machinery and equipment operating profitably."[26] Although this sounds very plausible, what precisely is it that occasions the shift to the factory mode? Presumably the factory and the prefactory modes both benefited by the development of a steady, all-weather source of supply of raw materials and intermediate products (as well as the shipment of final product to customers). If the prefactory mode had been superior to the factory previously, what explains the shift?

The answer, presumably, is that the appearance of infrastructure had a *differential* effect on the costs of the two modes. This would result if, as I conjecture, the factory mode involved more highly specialized labor and capital than the prefactory mode.[27] An interruption in supply would then have more severe cost consequences for the factory than the prefactory mode—since the (unspecialized) labor and capital employed by the latter could easily be turned to other productive uses. So as to better assure continuous utilization and realize the benefits of specialization in the period prior to the appearance of a reliable supply technology, least-cost operation of the factory entailed carrying relatively large raw-material and intermediate-product inventories. Once a steady, all-weather flow of goods was assured, however, these inventories could be drastically cut back and the advantages of specialization realized. Thus it is the joining of differential inventory economies (made possible by the development of infrastructure) with greater specialization that explains the overall result.

It was not merely manufacturing that was affected by this process. "In the 1850's and 1860's the modern commodity dealer, who purchased directly from the farmer and sold directly to the processor, took over the marketing and distribution of agricultural products. In the same years the full-line, full-service wholesaler began to market most standardized consumer goods. Then in the 1870's and 1880's the modern mass retailer—the department store, the mail-order house, and the chain store—started to make inroads on the wholesaler's markets."[28] All of these relied on the prior development of railroad and communications infrastructure for their viability.

The development of mass distribution, in turn, had ramifications for manufacturing. Not only could economies of scale be more fully exploited—since efficient plant size increases as the cost of moving goods from factory to user falls as a fraction of the total cost,[29] but vertical integration of production with distribution frequently resulted. Although economists commonly emphasize production and neglect distribution, the latter is plainly an important part of the productive process and needs to be taken into account if the private sector is to be accurately understood. To suppose that the organization of production and distribution can be addressed independently can and sometimes does occasion error. Forward vertical integration into distribution is preeminently a transaction-cost issue.[30]

One of the most intriguing subjects Chandler addresses is the difficulty of organizing effective cartels. Whereas there is a widespread tendency to suppose that express or tacit collusion is easy to effectuate—thus John Kenneth Galbraith opines that "the firm, in tacit collaboration with other firms in the industry, has wholly sufficient power to set and maintain prices"[31] —there are transaction-cost reasons to believe otherwise.[32] Chandler's evidence supports the transaction-cost thesis.

The history of cartel failures among the railroads is especially instructive. The early railroads evolved a series of progressively more elaborate interfirm structures in an effort to curb competitive pricing. The first of these involved informal alliances, which worked well until "the volume of through traffic began to fall off and competitive pressures increased." With the onset of the depression in 1873 there began an "increasingly desperate search for traffic . . . Secret rebating intensified. Soon roads were openly reducing rates." The railroads thereupon decided to "transform weak, tenuous alliances into strong, carefully organized, well-managed federations."[33] The membership of the federations was expanded and other federations in other geographic regions appeared. As Albert Fink, who headed up the largest such federation realized, however, "the only bond which holds this government together is the intelligence and good faith of the parties composing it."[34] To rectify this weakness, he urged the railroads to seek legislation that would give the actions of the federation legal standing.

Lack of legal sanctions means that loyal members of the cartel must exact penalties against deviants in the marketplace.[35] Unless such disciplinary actions (mainly price cuts) can be localized, every member of the cartel, loyalist and defector alike, suffers. This is a very severe (if little remarked) limitation on the efficacy of cartels. Inasmuch as national legislation was not forthcoming, Fink and his associates "found to their sorrow that they could not rely on the intelligence and good faith of railroad executives." In the end, the railroads turned to merger.[36] Cartel experience in the telegraph industry ran a similar course. Limited cooperative arrangements in the 1850s proved ineffective. Market division was then attempted by creating six operating regions, with one company assigned to each. Business was pooled where the lines overlapped, but implementation problems arose. The six firms were reduced first to three and then, in 1866, to a single company, Western Union.[37]

Manufacturers in the 1870s and 1880s used trade associations to devise "increasingly complex techniques to maintain industry-wide price schedules and production quotas." When these failed the manufacturers resorted to the purchase of stock in each others' companies, which ownership "permitted them to look at the books of their associates and thus better enforce their cartel agreement." But they could not be certain that the company accounts to which they were given access were accurate, and neither investment nor operating decisions of member firms were subject to common control. As with rail and telegraph, effective control required the next step, merger.[38]

The lesson in all of this is that, joint profit-maximizing

aspirations to the contrary notwithstanding, interfirm (cartel) organization is not to be uncritically equated with internal organization. Merger is a much more effective vehicle by which to control mutually unwanted competition. The reasons for this have been set out elsewhere.[39]

First mover issues arise where significant cost savings accrue to experience. The matter is not, as Richard A. Posner and others have stated, one of cost *avoidance*.[40] Rather, although early and late entrants may incur identical costs, the difference in *timing* can have cost-bearing consequences. If early entrants are able to recover their costs more easily than late entrants, the former may be said to enjoy an advantage. This can have public policy ramifications in dominant-firm industries.[41]

Cost-bearing consequences of two kinds are of special interest: capital costs and labor costs. The first of these is expressly identified by Chandler and the second can be inferred. Thus Chandler observes that whereas "the pioneer could finance the building of [his marketing organization] . . . out of cash flow, generated by high volume," the viable newcomer had to set up a competing network from the outset.[42] Capital-requirements consequences of a discreteness kind thereby result. Differential costs then appear if, as is generally true, the rate of return that investors require is an increasing function of the amount of capital required. First mover advantages can also arise in connection with learning by doing if human assets are imperfectly transferable. Chandler observes that the economic advantage of the Singer Company, for instance, lay in its organization—much of which took the form of relatively specific human capital.[43] Although the arguments here are somewhat more involved,[44] the fact that human-asset cost consequences of importance sometimes arise in the course of an industry's history is noteworthy.

CONCEPTUAL PROBLEMS

The modern corporation, according to Galbraith, has progressively supplanted functions previously assigned to markets. Internal organization and planning are now purportedly supreme.[45] The central theme of *The Visible Hand* is that this transformation was already well advanced by the turn of the century. To be sure, internal organization has taken on many intermediate process and distribution functions, which were mediated by the market in an earlier era, and the same is true of certain capital-market functions. But no firm is fully integrated (it is mind-boggling to contemplate), and it is the rare firm that is not subject to the discipline of the capital market to some degree, however attenuated its influence may be.[46] Thus internal organization and market organization coexist in active juxtaposition with one another. It is incorrect to suggest otherwise. Intentionally or not, Chandler's visible hand theme sometimes reads as though, final product markets excepted, market mechanisms have been rather fully displaced by internal organization.[47]

To be more specific, consider the organization of the automobile industry today as compared with the carriage industry in the late nineteenth century. Although automobile firms are much larger and incur considerable administrative expense in coordinating the manufacture and marketing of cars, it is not clear that the *proportion* of activity that is administratively coordinated by the automobile manufacturers is greater than that which characterized carriage manufacture. Rather, as the complexity of the product increased, the number of transactions that are processed through intermediate product markets and the number that are processed administratively *both* increased. The hazard to be avoided is one of salience. Increases in administrative activity are immediately evident; increases in the number or importance of market-mediated transactions, by contrast, can only be discerned by careful examination. The "marvel" of the price system to which Friedrich Hayek referred in 1945 is that markets operate in such a subtle way.[48] The economic significance of markets does not turn on saliency.

Unfortunately, Chandler's theme that "modern business enterprise took the place of market mechanisms in coordinating the activities of the economy and allocating its resources"[49] leaves little room for intermediate product markets and capital markets to operate. Final product markets excepted, the displacement of the market is very extensive if not complete. If internal organization is subject to limits, these are not disclosed. Instead we are informed that "because they *internalized more* market transactions than did the wholesalers, the new mass retailers still further increased the productivity and reduced the costs of the distribution of consumer goods in the United States."[50] Although this is consistent with the visible hand theme, internalization should not be mistaken for a cost panacea. More generally, the issue is what are the distinctive transaction-cost properties of different types of forward integration and how do these relate to product and customer characteristics? The underlying microanalytics need to be exposed if organization form is to be matched to circumstances in a discriminating way.

The importance of technology to the industrial revolution in Europe is made clear by David S. Landes.[51] Chandler carries this forward with respect to the managerial revolution in the United States. But the relative importance of technological and organizational innovations remains to be established. Although Chandler gives serious attention to innovations of the latter kind, it is sometimes difficult to resist the view that technology really is determinative. Flow processes—whether natural (liquids, gases, grains) or devised (assembly lines)—appear simply to dictate organizational outcomes. I submit, however, that tight linkages among processes are technologically determined only if technological nonseparabilities are significant. Otherwise, decisions to forge such linkages reflect transaction-cost savings rather than technological imperatives.

In petroleum refining, for instance, is the process really continuous, in the sense that all of the storage tanks are used exclusively for crude oil or completely refined products, or do some tanks represent intermediate product inventories? With respect to the latter, why is it that successive processing operations are not market-mediated rather than coordinated by administrative fiat? Is it merely a savings on buffer inventories that explains why the refining process is not more fully decomposed into separable parts? Or consider what is perhaps a more familiar example: the purported thermal economies that are said to be available by integrating iron with steel making. It is widely believed that cost savings can be realized where integration has this "physical or technical aspect."[52] The integration of these activities would be unnecessary, however, if it were possible to write and enforce a complex contingent claims contract between blast-furnace and rolling-mill stages. The prohibitive cost of such contracting is what explains the decision to integrate.[53]

Omissions

Any book dealing with such a large subject as *The Visible Hand* must necessarily omit certain important issues. Some of these Chandler neglects by design; in other cases the reasons for the omission are unclear. An example of the first kind is Chandler's decision not to "describe the work done by the labor force . . . or the organization and aspirations of the workers."[54] While I respect his decision not to address these issues, I would observe that they are important and at some stage need to be treated if the organizational changes that Chandler so effectively describes are to be more fully placed in perspective. More troublesome, though related to the above, is Chandler's failure to describe the labor strife that was associated with the evolution of the modern business enterprise. The organizational changes that Andrew Carnegie and his associates introduced into steel making, for example, are discussed without so much as a mention of the Homestead strike.[55]

Although Chandler's emphasis on successful organizational innovations is understandable, there are real advantages, especially when dealing with an institution as complex as the business firm, in identifying organizational failures and examining the underlying defects in microanalytic detail. Chandler's discussions of cartels and holding companies, of the committee system for organizing an integrated, consolidated enterprise, and of inside contracting could all benefit from explication. And presumably there were other failures that, though unidentified, would likewise merit the same type of investigation. Follow-on research to *The Visible Hand* could usefully address itself to these issues.

Focusing more attention on failures might also forestall the risk that an unwary reader will conclude that the modern business enterprise was an uninterrupted sequence of successful refinements. What were the aberrations? Were the failures predictable, in that organizational flaws could have been identified ex ante, or were these innovations undone by events of an unforeseeable kind? The role of competition in sorting out innovations according to their economic merits also warrants more complete treatment.[56]

Public Policy

The main public policy implication that should be associated with Chandler's study is that organizational innovation has been and prospectively will be vitally important to the economic well-being of the United States. It suggests that, when faced with an organizational change that is imperfectly understood—for example, the conglomerate in the 1960s—public policy officials and analysts should not leap to the conclusion that it has an anticompetitive purpose and effect but instead should examine the transaction-cost effects thereof. Often, though not always, significant organizational innovations are driven by the prospect of realizing transaction-cost economies. Unless related anticompetitive effects are more than offsetting, such innovations should be sympathetically received.

The history of legislative efforts to arrest organizational innovations is interesting in this connection. Although many such efforts met with little success, specialized urban retailers sought in the 1880s to prevent the spread of department stores by seeking "legislation to protect them from the department stores' lower prices."[57] Mail-order houses were made the target of such legislative efforts in the decade after 1900 and the chain stores in the 1920s. Antitrust legislation in the 1890s is an entirely different matter, however, as well it should be. Although claims to the contrary were made, the trusts were a blatant effort to achieve monopoly power with predictable antisocial consequences. Thus it is not that the private sector is a perfectly self-regulating mechanism and requires no legislative intervention whatsoever; rather, the message is that intervention needs to be done in a discriminating way. Efforts to evaluate organizational innovation in transaction-cost terms should help to accomplish this objective.

I am apprehensive, however, that this central public policy message may be lost and that Chandler's book will contribute instead to continuing confusion in the area of antitrust enforcement. Statements to the effect that "vertical integration led to industrial concentration" may be seized on by those who have a special animus toward vertical integration and who will not ask the necessary questions. What amount of concentration resulted from integration? Was it of a worrisome kind? What are the preconditions for vertical integration to pose public policy issues, and when can it be presumed to be of a procompetitive, efficiency-enhancing kind? These issues are never addressed. On the contrary, Chandler encourages adverse public policy reaction by broad statements that integration "created formidable barriers to entry" and that the firms that were "first to integrate continued to dominate"—where domination is left undefined.[58]

Experience demonstrates, however, that domination claims are incautious. The once-dominant Ford (which was much more highly integrated) was overtaken by General Motors. The steam-locomotive companies were unable to adapt altogether to the new diesel technology; instead of Baldwin, we have General Motors and General Electric. Whereas United States Steel accounted for 65 percent of United States ingot capacity at the turn of the century, its share of capacity had fallen below 25 percent in 1968, and other dominant firms have experienced a similar decline.[59] The xerography industry is currently undergoing changes of this sort; even regulated industries, such as the telephone, are not immune to encroachments; and Douglas Aircraft has been digested by McDonnell. More generally, the composition of the 200 largest firms changes significantly over any 50-year period.[60] It is no answer, moreover, to observe that only rarely are the assets of large corporations liquidated. Going-concern values normally exceed liquidation values, so merger has often been the device by which the assets of a faltering firm are preserved.

Unless insulated against entry by patents or government regulations, it is the rare dominant firm that, over a period of thirty years, does not lose significant market share to new entrants or aggressive rivals. Chandler's discussion of dominance is troublesome precisely because it easily leads to the opposite inference—that dominance, once achieved, is durable almost indefinitely.[61] To be sure, there are industries where unassisted market processes have not and, in the near-term future, prospectively will not alter a dominant-firm outcome. A case for government intervention then arguably exists.[62] Public policy is better served, however, if persistent dominance is regarded (and dealt with) as the exception rather than the rule. Intervention in dominant-firm markets is thus warranted only on a showing that the market processes on which an enterprise system relies have repeatedly failed to perform their self-policing functions.

The Visible Hand significantly alters our understanding of the modern corporation. Any residual tendency of historians to study business history in good fellow–bad fellow terms should have been permanently put to rest. At the same time, much remains to be done to deepen our understanding of the nature and importance of organizational innovation. A comparative institutional approach in which transaction costs are featured is, I believe, a promising research strategy. Such future research will benefit from the complementary efforts of both business historians and specialists in industrial organization.

NOTES

1. See Alfred D. Chandler, Jr., *The Visible Hand: The Managerial Revolution in American Business* (Cambridge, Mass., 1977); idem, *Strategy and Structure* (New York, 1966). Recent surveys of the theory of the firm include Armen A. Alchian, "The Basis of Some Recent Advances in the Theory of Management of the Firm," *Journal of Industrial Economics* 14 (February 1965): 30–41; Richard M. Cyert and D. L. Hedrick, "Theory of the Firm: Past, Present, and Future," *Journal of Economic Literature* 10 (June 1972): 398–412; Lee E. Preston, "Corporation and Society: The Search for a Paradigm," ibid., 13 (June 1975): 434–453; Michael A. Crew, *Theory of the Firm* (New York, 1975). For an important summary and interpretation of the literature on market failure, see Kenneth J. Arrow, "Political and Economic Evaluation of Social Effects and Externalities," in *The Analysis of Public Output*, ed. Julius Margolis (New York, 1970), pp. 1–23; related contributions to the field are discussed in Oliver E. Williamson, *Markets and Hierarchies: Analysis and Antitrust Implications* (New York, 1975), chap. 1.

2. Arthur H. Cole, "The Entrepreneur: Introductory Remarks," *American Economic Review* 58 (May 1968): 61–62; Thomas Cochran, "The Business Revolution," *American Historical Review* 79 (December 1974): 1450; Kenneth J. Arrow, *Essays in the Theory of Risk Planning* (Chicago, 1971), p. 224. For some of the reasons for this neglect, see Williamson, *Markets and Hierarchies*, pp. 192–193.

3. Differential entrepreneurial ability "can hardly account for the clustering of giant enterprises in some industries and not in others. The most brilliant industrial statesmen or the most ruthless robber barons were unable to create giant multinational companies in the furniture, apparel, leather, or textile industries" (Chandler, *Visible Hand*, p. 373).

4. "Enterprises did not grow large and industries become concentrated because the entrepreneurs who built them had [differentially] privileged access to capital" (Chandler, *Visible Hand*, p. 373).

5. Ibid., p. 376.

6. Ibid., p. 490.

7. Ibid., pp. 87, 133.

8. Cochran, "Business Revolution," pp. 1464–65; Chandler, *Visible Hand,* chap. 2.

9. *Chandler, Visible Hand,* p. 72.

10. Ibid., p. 75.

11. Ibid., p. 120.

12. Williamson, *Markets and Hierarchies,* pp. 133–136, 152.

13. Chandler, *Visible Hand,* pp. 290–293, 299–309.

14. Ibid., p. 449.

15. Ibid., pp. 286, 417, 453, 456–463.

16. Chandler has discussed the development of the multidivisional, or M-form, structure at length in *Strategy and Structure;* see especially chaps. 1–3, 6.

17. For a discussion of the remarkable control properties of the M-form organization, see Williamson, *Markets and Hierarchies,* chaps. 8–9.

18. Oliver E. Williamson, "The Vertical Integration of Production: Market Failure Considerations," *American Economic Review* 61 (May 1971):112.

19. Chandler, *Visible Hand,* p. 14 (italics added).

20. Note that those who had very strong preferences for traditional modes of organization might be "squeezed" to adapt. Thus, suppose that the competitive market price associated with traditional manufacture (which price covered full costs, including a living wage) falls when steam is used and work is both concentrated at a central location and regularized. Those who prefer the prefactory method of production may find that this older mode is no longer viable. Workers who have weak work-mode preferences will be induced to shift to the factory mode by the offer of a very modest wage premium. Workers with stronger preferences for the traditional mode and for whom the same wage premium would not, by itself, induce a shift may find that their preferred mode is no longer viable at the new set of market prices.

21. Chandler, *Visible Hand,* p. 246.

22. Ibid., p. 76.

23. Ibid., pp. 76, 280.

24. Ibid., pp. 240, 280.

25. See Williamson, *Markets and Hierarchies,* pp. 34–35, 216.

26. Chandler, *Visible Hand,* p. 245.

27. For many purposes it may be useful to hold technology constant in making comparisons among different methods of organization; this is not such a case, however, since the factory was more than the aggregation in a single location of autonomous work stations that had previously been dispersed.

28. Chandler, *Visible Hand,* p. 209.

29. This statement is based on the assumption that economies of scale had not yet been fully realized.

30. See Oliver E. Williamson, "Assessing Vertical Market Restrictions," *University of Pennsylvania Law Review* 127 (April 1979).

31. John Kenneth Galbraith, *The New Industrial State* (Boston, 1967), p. 200.

32. Williamson, *Markets and Hierarchies,* chap. 12.

33. Chandler, *Visible Hand,* pp. 134, 137.

34. Quoted in ibid., p. 140.

35. Williamson, *Markets and Hierarchies,* pp. 243–244.

36. Chandler, *Visible Hand,* chap. 5. The quotation is from p. 141.

37. Ibid., p. 197.

38. Ibid., pp. 317–319.

39. Ibid., p. 141. The failure of the railroad cartels may be partly attributable to the dilemma faced by middle managers. They were expected to maintain both rates and the volume of traffic; when traffic fell off, however, the rate structure was apt to be compromised.

40. Richard A. Posner, *Antitrust Law: An Economic Perspective* (Chicago, 1976), p. 59.

41. For stronger views on the historical importance of "firstness," see F. M. Scherer's review of Posner, *Antitrust Law* in *Yale Law Journal* 86 (April 1977): 966–997.

42. Chandler, *Visible Hand,* p. 299.

43. Ibid., p. 405.

44. See Williamson, *Markets and Hierarchies,* pp. 215–218.

45. See Galbraith, *New Industrial State,* for the technostructure theory of the firm.

46. Galbraith frequently responds to statements that many business efforts end up as expensive failures by challenging his critics to enumerate them. After the Edsel, what else? Is the Edsel the exception that proves the rule? Unfortunately, though understandably, business failures are not documented so fully as successes. A partial remedy for this condition is afforded by Thomas Berg's *Mismarketing* (New York, 1970), in which a number of expensive marketing failures are described; R. A. Smith's *Corporations in Crisis* (New York, 1966) is also noteworthy. To be sure, consumers are not beyond manipulation, but there are limits. Donald Kanter, a professor of marketing at the University of Southern California "notes that 80% of new products fail every year, despite television advertising" (*Wall Street Journal,* November 1, 1976, p. .1).

47. Chandler, *Visible Hand,* pp. 1, 286, 455.

48. Friedrich Hayek, "The Use of Knowledge in Society," *American Economic Review* 35 (September 1945): 510–530.

49. Chandler, *Visible Hand,* p. 1.

50. Ibid., p. 237 (italics added).

51. David S. Landes, *The Unbound Prometheus: Technological Change, 1750 to the Present* (New York, 1969).

52. Joe Bain, *Industrial Organization* (New York, 1968), p. 381.

53. See Williamson, "Vertical Integration," p. 113.

202 / OLIVER E. WILLIAMSON

54. Chandler, *Visible Hand,* p. 6.

55. For an interesting treatment of these issues, see Katherine Stone, "The Origins of Job Structures in the Steel Industry," *Review of Radical Political Economics* (summer 1974), pp. 61–97; see also my own interpretation of the reorganization of the steel industry in terms of transaction costs in Oliver E. Williamson, "The Modern Corporation as an Efficiency Instrument," in *Governmental Controls and the Free Market,* ed. S. Pejovich (College Station, Texas, 1976), pp. 163–194.

56. Chandler briefly notes the absence of competition in connection with the organizations of the railroads at the turn of the century but does not elaborate on the point; see *Visible Hand,* p. 186.

57. Ibid., pp. 229, also 232–233.

58. Ibid., pp. 363, 364, 365.

59. F. M. Scherer, *Industrial Market Structure and Economic Performance* (Chicago, 1970), pp. 217–218.

60. Norman R. Collins and Lee E. Preston, "The Size Structure of the Largest Industrial Firms," *American Economic Review* 51 (December 1961): 986–1011; Scherer, *Industrial Market Structure,* pp. 47–50. To be sure, the dominance to which Chandler refers is within a single industry, while Collins and Preston and Scherer have studied size changes within the 100 or 200 largest firms in all industrial areas. It is nonetheless sobering to realize that only 36 of the 100 largest firms in 1909 remained among the top 100 in 1958.

61. Chandler, *Visible Hand,* pp. 250, 297, 302, 365.

62. Williamson, *Markets and Hierarchies,* chap. 11.

7 / The Rise of the Modern Industrial Enterprise: A New Perspective

Herman Daems

THE PURPOSE of this essay is to highlight the central issues in the rise of the modern industrial enterprise and, on the basis of the historical findings reported in this volume, to sketch a broad explanation of the evolution of the multiunit hierarchical firm. The foregoing essays have dealt primarily with several fundamental questions. First, what defines the modern industrial enterprise and what are its functions in a market economy? Second, when and under what circumstances did this new instituition develop? Third, why did the modern multiunit hierarchical firm come to dominate certain industries when it did? Finally, what effects has this institution had on the performance of modern economies and on the structure of modern societies? Many more questions might be asked about the evolution of big business, some more speculative, others more practical. One speculative question concerns the value of historical knowledge about the growth of the modern enterprise in understanding the future of contemporary business giants. A more practical question, raised by the insights provided in this volume, is where research efforts should be directed in the future. In this summary, I shall concentrate on exploring the four basic questions listed above.

DEFINITION AND FUNCTIONS

Alfred D. Chandler, Jr., defines the modern business enterprise as an economic institution that owns and operates a multiunit system and that relies on a multilevel managerial hierarchy to administer it.[1] The definition is not only simple but also powerful; it clearly brings out the essential nature of the modern firm, namely, its hierarchical structure, hints at the resulting centralization of assets within a few large industrial companies, and focuses sharply on the basic research questions. When this definition is accepted, the study of the modern firm becomes a study of when, where, and why business hierarchies were established to manage functional and vertical integration and product diversification, with a resulting increase in aggregate concentration of assets. This focus makes its possible to view the modern firm as one institutional arrangement among others for coordinating the activities of production and distribution units. The two other institutional arrangements most often used to coordinate production and distribution in modern industrialized economies are markets and federations.[2] Markets allow autonomous production and distribution units to coordinate their activities by means of price-guided exchange. Federations such as trade associations, business interest groups, certain industrial combines, and cartels allow the members to coordinate their activities through negotiated agreements.[3]

Chandler's definition thus allows us to view the modern firm as involved in a rivalry with markets and federations, a rivalry that might be labeled an institutional competition. Indeed, institutional structures compete in much the same way as technological processes compete for the utilization of scarce resources. By implication, the modern business firm became predominant when its particular form of institutional organization, its hierarchical structure and centralized control over industrial property, gained a competitive advantage over other forms. Thus tracing its history is equivalent to explaining when, where, how, and why business hierarchies were able to coordinate economic activity more efficiently than markets and federations.

In essence, coordination of economic activities requires the scheduling of orders and the specification of standards. Such coordination cannot be effective unless arrangements exist to enforce the carrying out of orders on time and according to specifications. Hierarchies, markets, and federations rely on different instruments for enforcing compliance with coordination commands. Their efficiency in dealing with coordination commands determines their competitive advantage in institutional competition.

The concept of institutional competition and the efficiency of the three alternative arrangements in dealing with a coordination command can best be illustrated by an example, which is also useful in defining the differences among the various institutions more sharply. Suppose a producer ships products from a plant to a warehouse. There are three ways to ensure execution of the shipment orders on schedule and under good conditions. The first way, relying on market mechanisms, is for the producer to contract with an independently owned transportation company. Although the relationship is not hierarchical, the producer does give a command, but he relies on market mechanisms for its execution. To secure correct delivery the producer writes a contingent contract that calls for the payment of a deposit from which fines can be paid if transportation is not on schedule or if goods are damaged. The producer may find it difficult to enforce the provisions of the contract, however, when he cannot prove that improper actions on the part of the transporter caused delayed delivery and damaged goods. Threat of withdrawal of future orders may not be very effective if the transportation company has other equally attractive business opportunities.

A second, hierarchical, way to organize compliance with the shipment order is for the producer to take full legal control over the transportation company. The manager of the transportation company will then have an incentive for carrying out the order correctly since failure to comply might result in his being fired and therefore the loss of his right to operate those assets. As long as the costs to the manager of finding a new job or entering the transportation industry on his own account are higher than for the independent transporter to find a new order after some of its older orders are withdrawn, the manager will have a strong incentive to execute orders correctly.[4] Hence the importance of consolidated ownership in enforcing authority structures. Failure to execute an order properly will lead to exclusion from the economic activity. With decentralized ownership, such exclusion is not possible unless the producer placing the order is the only buyer of transportation services. Consolidated ownership is an important precondition for the enforcement of coordination commands by means of hierarchy, but it is not sufficient. As important as full legal control is the development of an internal monitoring system. Such a monitoring system will allow the producer to supervise the transportation manager's action more closely and detect whether failure to deliver the goods on schedule is the result of improper action by the transportation manager or of environmental conditions beyond his control.

A third way to organize coordination is for the producer and transporter to offer each other exclusive rights in transporting goods during a certain period and to negotiate the specific conditions afterward, shipment by shipment. Producer and transporter agree to be the only partners in future transportation deals, but they leave unspecified the details of the orders. Thus coordination is obtained by an agreement to negotiate commands in the future. One way to ensure compliance with the agreement is by pooling profits. A profit-pooling plan calls for the producer and transporter to have a fixed share in the joint profits of both companies. Under these conditions the companies will have an incentive to honor the agreement and to negotiate coordination.[5] Agreements to negotiate coordination will be referred to as federations. In federations, ownership is not necessarily consolidated and monitoring systems are not imposed. Shirking remains possible, and enforcement is more difficult and thus more costly than within hierarchies.

The foregoing example illustrates three alternative institutional arrangements for organizing compliance with scheduling orders and quality standards: the market, the hierarchy, and the federation. Hierarchies differ from markets and federations in the consolidation of ownership and legal control and in the development of a monitoring system. Federations differ from markets in that they define in advance who the parties will be in future negotiations about certain decisions.

Each institutional arrangement has its own instruments for ensuring compliance with a coordinated activity. Hierarchies rely on supervision and exclusion from future participation to implement coordination. Markets achieve coordination by means of bonding. Federations obtain coordination by tying members to an agreement and by excluding others. The efficiency of these arrangements in dealing with the coordination of economic activity varies in a complex way with the nature of the activity.

The rapid growth of the multiunit modern business firm in some industrial sectors suggests that the hierarchical structure proved more efficient than market mechanisms and federations in coordinating the activities of production and distribution units in those sectors. The hierarchical coordination of units within the modern business firm relies on the consolidation of ownership and also, more significantly, on the development of sophisticated control instruments for supervision and monitoring. The modern firm also obtains resources, capital funds, and personnel for the various units it coordinates and monitors. The firm's efficiency in allocating such funds and personnel over its distribution and production units influences its competitive advantage over other institutional arrangements. The functions of the modern firm, then, are coordination, monitoring, and the allocation of resources. It is in carrying out these crucial functions in combination that the managerial hierarchy proved, under certain conditions, to be more efficient than other institutional arrangements. From this perspective, I shall examine the conditions that made the rise of the modern business enterprise possible.

TIMING AND CONDITIONS

Unlike state hierarchies and military hierarchies, managerial hierarchies are relatively new in the history of the industrialized market economies. In the United States, for instance, giant industrial enterprises staffed by salaried managers first appeared during the 1880s. They developed in four industrial groups. Three produced consumer goods (perishable food products, semiperishable branded packaged products, and light assembled machinery), and the fourth manufactured producer goods, primarily standardized heavy machinery (boilers, printing presses, and shoe machinery). In designing their extensive hierarchies, these companies benefited from the organizational innovations made two or three decades earlier by the railroad and telegraph companies, mass marketers, and mass producers. They were soon joined by the producers and refiners of chemicals, especially organic chemicals, and, early in the twentieth century, by the manufacturers of new assembled machinery—automobiles and household appliances. The modern business enterprise in these industrial groups proved to be a highly stable institution—that is, the companies and their hierarchies have continued to manage vertical integration and product diversification successfully to the present day. In other industries, however, hierarchical structures, disintegrated when they could not survive competition with other institutions, and the firms disappeared from the lists of the 100 largest United States corporations. Except for those that were consolidated with another enterprise through acquisition and merger, those that dropped out of this group before World War II did so because they were operating in a sector where hierarchies had no competitive advantage for coordinating production and distribution.[6]

Chandler's analysis of United States firms leads to four conclusions. First, giant managerial hierarchies were built almost wholly by linking high-volume production with mass marketing and then integrating backward; both actions often led firms to take up operations overseas. Second, vertical integration, through the development of a managerial hierarchy, took place only in industries where capital- and energy-intensive technology allowed economies of scale in processing and assembling a large volume of raw materials and semifinished goods into an equally large volume of consumer goods or standardized producer goods. Third, as noted above, the modern business firm that evolved in these industrial sectors proved to be extremely stable over the course of a century. Fourth, hierarchical management of product diversification was important first in industries where technology was advancing rapidly, as in organic chemicals and electrical engineering. Although Chandler's findings apply to the United States economy, the preceding chapters suggest that they are relevant to the events in other Western countries.

A comparison of the largest companies in the United States, Great Britain, Germany, and France indicates the similarities in the development of big business. In all four countries, giant business hierarchies seem always to have appeared in the same type of industry, but in each managerial hierarchies appeared at different times, producing variations in the composition of the list of largest companies. French and British chemical companies were slower to integrate and diversify than their German counterparts, Bayer, Hoechst, BASF, and AGFA, which were already among the world's largest companies before World War I. Food companies became much larger much sooner in Britain and the United States than in Germany and France. Regardless of timing, however, large managerial hierarchies disappeared whenever they could not face competition from other institutional arrangements or when they could not significantly improve industrial performance. For instance, the United States Leather Company, an amalgamation of a number of American leather companies, and Siemens-Rheinelbe-Schuckert Union, the giant enterprise formed by the merger of the electrical-engineering firm Siemens-Schuckert and the coal, iron, and steel combine Rheinelbe in Germany, were short-lived combinations. The benefits of managerial coordination appear to have been small for those companies, since they rapidly disintegrated when faced with competition. The broad historical picture, then, supports Chandler's findings that the rise of the modern business enterprise was limited largely to the so-called new-product industries. A more detailed examination of the history of the modern firm in Germany, Britain, and France will confirm this conclusion.

The shift from markets to federations and managerial hierarchies in Germany, described by Jürgen Kocka, is particularly interesting.[7] During the 1920s, the institutional choices for organizing industry in Germany were wide open; no legal obstacles had been posed to such federations as cartels, trade associations, and business-interest groups. Nevertheless, giant managerial hierarchies evolved in the chemicals and electrical-engineering industries.[8] During the late nineteenth century and the early decades of the twentieth century, they were among the largest companies in the world, as they remain today; these firms were designed to coordinate the integration of research and development with production and marketing and to manage diversification of a greater number of product lines. At the same time, similar developments were taking place in the German metal-making and metal-working industries, where coordination was first accomplished by means of federations—tight cartels with a central agency both acting as a sales organization for the cartel members and allocating orders to the different producers. In the mid-1920s, however, cartels lost ground to hierarchical co-ordination, and such giant integrated enterprises as Vereinigte Stahlwerke were formed.[9]

The development of the modern firm in Britain is instructive because it differs from that in Germany and France. Food companies were among the first giants. The more rapid development of large British food enterprises may have resulted from the denser population and the larger size of the urban areas, which lowered the cost of transporting consumer goods.[10] Nevertheless, British firms were slower to adopt hierarchical organization than those in the United States. The loose holding company, a federation that consolidated legal control somewhat but did not introduce monitoring systems, remained the preferred form. As Leslie Hannah has suggested, managerial hierarchies were slower to be utilized than elsewhere, since the British market system was so well developed that it remained longer as a viable institutional arrangement for organizing industrial activity.[11] Starting in the 1920s and continuing more rapidly in the 1950s and 1960s, managerial hierarchies took over the functions of coordinating and monitoring economic activities and the allocation of resources from the markets for one of two reasons. Either the complexity of industrial activity increased because technological development made possible economies of scale and new products, or international competition became more intensive, forcing rationalization of production and distribution.

At first sight, France suggests a completely different story. Until the early 1920s, most of the largest French corporations were coal-mining and metal-producing firms, certainly not the situation typical in the United States or Germany at the time. Beginning in the mid-1920s, however, managerial hierarchies came to dominate such industries as chemicals. French corporations also formed loose industrial groups. The French experience was probably similar to the situations in Japan and Belgium. In all three nations, group structures were built by holding companies, a phenomenon that contributed to an enormous expansion of interlocking stockholdings. Such groups consolidated ownership but were not operated through managerial hierarchies, and their instruments for coordination, supervision, and allocation of resources were not well developed. The French industrial group can be considered a transitional form between federation and pure hierarchy. Maurice Lévy-Leboyer suggests that the rise of group structures in France was an institutional innovation intended to overcome the fundamental imperfections of allocating capital by means of capital markets. A similar explanation has been advanced for group structures in Japan and Belgium.[12] After World War II, French groups, as well as those in other European nations, shifted rapidly to sophisticated hierarchical structures; companies discovered that the loose prewar combinations needed reorganization and quickly established managerial hierarchies to administer vertical integration and product and geographic diversification.[13] These structures were often innovative. Europeans may have moved so fast to catch up in the hierarchical organization of industry that they actually expanded beyond the size of United States businesses.[14]

Thus, except for the question of timing, Chandler's findings appear to be generally valid for business in Great Britain and on the Continent. On the basis of this picture of when and where the business hierarchy and, with it, the modern business firm gained a competitive advantage over federations and market mechanisms, it is now possible to examine the reasons for its predominance.

COMPETITIVE ADVANTAGES

The rise of the giant business firm in certain industrial sectors sometimes appears to have been inevitable; the notion that managerial hierarchies evolved because they had to is of little value, however, in understanding and evaluating the hierarchical organization of industrial activity. Unless the reasons for its development are formulated in a manner that allows hypotheses to be tested, the history of the modern business firm remains unexplained. In essence, Chandler argues that coordination and monitoring of industrial processes by managerial hierarchies had a significant positive effect on performance in some industries and a minor or negative effect in others. This theory is logically identical with the hypothesis that without managerial hierarchies economic performance would have been worse in certain industries. The reasons why performance necessitates the hierarchical integration of units in one industry but not in another remain to be specified. On the basis of the earlier essays in this volume, I shall attempt in this section to explain why hierarchical coordination and monitoring gained a competitive advantage in organizing industrial activity. First, however, it is useful to review the conventional paradigms in the field of industrial organization.

Scholars of industrial organization have traditionally been concerned with the impact of the structure of an industry on business conduct and performance. Industrial structure is generally regarded as dependent on concentration, technology, product differentiation, and barriers to mobility within and among sectors. I shall take a somewhat different view, adding the concept of the institutional mode to the three traditional concepts of structure, conduct, and performance. Institutional mode may be defined as the institutional arrangement that determines the organization of coordination among units—that is, whether coordination is organized by means of market mechanisms, federations, or hierarchies. In this discussion, I shall consider institutional mode a variable that is subject to an individual firm's choice—that is, a decision variable—and not as a given parameter as in conventional paradigms.[15] Thus concentration, technology, production differentiation, and barriers to entry in an industry are viewed as depending partly on the institutional mode chosen.[16]

Marketing Instruments and Product Differentiation

The first step in building a giant hierarchical, integrated enterprise has always been the integration of high-volume production with mass marketing—a step that was first taken in the major industrial groups already described. An underdstanding of the mechanisms by which goods are marketed and of the effects of marketing instruments on the volume of a firm's sales is thus essential to any explanation of why hierarchies gained a competitive advantage over markets and federations in coordinating economic activity. Marketing instruments are the factors other than price that a firm can use to influence unit sales; among them are advertising, branding, packaging, location of distribution outlets, and provision of such specialized services as demonstration, analysis of user needs, expert advice, aftersales maintenance, and consumer credit. Some markets are sensitive to such instruments, while others are not.

The effect of marketing instruments on sales volume, then, varies considerably among product types. Historically, sensitivity to marketing instruments has been strongest in food and in the so-called new industries such as chemicals, electrical engineering and equipment, light machinery, and automobiles. In those same industries, opportunities for product differentiation were greatest when marketing instruments were able to have a significant impact on volume.[17] Marketing decisions thus became interdependent, or complementary, with production decisions, and economies achieved in production through a major expansion in capacity could be realized only by making the appropriate decisions about marketing instruments. At the same time, there was no point in developing a marketing network capable of handling high volumes—certainly not a specialized marketing network—unless high-volume production lowered unit costs and thus lowered selling prices to exploit price elasticity. Because marketing decisions and production decisions were complementary, a rational incentive encouraged businesses to centralize these formerly independent decisions.[18]

The complementarity between marketing and production did not, however, lead to a full hierarchical coordination of marketing with production units unless careful coordination—that is, scheduling and standardization of the flow of raw materials and finished goods—promised a substantial decrease in unit costs and reduced uncertainty about the fluctuations of unit costs by eliminating the need for buffer inventories, by reducing time necessary for goods to flow through the vertically interrelated units, and by permitting a steadier and more stable utilization of production and marketing facilities. I believe that the last factor was particularly important. Indeed, such stabilization of capacity utilization was especially useful in reducing profit fluctuations in industries where capital-intensive technological processes resulted in high fixed costs.[19]

This discussion leads to a hypothesis that I shall express, for the sake of precision, in the terms used by economists working in the field of industrial organization. The need for product differentiation by means of marketing instruments and the need for hierarchical coordination between production and marketing increase when economies of scale can be obtained in production. Indeed, product differentiation helps sustain large-scale production in three ways. First, it reduces brand switching among customers and consequently eliminates an important element of demand uncertainty at the level of the firm, which is then subject only to fluctuations in the market as a whole. Second, because barriers to entry and to mobility within industries are strengthened, the long-term return on a firm's investment in capital-intensive capacity is protected; such tendencies to erect barriers to mobility are particularly strong when the costs of capacity adjustment are high. Third, utilization of the capacity of a production unit can be stabilized, since production differentiation allows the firm to adjust the sales volume for its brands appropriately by means of advertising. A possible corollary to this hypothesis is that such production economies are undertaken more readily in sectors where sales volume can be coordinated with production volume through marketing instruments and product differentiation.

The coordination became necessary because of the complementarity between production and marketing decisions. Why, then, was this coordination organized by means of a hierarchy, and why were markets and federations not relied on to coordinate independently owned sales agencies with production units? The daily scheduling of flows required the consolidation of accurate information and centralized decision making. As a result, little room was left for independent action on the part of the sales agents, especially when they had to be specialized to sell effectively. It is hard to imagine, then, that individuals could be found to run the risks of an independently owned and specialized sales operation; indeed, market mechanisms and federations could hardly be efficient under these circumstances. With constantly varying demand conditions and product innovations, the arrangements would have required such an elaborate system of contingent contracting and negotiating that the costs of writing, enforcing, and renewing the necessary contracts and agreements would have been much higher and the benefits of scheduling much more limited than with hierarchical scheduling.[20]

Furthermore, as indicated earlier, with nonhierarchical coordination it would have been difficult to control what can be called the entry and exit behavior of sales agents; decisions about starting or discontinuing marketing activity would have depended solely on the availability of skilled individuals who were willing to operate independently owned sales agencies. Certainly such freedom of action might have threatened the efficient scheduling that required a high degree of discipline, to use an ugly word—discipline that was difficult to enforce without consolidation of legal control and supervision. By owning distribution outlets or by granting exclusive distribution rights, moreover, the modern firm protected itself from having the distributor switch to other suppliers. Given the investments of the forward integrated firm in the distribution sector, the sales agent who wanted to start distributing on his own account or for another manufacturer would have found profit opportunities reduced because of the preexisting distribution capacity in the market. Owning distribution units, then, served as a strategy of preemptive entry.

Hierarchical scheduling was not a free good, to be sure. On the contrary, it was expensive, with extra costs arising mainly from the need to monitor individual units. Moreover, fixed costs came to make up a higher proportion of total costs in the hierarchically integrated firm, which thus risked greater losses when downturns in sales turnover occurred. As all historical evidence suggests, however, the benefits derived from hierarchical scheduling were enormous. Such scheduling resulted not only in lowering unit costs but also, in these marketing-intensive sectors, in reinforcing the formidable barriers to entry created by the large production and distribution organization of the integrated managerial firm. If barriers to entry are indeed erected by integration, then they provide, in my view, the best evidence that the benefits and efficiencies of hierarchical scheduling were real; if they were fiction, nonintegrated producers would have invaded the sector and could have competed successfully with the integrated giants.

One of the most difficult problems of economics is determining the effect of the hierarchical integration of vertically interrelated units on allocative efficiency and on wealth. No easy answer exists. If product differentiation and hierarchical integration are necessary for production economies and for the stabilization of capacity utilization, it may well be that the resulting lower unit costs improve allocative efficiency. If product differentiation and hierarchical integration lead to market power, as is commonly assumed, it may well be the other way around. Further research into this problem is necessary.

PROCESSING TIME AND SELLING VALUE OF PRODUCTS

The need to control flow time, or the speed of processing, was another powerful determinant of hierarchical integration. For such goods as perishables and semiperishables, the selling value of a product is inversely related to the time it spends in the production and distribution cycle; the longer the goods are held up in processing and distribution, the more they lose their freshness and the lower their selling value in the market will be. Efforts will then be made to reduce flow time—that is, to increase the speed of processing and distribution—by eliminating as many steps as possible and by either avoiding the accumulation of inventories altogether or holding them at the lowest possible level. The pressure to schedule flows is even greater when economies of scale can be realized in production or basic processing. This was the case with perishable and semiperishable consumer goods;[21] at the same time, however, this process explains the need for scheduling in such industries as the manufacture of organic chemicals, where the development of new products can make inventory obsolete overnight. In the latter case, the argument must be seen as reinforcing existing tendencies toward scheduling and not as a primary incentive, particularly when production equipment is not easily converted to the production of new products. As it turned out, the benefits of scheduling were realized only when marketing was coordinated with processing or production in a managerial hierarchy; federations and market mechanisms could not handle the scheduling efficiently.

OTHER FACTORS

In industrial areas such as electrical engineering and chemicals, especially organic chemicals, where technological frontiers were expanding rapidly and where patents protected products and processes, huge industrial research laboratories were established. They proved to be efficient and effective only when their work was tied closely to the marketing and production operations of the firm. Indeed, the laboratories of the electrical and chemical giants had the task of discovering new products and processes and were also charged with carrying out testing so that a water-tight patent application could be filed. Moreover, they had to be on guard against infringements on the company's patents; they had to check the validity of their competitors' patent applications; and they had to counter these patents with new discoveries. Equally important, they had to respond to the questions and needs of the company's customers. Because a company's profitability or even survival depended on its ability to meet customer needs with products and to match its competitors' moves, careful planning and scheduling of the work of the industrial laboratory, in order to make it operate efficiently and effectively, was not a luxury but a necessity. Once again, an opportunity existed for scheduling, and it had to be hierarchical because market scheduling would have left too much room for opportunistic behavior and strategic maneuvering.[22]

History demonstrates, however, that opportunities for improving and stabilizing profits through hierarchical coordination did not depend totally on the conditions just described. Markets had to be of sufficient size to make large-scale marketing and production economical. They also had to be geographically concentrated. When markets were dispersed, as in Germany and France, increased transportation costs—even with such modern means of transportation as railroads—wiped out the advantages of careful scheduling when other factors were constant. The result was that development of the modern business firm, especially in the production of perishable consumer goods, was delayed until cities expanded and the advent of the truck, the automobile, and the airplane reduced transportation costs.

The Emergence of the Modern Firm

This chapter so far has summarized what I believe to be the basic reasons for the hierarchical integration of marketing with production. Fundamentally, scheduling through managerial hierarchy promised higher and more stable profits than earlier arrangements, mostly by lowering unit costs and stabilizing capacity utilization. Modern firms did not stop there, however. They moved backward to schedule and standardize the inflow of raw materials and semifinished products. Hierarchical scheduling of multiunit systems, in turn, led to the development of organizational structures and control systems to monitor the units. Much of the competitive advantage of hierarchies over markets and federations, I believe, depends on their ability to provide effective and relatively cheap supervision of performance and the use of resources. As the modern firm coordinated and monitored the activities of more units, their competition for funds within the hierarchical structure made allocation and planning necessary. Thus executives in modern firms came to design measures to allocate resources rationally and to internalize even more the functions of the market. The picture is now complete: the modern hierarchical firm evolved to coordinate the flow of goods, to monitor the units, and to allocate resources to them; it carried out all these functions by means of a hierarchical management structure.

In reviewing the development of the modern firm, I have focused on economic and technological determinants such as the sensitivity of market demand to marketing instruments, the resulting interdependencies of marketing and production decisions, the relatively high share of fixed costs, making profits more volatile under fluctuations in volume, the perishability of the product, the economic advantages of higher flow speed, the effect of new efforts in research and development, the regional concentration and size of markets, and, finally, transportation costs. I have ignored the legal and cultural determinants here. They are undoubtedly important, but history suggests that even in countries where cultural and legal differences from the United States were significant, as in Germany, the large hierarchical firm evolved if the "right" economic and technological circumstances prevailed.

Historians and economists may remain skeptical about the hypothesis I have just described; the former may feel that too little historical detail has been provided, while the latter may argue that the statistical tests have yet to be carried out. Their reservations may be justified, and it is certainly to be hoped that more comparative evidence will be forthcoming. In the absence of further data, however, the emerging pattern of the appearance and growth of hierarchical business structures appears to be comparable in the nations of the industrialized Western world.

ECONOMIC AND SOCIAL EFFECTS

Hundreds, probably even thousands, of books and articles have been written about the effect of large hierarchical structures on economic performance. They deal with the impact of the large corporation on economic growth, allocative efficiency, the business cycle, and monetary stability, to name only a few of the issues economists have discussed. Nor have its effects on the structure of society and the conditions of work been ignored. Most of the literature has been academic and scholarly; some of it is ideological. Whatever the reason, the latter type seems to have been read far more widely than the former, despite the fact that social issues cannot be reduced to black and white.

An analysis of the economic and social effects of the large managerial hierarchy is difficult because, as suggested earlier, it is really a counterfactual problem. Such an analysis requires a precise picture either of what the world would look like without business hierarchies to manage the flow of goods or of what it ought ideally to look like. As Oliver E. Williamson and others have pointed out, however, there is no good "model" or ideal world with which we can compare our real world.[23] While economists have tended to use the perfect competition model in evaluating the allocative efficiency of the large corporation, it is a valid reference point only if a number of stringent conditions are fulfilled. The only objective way to evaluate the role of the large business hierarchy is to engage in large-scale social experimentation with alternative modes of organizing economic activity, which is possible only in fantasy.

What remains is the traditional historical method of carefully comparing economic and social conditions before and after the evolution of the giant business hierarchy and meticulously analyzing the conditions in different industrial sectors and countries. As noted earlier, the business hierarchy fulfills the functions of coordinating and monitoring economic activity and allocating resources. Plausibly, these services were socially desirable. While the fact that business hierarchy has appeared, prospered, and developed in all market economies in the face of the institutional competition suggests that it carried out these functions efficiently, the social costs of its predominance cannot be ignored. These costs include the allocative inefficiency of market power and alienation and bureaucratization of modern work.

As Morton Keller has pointed out, the threats perceived to the economic interests, the distrust engendered by the vast size of hierarchical business, and the desire to share some of the corporate power led to new regulatory legislation.[24] Traditional values were also shaken; uniformity and homogeneity came to be valued more highly than individualism and variety; power shifted to professionals. Today the debate over the effect of the business hierarchy continues, although new avenues are opening and allow the questions to be explored with greater scholarly vigor.

CONCLUSION

Today, interest in the rise of the modern industrial firm is being renewed, and scholars are focusing on the institutional organization of the economy and of society. Economists and historians have rediscovered the importance of institutions for economic and social life. For a long time, however, institutional economics has been outside the mainstream of economics. Some economists have even concluded that institutions, such as hierarchies and federations, were irrelevant for coordination and the allocation of resources because the price mechanism could deal with these functions more efficiently. This bold conclusion is valid only when the price mechanism can deal with every possible contingency and when the costs of operating the price system and of collecting information are low. If these assumptions are not realized, as is very likely, economic activities can be coordinated by price mechanisms only at great cost, since it will prove difficult to enforce the coordination commands. Institutional arrangements, then, are a way to organize coordination, monitoring, and resource allocation efficiently. Rivalry among such arrangements ensures that these functions are organized efficiently. Recently, economists have come to realize the importance of institutional competition for the performance of the economy and have started to lay the foundations for new theoretical developments. This school of thought is sometimes referred to as the new institutional economics.

Institutional history had fared no better than institutional economics until recently, but here, too, the tide is turning. Historians have broken new ground and are accumulating a wealth of information on the formation and functioning of the various institutions that make up modern society. It is to be hoped that economists and historians can benefit from each other's insights. Economists are trained to think analytically about problems; historians are used to adding perspective and synthesis. Close cooperation between economists and historians can certainly contribute to a better understanding of the institutional structure of the modern world.

NOTES

1. Alfred D. Chandler, Jr., "The United States: Seedbed of Managerial Capitalism," this volume.

2. For a similar distinction, see G. B. Richardson, "The Organization of Industry," *The Economic Journal* 82 (1972): 882–896; Alfred D. Chandler, Jr., and Herman Daems, "Administrative Coordination, Allocation and Monitoring: Concepts and Comparisons," *Recht und Entwicklung der Grossunternehmen*, ed. Norbert Horn and Jürgen Kocka (Göttingen, 1979).

3. In some industrial countries interlocking ownership structure and interlocking directorates have not resulted in a clear hierarchical control relationship, and decisions tend to be decentralized or negotiated among the firms in the network. Examples are the French and Belgian industrial groups and some of the early German combines such as the Siemens-Rheinelbe-Schuckert Union in the 1920s. The prewar Japanese Zaibatsu may also fall into this category.

4. Armen A. Alchian and Harold Demsetz have argued that firing a manager is the same as withdrawing future orders for the enforcement of commands. Their argument is only correct when the costs of finding a new job or finding new business orders are the same. It seems to me that, in general, these costs will be higher for the new job than for the new orders. One difference is in the new start-up costs. See Alchian and Demsetz's "Production, Information Costs, and Economic Organization," *American Economic Review* 62 (1972):777–795.

5. Failure to ship products on schedule in good condition may lead to a loss of income for the producer only, but with the profit-pooling plan the transporter will have to share in that loss. Thus the profit pool provides an incentive for the transporter. If, however, he can make up for the loss by making more profit for himself if he does not execute the order and employs his resources elsewhere in a more lucrative opportunity, the incentive to comply with the agreement is impaired.

6. For studies dealing with turnover among the largest United States companies, see Norman R. Collins and Lee E. Preston, "The Size Structure of the Largest Industrial Firms, 1909–1958," *American Economic Review*

51 (1961):986–1011; Frederick M. Scherer, *Industrial Market Structure and Economic Performance* (Chicago, 1970); R. C. Edwards, "Stages in Corporate Stability and the Risks of Corporate Failure," *Journal of Economic History* 35 (July 1975):428–457.

7. Jürgen Kocka, "The Rise of the Modern Industrial Enterprise in Germany," this volume.

8. An excellent illustration of this evolution is the formation of the controversial I. G. Farben Aletien Gesellschaft in 1925. This huge chemical company was founded as an amalgamation of the six leading chemical companies in Germany, which had been operating as a federation between 1916 and 1925. The federation was a business-interest group, referred to as Interessengemeinschaft der deutschen Teerfarbenfabriken; it did not consolidate ownership, and decisions were reached after lengthy negotiations. By 1925 the companies had realized that they could not negotiate the rationalization of production and marketing of chemicals. They decided to consolidate ownership and to start building a new organization to coordinate the activities of the production and marketing units and the research laboratories.

9. Kocka, "Modern Industrial Enterprise in Germany," this volume.

10. In the 1920s German and French cities were much smaller than those in Britain and the United States. In 1925 the population of Berlin was a little over 4 million; Paris was only slightly larger, with 4.8 million, while London and New York each had populations of 7.7 million.

11. See Leslie Hannah, "Visible and Invisible Hands in Great Britain," this volume.

12. See Maurice Lévy-Leboyer, "The Large Corporation in Modern France," this volume. On Japan, see M. Yoshino, *Japan's Managerial System: Tradition and Innovation* (Cambridge, Mass., 1968), chap. 5. On Belgium, see Herman Daems, *The Holding Company and Corporate Control* (Boston, 1977).

13. See Gareth P. Dyas and Heinz T. Thanheiser, *The Emerging European Enterprise: Strategy and Structure of French and German Industry* (Boulder, Colo., 1976); L. C. Franko, *The European Multinationals: A Renewed Challenge to American and British Big Business* (New York, 1976).

14. In 1975 the 50 largest European companies employed 6,592,829 people, while 5,770,844 were employed by the 50 largest United States companies. Differences in factor prices naturally play a role in this difference, although the rapidly rising wages in the 1970s and the generous investment subsidies of the European governments may have favored capital-intensive production in Europe. The basic point, however, is that European managers were dealing with larger organizations than managers in the United States.

15. In a recent paper, Richard E. Caves and Michael Porter have also made industrial structure partly dependent on strategic divisions of the firm; see their "From Entry Barriers to Mobility Barriers," *Quarterly Journal of Economics* 91.2 (1977):241–262.

16. My approach thus has much in common with the pathbreaking con-

ceptual work of Ronald Coase, Harold B. Malmgren, Oliver E. Williamson, and G. B. Richardson. The main difference is that I shall pay close attention both to the modern, hierarchical, multiunit firm as one of several possible institutional arrangements for organizing interaction and to formulating a theory that can be tested and that depends on the specifics of various industries. See Coase, "The Nature of the Firm," *Economica,* n.s. 4 (1937): 386–405; Williamson, *Markets and Hierarchies* (New York, 1975); Malmgren, "Information, Expectations and the Theory of the Firm," *Quarterly Journal of Economics* 75 (1962):399–421; Richardson, "Organization of Industry."

17. In a very interesting study of product differentiation, Michael E. Porter makes a distinction between convenience goods and nonconvenience goods. Since I discuss consumer-goods markets as well as producer-goods markets, I have not adopted his classification. See Michael E. Porter, *Interbrand Choice, Strategy, and Bilateral Market Power* (Cambridge, Mass., 1976).

18. For a theoretical demonstration, see Kenneth T. Arrow, *Limits to Organizations* (New York, 1974), pp. 33–34.

19. See Frederick M. Scherer, *Industrial Market Structure and Economic Performance* (New York, 1970), pp. 192–198.

20. See Williamson, *Markets and Hierarchies,* p. 91.

21. The cigarette industry in the United States at the end of the nineteenth century illustrates this point very well. The invention of the Bonsack cigarette-making machine allowed for enormous economies of scale in production. Since cigarettes are semiperishable, it was important to move the goods as fast as possible to the buyers. Failure to schedule this flow carefully would periodically have led to huge inventories that would diminish the selling value after a while. Deteriorated quality would also have harmed the brand image.

22. Williamson, *Markets and Hierarchies,* p. 47.

23. Ibid.

24. Morton Keller, "Regulation of Large Enterprise: The United States Experience in Comparative Perspective," this volume.

Contributors

ALFRED D. CHANDLER, JR.
Isidor Straus Professor of Business History
Harvard University

HERMAN DAEMS
Professor of Management
University Facility of St. Aloysius, Brussels,
and The European Institute for
Advanced Studies in Management

LESLIE HANNAH
Director of the Business History Unit
London School of Economics

MORTON KELLER
Samuel J. and Augusta Spector Professor of History
Brandeis University

JÜRGEN KOCKA
Professor of History
University of Bielefeld

MAURICE LÉVY-LEBOYER
Professor of Contemporary Economic History
University of Paris X

OLIVER E. WILLIAMSON
Charles and William L. Day Professor
of Economics and Social Science
University of Pennsylvania

Index

HARVARD STUDIES IN BUSINESS HISTORY

*Out of print